A Football Fan's
Guide to Europe

ACKNOWLEDGEMENTS

Additional research by Gabriela Berrios, Hugo Ripley, Claudia Ressler and Ryan van Huyssteen. Thanks to the football clubs, tourist offices, bars, clubs and restaurants that responded to requests for information and to the many people who assisted with information on the city guides, in particular Angus Perry-Macleod, Cameron Hall, Tom Morton, Mike and Annie Bayliss, Mark Griffiths, Manuel Moguer Terol, Phil Whitehead, Matthijs Goes, Amanda Gowing, Angelica Johansson and Ray Murphy. The photographers showcased in this book reserve their rights as the authors and owners of their photographic works. All photographers and photo agencies were contacted regarding the use of their works. Should any errors or inconsistencies be apparent please contact the publisher.

PICTURE CREDITS

Pg 8: Christa Richert /www.sxc.hu. Pg 9: PA Photos (top), Nils-Erik Bjørholt/Innovation Norway. Pg10: Terje Rakke/Innovation Norway, Niels Jørgensen/Innovation Norway (1) C.H./Innovation Norway (2) Nils-Erik Bjørholt/Innovation Norway (3). Pg 11: Mike Egerton/PA Photos. Pg 12: Malmö Turism/www.imagebank.sweden.se. Pg 13: Oscar Dahl/www.sxc.hu (top), Peter Grant/www.imagebank.sweden.se. Pg 14: Göran Assner/Swedish Travel and Tourism Council/www.imagebank.sweden.se. Pg 15: Johan Palmborg/ www.imagebank.sweden.se, Sig Kälvelid/www.imagebank.sweden.se (1) Bo Lind/VisitSweden/www.imagebank.sweden.se (2) Ann Lindberg/www.imagebank.sweden.se (3) Pg 16: Martin Olsson/Wikimedia, Mangan2002/wikimedia (Gren), Barry Coombs/PA Photos (Mild). Pg 17: Steve Morton/PA Photos (top), Wikimedia. Pg 18: Armin Hanisch/www.sxc.hu. Pg 19: Andrew Milligan/PA Photos (top), Scott Liddell/www.sxc.hu Pg 20: www.seeglasgow.com/Glasgow City Marketing Bureau. Pg 21: www.seeglasgow.com/Glasgow City Marketing Bureau, Auchentoshan Distillery (1) www.seeglasgow.com/Glasgow City Marketing Bureau (2) www.seeglasgow.com/Glasgow City Marketing Bureau (3) Pg 22: John Walton/PA Photos, Darz Mol/Wikimedia (Larsson), Peter Robinson/PA Photos (Johnstone). Pg 23: Chris Clark/PA Photos (top), SMG/PA Photos. Pg 24: Gordon MacDonald/wWikimedia, Peter Robinson/PA Photos (Greig), Tony Marshall//PA Photos (Laudrup). Pg 25: Lynne Cameron/PA Photos (top), Steve Woods/www.sxc.hu. Pg 26: www.visitcopenhagen.com Pg 27: Ossian Engmark/www.sxc.hu (top), www.visitcopenhagen.com. Pg 28: Wonderful Copenhagen. Pg: 29 Wonderful Copenhagen (1) Wonderful Copenhagen (2) Fritz Hansen/Wonderful Copenhagen (3) Morten Bjarnhof/Wonderful Copenhagen. Pg 30: Tony Marshall/PA Photos, Matthew Ashton/PA Photos (Zuma), Nigel French/PA Photos (Poulsen). Pg 31: Tony Marshall/PA Photos (top), Benjamin Earwicker/www.sxc.hu. Pg 32: Andreas Hunziker/www.sxc.hu. Pg 33: Richard Styles/www.sxc.hu (top), Mike Vam/www.sxc.hu. Pg 34: britainonview/McCormick-McAdam. Pg 35: Claridges Hotel, Paul Egan/www.sxc.hu (1) Sat Singh/www.sxc.hu (2) Paul Duffett/www.flamephotos.co.uk (3) Pg 36: Mike Egerton/PA Photos, Tony Marshal/PA Photos (Henry), Barratts/PA Photos (James). Pg 37: Teun van Thiel/www.sxc.hu (top), Wikimedia. Pg 38: Nick Potts/PA Photos, Tony Marshall/PA Photos (Lampard), Neal Simpson/PA Photos (Terry). Pg 39: Chris Eyles/www.sxc.hu (top), Lars Sundström/www.sxc.hu. Pg 40: Alasdair Ferguson/www.sxc.hu. Pg 41: Radek Bayek/www.sxc.hu, Britta Kuhnen/www.sxc.hu (1) Ruth Harris/www.sxc.hu (2) Harry McCord/www.sxc.hu (3). Pg 42: John Walton/PA Photos, Michael Steele/PA Photos (Dalglish), Steve Drew/PA Photos (Gerrard). Pg 43: Oli Mohd/www.sxc.hu (top), Martin Rickett/PA Photos. Pg 44: Stephen D Gibson/www.sxc.hu. Pg 45: Stephen D Gibson/ photoeverywhere.co.uk, Paul Gwyther/www.sxc.hu (1) Jas/Wikimedia (2) Comedy Store (3). Pg 46: Peter Byrne/PA Photos, PA Photos (Best), Matthew Ashton/PA Photos (Cantona). Pg 47: Martin Rickett/PA Photos (top), Jean Scheijen/www.sxc.hu. Pg 48: Belgian Tourist Office NYC/USA. Pg 49: Belgian Tourist Office NYC/USA. Pg 50: Pierre Benker/www.sxc.hu, JP de Swart (1) Ilker/www.sxc.hu (2) Belgium Comic Strip Centre (3). Pg 51: Adam Davy/PA Photos. Pg 52: Wolfgang Staudt/www.sxc.hu, Brouwerij De Halve Maan (1) Hendrik de Leyn (2) LittleMan/www.sxc.hu (3). Pg 53: PA Photos. Pg 54: Belgian Tourist Office NYC/USA, Province de Liège (1) Wikimedia (2) Belgian Tourist Office NYC/USA (3). Pg 55: V4nco/Wikimedia. Pg 56: Herman Brinkman/www.sxc.hu. Pg 57: Netherlands Board of Tourism & Convention (top), Wikimedia. Pg 58: Netherlands Board of Tourism & Conventions. Pg 59: Ben Deiman Fotografie/Netherlands Board of Tourism & Conventions, Wikimedia (1) The Hash Museum (2) Zaanse Schans/Netherlands Board of Tourism & Conventions (3). Pg 60: Paul van Vlodjaer/Wikimedia, PA Photos (Cruyff), Peter Robinson/PA Photos (Neeskens). Pg 61: Nick Potts/PA Photos (top), Adrian Dennis/PA Photos. Pg 62: Jurjen Drenth/Netherlands Board of Tourism & Conventions, DAF Museum (1) ReinVM/Wikimedia (2) Netherlands Board of Tourism & Conventions (3). Pg 63: Wikimedia. Pg 64: Fred Ernst/Netherlands Board of Tourism & Conventions (top), Luider/Imago Fotobureau/Netherlands Board of Tourism & Conventions, Marc Nolte/WATT (1) Spido Havenrondvaarten/Netherlands Board of Tourism & Conventions (2) Maar/Netherlands Board of Tourism & Conventions (3). Pg 65: Knurftendans/Wikimedia. Pg 66: Abdulaziz Almansour/www.sxc.hu. Pg 67: Vladimir Stojkovic/www.sxc.hu (top), Konrad Mostert/www.sxc.hu. Pg 68: BTZ Bremer Touristik-Zentrale. Pg 69: Stubu Dancehouse, InBev Deutschland (1) BTZ Bremer Touristik-Zentrale (2) Universumâ Bremen (3). Pg 70: Daniel FR/Wikimedia, PA Photos (Höttges), David Davies /PA Photos (Bode). Pg 71: Mike Egerton/PA Photos (top), Sander van der Veen/www.sxc.hu. Pg 72: Stadt Dortmund/GPM Foto/GP Müller, Patryk Specjal/www.sxc.hu (1) Dortmund Brewery Museum/ Jan Heinze (2) Stadt Dortmund/Zielske Photographie (3). Pg 73: John Walton/PA Photos. Pg 74: Florian K/Wikimedia, Dirk Herrmann/www.sxc.hu (1) Bayer AG (2) Sanja Gjenero/www.sxc.hu (3). Pg 75: Mike Egerton/PA Photos. Pg 76: Christl Reiter/The Munich City Tourist Office Pg 77: The Munich City Tourist Office, Robert Hertz/ The Tourist Office Munich (1) Michael Nagy/The Munich City Tourist Office (2) Michael Nagy/The Munich City Tourist Office (3). Pg 78: Michael Nagy/The Munich City Tourist Office, PA Photos (Beckenbauer), PA Photos (Müller). Pg 79: Mike Egerton/PA Photos (top) Svilen Mushkatov/www.sxc.hu. Pg 80: Raenmaen/Wikimedia, Tracy Olson/www.sxc.hu (1) Gelsenkirchen Tourism (2) Will Watt/www.sxc.hu (3). Pg 81: John Walton/PA Photos. Pg 82: Marc Bertrand/www.photos.parisinfo.com. Pg 83: Stef Goedhart/www.sxc.hu (top), Amélle Dupont/Paris Tourist Office. Pg 84: David Lefranc/Paris Tourist Office. Pg 85: Marc Bertrand/Paris Toùrist Office, Thomas Faivre-Duboz (1) Amélle Dupont/Paris Tourist Office (2) Marc Bertrand/Paris Tourist Office (3). Pg 86: Tara0/Wikimedia, Peter Robinson/PA Photos (Fernández), Peter Jordan/PA Photos (Ginola). Pg 87: Paul Faith/PA Photos (top), Craig Jewell/www.sxc.hu. Pg 88: Paris Tourist Office/Alain Potignon, Samuel Rosa/www.sxc.hu (1) Paris Tourist Office/Marc Bertrand (2) Thomas Sanson/Mairie de Bordeaux (3). Pg 89: David Cheskin/PA Photos. Pg 90: Stephen Pond/PA Photos, Ninkasi Entreprises (1) Centre d'histoire de la résistance et de la déportation/Pierre Verrier (2) Marie Perrin/Lyon Tourist Office (3). Pg 91: Andrew Milligan/PA Photos. Pg 92: OTC Marseille. Pg 93: OTC Marseille. Pg 94: Jon Buckle/PA Photos, museuvirtualdofutebol.blogspot.com (Skoblar), Neal Simpson/PA Photos (Papin). Pg 95: Neal Simpson/PA Photos (top), Alexander Korabelnikov/www.sxc.hu. Pg 96: David Chambers/www.sxc.hu. Pg 97: Joe Giddens/PA Photos (top), Michaël Claude/www.sxc.hu. Pg 98: Basel Tourism, vecteezy.com (1) Basel Tourism (2) Swatch (3). Pg 99: Otto Normalverbraucher/Wikimedia. Pg 100: Laura Shreck/www.sxc.hu. Pg 101: Remy van Donk/www.sxc.hu (top), Colin Nixon/www.sxc.hu. Pg 102: Irum Shahid/www.sxc.hu, Malina/www.sxc.hu (1) Kunsthistorisches Museum, Vienna (2) Jan Zabroda/www.sxc.hu (3). Pg 103: Piedro/Wikimedia. Pg 104: Jaak Nilson/visitestonia.com. Pg 105: Sean Dempsey/PA Photos (top), Jaak Nilson/ visitestonia.com. Pg 106: Jaak Nilson/ visitestonia.com, Onnela Anne (1) Jarek Jõepera (2) Toomas Tuul (3). Pg 107: Tom Buist/PA Photos. Pg 108: Matthijs Mejan/www.sxc.hu. Pg 109: PA Photos (top), Jay Simmons/www.sxc.hu. Pg 110: Matthijs Mejan/www.sxc.hu. Pg 111: Greg Hennigan/www.sxc.hu, Paula Pandey Chetri/www.sxc.hu (1) Ugur Can/www.sxc.hu (2) Peter Hamza (3) Pg 112: Lightning/Wikimedia. Pg 113: 123rf.com. Pg 114: Matthijs Mejan/www.sxc.hu, Museum of Circus Art (1) Jory Krüspe/www.sxc.hu (2) Grand Hotel Europe, St petersburg (3). Pg 115: Neal Simpson/ PA Photos. Pg 116: Janusz Gawron/www.sxc.hu. Pg 117: Michal Zacharzewski/www.sxc.hu. Pg 118: Piotr Wachowicz/www.sxc.hu, Marcin Jochimczyk/www.sxc.hu (1) Rafal Stachurski/The Wieliczka (2) Fantasy Park (3). Pg 119: Tomas Markowski/PA Photos. Pg 120: Orlando Pinto/www.sxc.hu. Pg 121: Mooncross/www.sxc.hu (top), Tony Marshall/PA Photos. Pg 122: Lavinia Marin/www.sxc.hu. Pg 123: Dirk Herrmann/www.sxc.hu, Hendrina Christian/www.sxc.hu (1) Biborné Veres Dorottya/www.sxc.hu (2) Norbert Langeder/www.sxc.hu (3). Pg 124: Cathal McNaughton/PA Photos, PA Photos (Nedvûd/Rosick). Pg 125: Mike Egerton/ PA Photos (top), Bob Smith/www.sxc.hu. Pg 126: Michaela Kobyakov/www.sxc.hu. Pg 127: Joe Giddens/ PA Photos (top) Matthew Ashton/PA Photos. Pg 128: Henk von Pickartz/www.photo-bytes.com, Henk von Pickartz/www.photo-bytes.com (1) Mils Drastich/www.sxc.hu (2) Matthew Ashton/PA Photos (3). Pg 129: Alexander Noskin/Wikimedia. Pg 130: Tatyana Postovyk/www.sxc.hu, Gary Scott/www.sxc.hu (1) SEA 'Artyomsol', Ukraine (2) Henk von Pickartz/photo-bytes.com (3). Pg 131: Jon Buckle/PA Photos. Pg 132: Sorina Bindea/www.sxc.hu. Pg 133: Sandor Pinter/www.sxc.hu (top), Attila Czigany/www.sxc.hu. Pg 134: Budapest Tourism/www.budapestinfo.hu, Szimpla, Budapest (3). Pg 135: Tony Marshall/PA Photos. Pg 136: Municipality of Debrecen, Oliver C Gruener (1). Pg 137: Phil Noble/PA Photos. Pg 138: Ivica Mezei/www.sxc.hu. Pg 139: Mike Egerton/PA Photos (top), Sanja Moharic Hehet/www.sxc.hu. Pg 140: Lidija Macej/www.sxc.hu, Wikimedia (1) Rodolfo Clix/www.sxc.hu (2) AntonU/www.sxc.hu (3). Pg 141: Adam Davy/PA Photos. Pg 142: Petar Pavlovic/www.sxc.hu. Pg 143: Dragan Sasic/www.sxc.hu (top), Vladimir P/www.sxc.hu. Pg 144: Belgrade Tourism. Pg 145: Belgrade Tourism. Pg 146: Steve Mitchell/ PA Photos. Pg 147: Matthew Ashton/PA Photos. Pg 148: José A Warletta/www.sxc.hu. Pg 149: Barry Coombs/PA Photos (top), Nick Potts/PA Photos. Pg 150: Hanka Lehmannova/www.sxc.hu. Pg 151: April Bell/www.sxc.hu, Margarit Ralev/www.sxc.hu(1) Chris Cockram/www.sxc.hu (2) Ivan Ivanov/Wikimedia (3). Pg 152: Martin Rickett/PA Photos. Pg 153: Paul Marriott/PA Photos. Pg 154: Lize Rixt/www.sxc.hu. Pg 155: Richard Fernandes/www.sxc.hu (top), Steve Woods/www.sxc.hu. Pg 156: Helvia Moreira/www.sxc.hu. Pg 157: Werner Braun/www.sxc.hu, Georges Jansoone/Wikimedia (1) Osvaldo Gago/Wikimedia (2) Davide Guglielmo/www.sxc.hu (3). Pg 158: António ML Cabral Esta/Wikimedia, PA Photos (Eusébio), Joe Giddens/PA Photos (Costa). Pg 159: P Fernandes/Wikimedia (top), Dan Colcer/www.sxc.hu. Pg 160: Barry Coombs/PA Photos, Martin Rickett/PA Photos (Figo), Wikimedia (Peyroteo). Pg 161: Paco Serinelli/Creative Photo Agency/PA Photos (top), Harris/PA Photos. Pg 162: Miguel Saavedra/www.sxc.hu. Pg 163: Holly McClellan/www.sxc.hu, Sofia Henriques/www.sxc.hu (1) Ivars Miezis/www.sxc.hu (2) Carla Pais/www.sxc.hu (3). Pg 164: Wikimedia, Matthew Ashton/PA Photos (Jardel), Peter Robinson/PA Photos (Gomes). Pg 165: Dave Thompson/PA Photos (top), Vivek Chugh/www.sxc.hu. Pg 166: Augustin Rodriguez/www.sxc.hu. Pg 167: Gisela Royo/www.sxc.hu (top), Marc Garrido i Puig/www.sxc.hu. Pg 168: Juan Carlos Rodriguez/www.sxc.hu. Pg 169: Wikimedia, Eva Serna/www.sxc.hu (1) Wikimedia (2) Marco Petrozzi/www.sxc.hu (3). Pg 170: Wikimedia, SMG/PA Photos (Adelardo), Cathal McNaughton/PA Photos (Torres). Pg 171: Paco Serinelli/Creative Photo Agency/PA Photos (top), Eyestar-Eileen /www.sxc.hu. Pg 172: Daniel Shroeder/Wikimedia, El Grafico/ImageForum/Wikimedia (Stefano), Katarzyna Cenian/Wikimedia (Zinedine). Pg 173: Solbaken/Wikimedia (top), Hector Blanco de Frutos/Wikimedia. Pg 174: Alexandre Casarin/www.sxc.hu. Pg 175: William23/www.sxc.hu, Wikimedia (1) Turespaña (2) Barcelona Tourism (3). Pg 176: Joan Tamora/PA Photos, Nick Potts/PA Photos (Ronaldinho), PA Photos (Cruyff). Pg 177: PA Photos (top), Wikimedia. Pg 178: Sue Anna Joe/www.sxc.hu. Pg 179: Lotus Head/www.pixelpusher.co.za, Rob Owen-Wahl/www.sxc.hu (1) Steve Woods/www.sxc.hu (2) Carlos Zaragoza/www.sxc.hu (3). Pg 180: Barrington Coombs/PA Photos, Wikimedia (Arza), Matthew Ashton/PA Photos (Suker). Pg 181: Martin Rickett/PA Photos (top), Henning Buchholz/www.sxc.hu. Pg 182: Peter Hall/www.sxc.hu. Pg 183: Charlie Lawrence/www.sxc.hu, Peter Hall/www.sxc.hu (1) Benjamin Siegel/www.sxc.hu (2) Daniela Martina/www.sxc.hu (3). Pg 184: Felivet/Wikimedia, Wikimedia (Kempes/Waldo). Pg 185: Felix Ordonez/PA Photos (top), Daniel Wildman/www.sxc.hu. Pg 186: H Assaf/www.sxc.hu, Wikimedia (1) Ronald Vern/www.sxc.hu (2) Ilona Kuusela/www.sxc.hu (3). Pg 187: Jose Breton/Creative Photo Agency/PA Photos. Pg 188: Alex Fittipaldi/www.sxc.hu. Pg 189: Juan Pablo Oitana/www.sxc.hu (top), Luca Cinacchio/www.sxc.hu. Pg 190: Victor Iglesias/www.sxc.hu. Pg 191: Duane Robinson/www.sxc.hu, Sorina Bindea/www.sxc.hu (1) Wojtek Kutyla/www.sxc.hu (2) Jim Goodrich/www.sxc.hu (3). Pg 192: Adam Davy/PA Photos. Pg 193: Lalupa/Wikimedia. Pg 194: Sander Klaver/www.sxc.hu. Pg 195: Enrico Corno/www.sxc.hu, Pierre Norraeus/www.sxc.hu (1) Lajla Borg Jensen/www.sxc.hu (2) Rodolfo Clix/www.sxc.hu (3). Pg 196: Nick Potts/PA Photos, Neal Simpson/PA Photos (van Basten), Barratts/PA Photos (Nordahl). Pg 197: Adam Davy/PA Photos (top), Dora Pete/www.sxc.hu. Pg 198: Xavoun/Wikimedia, Inter Club Sydney/Wikimedia (Meazza), Peter Robinson/PA Photos (Facchetti). Pg 199: Stephen Pond/PA Photos (top), Davide Gugliemo/www.sxc.hu. Pg 200: Rodolfo Belloli/www.sxc.hu. Pg 201: Lukasz Fus/www.sxc.hu, Rita Mezzela/www.sxc.hu (1) Rodolfo Belloli/www.sxc.hu (2) Neco Garnica/www.sxc.hu (3). Pg 202: John Walton/PA Photos, Peter Robinson/PA Photos (Platini), Tony Marshall/PA Photos (Zidane). Pg 203: Neal Simpson/PA Photos (top), Bonvivant/www.sxc.hu. Pg 204: Cristi Modoran/www.sxc.hu. Pg 205: George Chrono/www.sxc.hu (top), George Georgiades/www.sxc.hu. Pg 206: Vangelis Thomaidis/www.sxc.hu. Pg 207: Paulo Meira/www.sxc.hu, Takis Kolokotronis/www.sxc.hu (1) Gabor Granat/www.sxc.hu (2) Takis Kolokotronis/www.sxc.hu (3). Pg 208: Nick Potts/PA Photos. Pg 209: Action Images Greece/PA Photos. Pg 210: Ephe Drin/www.sxc.hu. Pg 211: Bulent Fahri Ince/www.sxc.hu (top), PA Photos. Pg 212: Ertugrul Murteza/www.sxc.hu. Pg 213: Tristan Jessurun/www.sxc.hu, Esther Ruzé/www.sxc.hu (1) Daniel Duchon/www.sxc.hu (2) Andre Veron/www.sxc.hu (3). Pg 214: Zoban Raftik/www.sxc.hu. Pg 215: Turksporfoto/PA Photos. Pg 216: Wikimedia, Tony Marshall/PA Photos (Hagi), Adam Davy/PA Photos (fiükür). Pg 217: Rebecca Naden/PA Photos (top), Wikimedia. Pg 218: Israel Ministry of Tourism/www.goisrael.com. Pg 219: Adam Davy/PA Photos (top), Owen Humphreys/PA Photos. Pg 220: Israel Ministry of Tourism/www.goisrael.com. Pg 221: Avi Ran/Wikimedia. Pg 222-223: Nina Chantrasmi/www.sxc.hu.

A Football Fan's
Guide to Europe

by DANIEL FORD and BILL EDGAR

NEW
HOLLAND

First published in 2009 by
New Holland Publishers (UK) Ltd
London • Cape Town • Sydney • Auckland
www.newhollandpublishers.com

Garfield House	80 McKenzie Street	Unit 1, 66 Gibbes	218 Lake Road
86–88 Edgware Road	Cape Town 8001	Street, Chatswood	Northcote
London W2 2EA	South Africa	NSW 2067	Auckland
United Kingdom		Australia	New Zealand

A catalogue record for this book is available from the British Library.

ISBN 978 1 84773 465 5

This book has been produced for New Holland Publishers by
SchreiberFord Publications Ltd
London • Cape Town

Project Manager: Daniel Ford
Designer: Francois Pretorius
Photo Editor: Grant Schreiber
Senior Editor: Sarah Greaney
Production: Marion Storz
Publisher: Ross Hilton
Publishing Director: Rosemary Wilkinson

2 4 6 8 10 9 7 5 3 1

Reproduction by PDQ Digital Media Solutions Ltd, UK
Printed and bound by Tien Wah Press (Pte) Ltd, Singapore

INTRODUCTION

The big concrete terracing at Akritas Chloraka (bottom of Cyprus Division 2) is baking hot so I'm sitting on a stray bit of cardboard. There are maybe 100 fans dotted around in the area where my cousin Lewis and I, and thousands of flies, have settled to watch the game against the second-placed side from Larnaca. Just in front of the children aiming toilet rolls quite accurately at the halfway line is a guy hopping about selling tickets. But whether they are for the match (the turnstiles were unmanned) or for a raffle is unclear. About the same number of people are dotted around on the terracing behind the goal, a bit of concrete that seems to hang on the hillside. Well, actually, it does hang on the hillside, as the whole stadium is cut into a massive drop from what is little more than a village, situated a few miles from the tourist town of Paphos. The stadium is rubbish, the football is rubbish and youngsters from the home side's youth team are throwing things at the opposition's big wigs who are sitting in front of me. But I love every minute of it because I am a football lover.

And if you love football, you know going to a game is about way more than football itself. It's about laughing at the opposition striker when he misses an easy chance (come on, that's the best bit), the beer before the game (hang on, maybe that's the best bit) and providing the perfect excuse for getting home late (sorry, that's the best bit). It's about discovering there's a second division team called Akritas Chloraka just up the road from where you are staying and astonishing the locals that you even care. And strolling up the road to watch them, then following their results on the internet for years to come.

Akritas Chloraka are not featured in this book. But football lovers across the world are always looking for any excuse for a beer, a plane trip and a chance to laugh at the opposition striker missing a sitter. So welcome to this offer of 26 countries, 49 cities and 61 clubs not a million miles from where you are sitting right now.

Featuring clubs from Barcelona and Real Madrid to IFK Gothenburg and Lyon; cities from London and Milan to Villarreal and Haifa; and countries from the east of Europe to the west, north and south. They've been chosen for their footballing ability and the city's visitability. And also because more of us than ever want to go away, watch a match and enjoy ourselves in a place that isn't where our season ticket tells us to go and who to watch. Of course there are some clubs missing. Is it anyone's fault Uefa has expanded more than the Roman Empire? But hopefully this is a list to tempt your taste buds and stretch your Easyjet account.

Daniel Ford

Note: The names of competitions have changed over the years. We have used, where possible, the titles of the competitions at the time that is relevant to the piece being written. So the Champions League was also the European Cup. The Uefa Cup was originally the Inter-Cities Fairs Cup, and from the 2009–10 season will be known as the Europa League. The Intertoto Cup was contested for the last time in 2008–09.

11 / Rosenborg

Norway

Sweden

115 / Zenit St Petersburg

107 / Levadia Tallinn

Estonia

Russia

112 / CSKA M
113 / Spartak

Scotland

22 / Celtic
24 / Rangers

16 / IFK Gothenburg

Denmark

30 / FC Copenhagen

46 / Manchester United
42 / Liverpool

70 / Werder Bremen

Poland

England

Netherlands

60 / Ajax
65 / Feyenoord
63 / PSV Eindhoven

75 / Bayer Leverkusen
73 / Borussia Dortmund
81 / Schalke 04

129 / Dynamo

36 / Arsenal
38 / Chelsea

53 / Bruges
51 / Anderlecht

Ukraine

124 / Sparta Prague

119 / Wisla Krakow

Belgium

55 / Standard Liège

131 / Shakhtar Donetsk

Germany

Czech Republic

86 / Paris St-Germain

78 / Bayern Munich
103 / Rapid Vienna

France

99 / FC Basle

Austria

135 / MTK Hungaria

Switzerland

Hungary

137 / Debrecen

91 / Lyon

141 / Dinamo Zagreb

89 / Bordeaux

196 / AC Milan
198 / Inter Milan

Croatia

202 / Juventus

146 / Red Star Belgrade
147 / Partizan Belgrade

Italy

164 / Porto

Spain

94 / Marseille

Serbia

Bulgaria

Portugal

170 / Atlético Madrid
172 / Real Madrid

176 / Barcelona

152 / CSKA Sofia
153 / Levski Sofia

158 / Benfica
160 / Sporting Lisbon

187 / Villarreal
184 / Valencia

214 / Beşiktaş
215 / Fenerbahçe
216 / Galatasaray

192 / Lazio
193 / Roma

180 / Sevilla

Greece

Turkey

Israel

208 / Olympiakos
209 / Panathinaikos

221 / Maccabi Haifa

● Club locations are approximately positioned only

CONTENTS

NORWAY

THE

3

MINUTE

GUIDE

Capital: *Oslo.* **Language:** *Norwegian (Nynorsk and Bokmål).* **Beer:** *Weizenbier.* **Food:** *Fish, smørrebrød (open sandwich), lamb.* **National anthem:** *Ja, Vi Elsker Dette Landet (Yes, We Love This Country).* **Population:** *4,644,000.* **Time zone:** *GMT +1.* **Emergency numbers:** *Police 112, medical 113, fire 110.* **Did you know?** *Hammerfest is Europe's northernmost city.* **Football body:** *Norges Fotballforbund Serviceboks, 1 Ullevaal Stadion Oslo 0840; tel: +47 2102 9300, fax: +47 2102 9301, email: nff@fotball.no, website: www.fotball.no. Founded 1902. Affiliated 1908.*

Below: The Norwegian city of Bergen.

Long wait, long-ball

Given that they had waited more than half a century since their only previous appearance at a major tournament, Norway fans could not object too strongly when coach Egil Olsen adopted a rudimentary long-ball style for the national team and took them to successive World Cups in the 1990s. They also reached Euro 2000 after his departure but since then have resumed their role as European also-rans.

Their only advance beyond an initial group stage at a tournament came in France in 1998, when they secured progress via their most famous result, a 2–1 victory over Brazil. The game featured their three big forwards named Flo – brothers Tore André and Jostein and their cousin Håvard – whose strong aerial presence suited the team's direct approach. Tore André scored, Håvard also started and Jostein appeared as a substitute to inspire the late comeback from a goal down.

Norway's star players in this period were typically functional and lacking flair, but at least the country had some top-class talent at last. As with the other Scandinavian nations, football development was slower than in the leading European leagues; Rosenborg, Norway's biggest club, only became fully professional in the late 1980s.

Not that this improved the spectacle of the domestic league, given the tedium of Rosenborg's unbroken title success from 1992 to 2004. However, there were four different champions in the next four years. A return to the glory days of Olsen for the national team would top it off nicely.

Above: The Norwegian World Cup team of 1998. *Below:* Beach football Norwegian style.

TRONDHEIM

In the dark midwinter

Drive a mere 460 km (285 miles) north from Trondheim, give or take the odd twist and turn to look at the mind-blowing scenery, and you'll reach the Arctic Circle. Just a little warning for you to bring a warm coat, that's all. But you'll be rewarded with a great little city, with cobbled alleyways and wooden buildings (not to mention the fjord) to stir images of the Viking history in this area.

In fact, although it was the base for kings as the capital of the country until 1380, when it was still called Nidaros, the city has really developed as the education and technology centre of the country. This is still true today — about a sixth of its population are students. Home to around 160,000 people, this port is nestled around the curves of the Nidelva River as it heads inland from the Trondheim Fjord.

Those looking for virtually round-the-clock light and midnight games of golf will be hoping the city's club Rosenborg have to play pre-season European qualifiers — being so close to the Arctic Circle the sun hardly sets during the summer. The downside? You'll hardly see any daylight at all, let alone the sun, if you are in Trondheim to watch a game in midwinter.

Weather	Low (°C)	High
January	-5	-1
February	-5	1
March	-2	4
April	0	7
May	5	13
June	8	16
July	12	17
August	10	17
September	6	13
October	3	9
November	-1	3
December	-4	1

Below: A stone relief on Trondheim Cathedral.

3 THINGS
YOU MUST DO...
(Apart from the football)

1 THE TRAMPE BICYCLE LIFT
Stick out your leg and try the nifty bicycle lift — the world's first — to head up the Brubakken hill towards Kristiansten Fort. Open: bikes available when winter snow clears until 31 Oct. Price: bikes Kr70 a day (and a Kr200 deposit or your credit card), lift Kr100 deposit from tourist office (Munkegata 19, tel: +47 7380 7660).

2 BAKKLANDET
This picturesque part of town on the east side of the river was first constructed in the 17th century. Originally home to working-class families, the painted wooden buildings now host shops, restaurants and cafés.

3 VAASFJELLET SKIING
Enjoy floodlit ski slopes (tel: +47 7283 0200). Open: varies. Price: adult day pass Kr280, adult evening pass Kr170. To get there: Christmas to Easter Mon–Fri, buses leave city 16.30 (also 11.30 on Wed and Fri) and return 21.00 (also 17.15 on Wed and Fri). Sat–Sun and hols buses leave the city 10.00 and 11.30 and return 16.30.

ROSENBORG

Above: Rosenborg fans in full flow at the Lerkendal Stadium.

MATTER OF FACT
Name: Rosenborg Ballklub
Stadium: Lerkendal Stadion
(capacity 21,166)
Address: Klaebuveien, 7492
To get there: Buses 3, 8, 20, 36, 55,
60, 66, 88
Telephone: +47 7382 2100
Email: info@rbk.no
Website: www.rbk.no

Stadium tours
Open: Mon–Thu 11.00, 14.30
Price: Depends on group size. About
75–100 NOK per person. Must book
(via www.rbk.no/incoming/
article58457.ece); minimum people
per group is five
Contact: Phone above number or
email: guide@rbk.no

| **Home** | **Away** |

Leading trophies
20   Norwegian League
9   Norwegian Cup

Main rivals
Trondheim has no other major clubs.
Historically Lillestrøm SK are the main
rivals but the nearest big club, around
300 km (186 miles) away, are
Molde FK.

TEN YEAR EURO RECORD

Season	Competition	Finished
1998–99	Champs League	Group
1999–00	Champs League	Group*
2000–01	Champs League	Group**
	Uefa Cup	Last 32
2001–02	Champs League	Group**
2002–03	Champs League	Group**
2003–04	Champs League	3rd qual rd
	Uefa Cup	Last 32
2004–05	Champs League	Group
2005–06	Champs League	Group
	Uefa Cup	Last 32
2006–07	DNQ	
2007–08	Champs League	Group
	Uefa Cup	Last 32

*2nd of two group stages
**1st of two group stages

Lucky thirteen

Given their overwhelming success, it could be argued Rosenborg *are* Norwegian football. Considering his role in their history, it could equally be claimed that Nils Arne Eggen is Rosenborg.

Eggen was part of their first title-winning side of 1967 but five coaching spells created his legend. He oversaw the club's first league and cup double in 1971, achieved a promotion during his third stint and then, returning in 1988, won two doubles. Finally, from 1992, he set in motion their 13 successive league titles, the world's second-best such sequence.

He also frightened Europe's elite, inspiring a Champions League victory over AC Milan at the San Siro in December 1996 *en route* to the quarter-finals and seeing off Real Madrid 2–0 a year later. Rosenborg spent eight successive seasons in the group stages and, by hogging Norway's Champions League riches, reinforced their domestic dominance. To emphasize the value of Eggen (who had taken a year off in 1998), a slow decline set in at home and abroad when he left for good in 2002.

SWEDEN

Capital: *Stockholm.* **Language:** *Swedish.* **Beer:** *Pils, Muechner, Juloel (Christmas).* **Food:** *Smorgasbord (buffet), reindeer,* köttbullar *(meatballs).* **National anthem:** *Sång till Norden (Song of the North).* **Population:** *9,045,000.* **Time zone:** *GMT +1.* **Emergency Number:** *112.* **Did you know?** *In 1989 Sweden had the first ice hotel and in 1973 Roland Ohisson of Falkenberg was buried in a coffin of chocolate.* **Football body:** *Svenska Fotbollförbundet, PO Box 1216, Solna 17 123; tel: +46 8735 0900, fax: +46 8735 0901, email: svff@svenskfotboll, website: svenskfotboll.se. Founded 1904. Affiliated 1904.*

Below: Swedish design is globally renowned.

Fulfilling Swede dreams

Although Denmark are the only Scandinavian country to have won a major tournament, triumphing at Euro '92, Sweden can lay a claim to being the strongest footballing power in the region, both at club and national level.

IFK Gothenburg are Scandinavia's only European club trophy winners, having lifted the Uefa Cup twice in the 1980s, while Malmö are alone in having reached a European Cup or Champions League final, their historic match bringing defeat to Nottingham Forest in 1979. Furthermore, unlike their neighbours, Sweden have hosted leading tournaments, staging the 1992 European championship and the 1958 World Cup. They were runners-up at the latter, the only time the region has provided a World Cup finalist.

Sweden made a significant impact on the world stage shortly after the Second World War. The forward trio of Gunnar Gren, Gunnar Nordahl and Nils Liedholm led them to an Olympic gold medal in 1948, earning them all moves to AC Milan. Then, despite missing these players because the Swedish football association would not pick anyone at a foreign club, the national team finished third at the 1950 World Cup.

Their march to the Euro '92 semi-finals was helped by home advantage but they also reached the last four at the World Cup in the United States two years later, losing only to a late goal by Brazil. They are often criticized as boring, but the yellow-clad fans who enjoy the team's habitual over-achievement do not seem to mind.

Above: The Råsunda Stadion in Solna, home of the national side. *Below:* The ice hotel.

THE TEN YEAR GUIDE

Allsvenskan

Season	Winner	Runner-up
1999	Helsingborgs	AIK
2000	Halmstads	Helsingborgs
2001	Hammarby	Djurgårdens
2002	Djurgårdens	Malmö
2003	Djurgårdens	Hammarby
2004	Malmö	Halmstads
2005	Djurgårdens	IFK Gothenburg
2006	Elfsborg	AIK
2007	IFK Gothenburg	Kalmar FF
2008	Kalmar FF	Elfsborg

*Seasons swapped to calendar years

Svenska Cupen

Season	Winner	Runner-up
1998–99	AIK	IFK Gothenburg
1999–00	Örgryte	AIK
2000–01	Elfsborg	AIK
2002*	Djurgårdens	AIK
2003	Elfsborg	Assyriska Föreningen
2004	Djurgårdens	IFK Gothenburg
2005	Djurgårdens	Atvidabergs
2006	Helsingborgs	Gefle
2007	Kalmar FF	IFK Gothenburg
2008	IFK Gothenburg	Kalmar FF

GOTHENBURG

Tongue-tripping down the Avenue

Gothenburg sits at the mouth of the River Göta on the west coast of Sweden facing Denmark, so is well situated for connections to that country (Frederikshavn) and Germany (Kiel) by sea. But it's such a relaxed place you won't want to leave once the football is over.

Head to the Avenue (officially the Kungsportsavenyn if you want to try and get your tongue around that, or more commonly Avenyn), the main strip of shops, bars, cafés is the city's main people magnet. If you walk its full length from its square (Kungsportsplatsen) in the old city centre, at the road's north end nearest the river, to Götasplatsen, the square that houses the city's theatre, concert hall and museum of art, you will have travelled about a kilometre. Your compass for heading north to south is the Poseidon statue, who as you will know from Greek mythology (or more likely the film) is the God of the Sea. Time for a beer to toast the country's largest port? Well, you are in the right street.

Today Gothenburg has a population of about 490,000. It was founded in 1621 and its location meant it developed rapidly as a trading city through the Swedish East India Company. Its population grew rapidly from 1800 heading into the 20th century, as the city built on its trading strength and grew into a modern industrial centre. The Dutch (who played a major role in planning the city), the Scottish and its Scandinavian neighbours have all added their influence to Gothenburg over the years, a mix which has probably contributed to the cosmopolitan air of tolerance that exists today. The friendliness of Gothenburg just about masks its high costs, which you'll soon notice on big nights out.

Below: Gothenburg marina with its conspicuous red and white office building nicknamed 'the lipstick'.

3 THINGS YOU MUST DO...
(Apart from the football)

1 LISEBERG AMUSEMENT PARK

Disney this isn't, but it's been around since 1923 and boasts millions of visitors a year so Liseberg (Örgrytevägen 5, tel: +46 31 400 100) has its attractions, with roller coasters, a log flume and many small stalls. Open: summer season plus Nov and Dec. Price: Kr70 if you are over seven. To get there: subway to Liseberg.

2 SOUTHERN GOTHENBURG ARCHIPELAGO

These islands lie just off the coast of the city and are famous for their natural beauty and Viking heritage. There are no cars and just 5,000 permanent residents. Contact tourist office (Kungsportsplatsen 2, tel: +46 31 612 500). To get there: tram to Salthomen, then ferry.

3 THE AVENUE

Walk along it, drink in its bars, eat in its restaurants and dance in its clubs. And if you're feeling in need of a dose of culture try the Gothenburg Museum of Art (Götaplatsen/Kungsportsavenyn 412 56, tel: +46 31 368 3500), which is famous for its collection of Nordic Art.

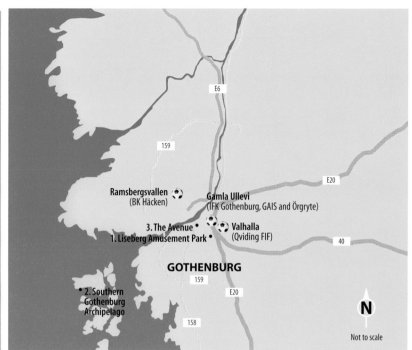

Ramsbergsvallen (BK Häcken)

Gamla Ullevi (IFK Gothenburg, GAIS and Örgryte)

3. The Avenue
1. Liseberg Amusement Park

Valhalla (Qviding FIF)

GOTHENBURG

2. Southern Gothenburg Archipelago

N

Not to scale

BARS > CLUBS > RESTAURANTS

Bars > If it's cocktails you want try **Bitter Bar & Matsal** (Linnegatan 59, tel: +46 31 249 120), a venue which also serves good food. This is a popular place on a popular street. For beer and live music head to **The Dubliner** (Östra Hamngatan 50B, tel: +46 3113 9020).

Clubs > The multi-roomed **Lounges** (Kungsportsavenyn 5, tel: +46 31 711 1541) and **Nivå** (Kungsportsavenyn 5, tel: +46 31 701 8090) are both close to each other on the Avenue. The Lounges offers a casino while Nivå has a barbecue restaurant, so take your pick.

Restaurants > Basement (Gotabergsgatan 28, tel: +46 31 282 729) is the place to go if you want to push the boat out. Chic and expensive are ways to describe this international cuisine restaurant.

Magnus & Magnus (Magasinsgatan 8, tel: +46 31 133 000) is a bar, eatery and club later on.

Below: Gothenburg at Christmas.

Weather	Low (°C)	High
January	-1	1
February	-1	1
March	0	5
April	1	9
May	6	15
June	10	18
July	12	19
August	12	18
September	8	15
October	6	11
November	0	6
December	-1	2

IFK GOTHENBURG

Above: Gamla Ullevi stadium.

TEN YEAR EURO RECORD		
Season	Competition	Finished
1998–99	Uefa Cup	2nd qual rd
1999–00	Uefa Cup	2nd round
2000–01	DNQ	
2001–02	DNQ	
2002–03	Uefa Cup	Qual rd*
2003–04	DNQ	
2004–05	DNQ	
2005–06	Intertoto Cup	3rd round
2006–07	Uefa Cup	1st qual rd
2007–08	DNQ	

*The only qualifying round

Peace and happiness

Sven-Goran Eriksson's renowned serenity and calm assurance was never better illustrated than when he coached IFK Gothenburg in the early 1980s. As the club faced bankruptcy, he kept his players focused and they conquered all, earning vital revenue. Whereas 1982 might have been the final year of Gothenburg's history, it is instead remembered as their finest.

The nadir came when Gothenburg borrowed money from their supporters for the Uefa Cup trip to Valencia in March 1982. Yet Eriksson's team ignored the distractions to eliminate the Spanish side and go on to lift Sweden's first European club trophy. He also secured Gothenburg's first league title for 13 seasons and added the domestic cup.

Eriksson ended his three-year stay by joining Benfica but the tone had been set as Gothenburg, free from financial worries, dominated at home and made strides across the continent. More impressive was Gothenburg's progress abroad. They reached the European Cup quarter-finals in 1985 and semi-finals the following year before securing the 1987 Uefa Cup, leaving them with Scandinavia's only two continental trophies. In the 1990s their Champions League victims included Barcelona, Manchester United and AC Milan.

Gothenburg have tested their fans' linguistic skills by flitting between grounds since moving into Ullevi stadium in 1916. They relocated to Nya Ullevi (new Ullevi) in 1958, although this changed to simply Ullevi; meanwhile the original stadium became Gamla Ullevi (old Ullevi). In 1992 they returned to Gamla Ullevi (still using the larger Ullevi for big games). The smaller ground, demolished and reconstructed for a scheduled 2009 opening, was to be called Nya Gamla Ullevi (new old Ullevi) but, mercifully, it will just be Gamla Ullevi.

GREATEST PLAYERS

> GUNNAR GREN (1941–49)
An inside forward with great ball control and a fine brain, Gren specialized in creating goals with inch-perfect passes but was still the club's leading scorer for three seasons before joining AC Milan.

> HAKAN MILD (1988–93; 1995–96; 1998–2001; 2002–05)
The midfielder made his debut at 16 and became an icon after his four spells at the club. Gothenburg fans sang his name throughout his last match for the club

MATTER OF FACT
Name: Idrottsföreningen Kamraterna Göteborg
Stadium: Gamla Ullevi (capacity 18,800, after scheduled 2009 re-opening)
Address: Skånegatan, SE 411 40, SE 416 55
To get there: Stadium is a few minutes' walk from central train station.
Telephone: +46 31 703 7300
Email: info@ifkgoteborg.se
Website: www.ifkgoteborg.se

Stadium tour
Open: No scheduled times – decided upon request
Contact: Tel: +46 31 335 7800

Home	Away

Trophies
2	Inter-Cities Fairs Cup/Uefa Cup
18	Swedish League
5	Spanish cup

Main rivals
Gothenburg ground-share with GAIS and Örgryte IS. BK Häcken (tel: +46 31 50 67 90, www.bkhacken.se) play at Ramsbergsvallen (Inlandsgatan 1, 417 15). Qviding FIF (www.qviding.se) play at Valhalla.

Above: IFK Gothenburg supporters wave their trademark chequered flags.

BERLIN BOYCOTTERS BLASTED
Three Gothenburg players – Ernst Andersson, Fritz Berg and Gunnar Löfgren – were criticized for refusing to represent Sweden at the 1936 Berlin Olympics in protest at the Nazi hosts. While their FA accepted the stance, Swedish football administrator Anton Johansson, claimed: "Gothenburgers aren't real Swedes".

SCOTLAND

THE **3** MINUTE GUIDE		**Capital:** *Edinburgh.* **Language:** *English.* **Beer:** *Tennents Lager, Deuchars IPA (Indian Pale Ale).* **Food:** *Shortbread, porridge, haggis.* **National anthem:** *Flower of Scotland.* **Population:** *5,144,200.* **Time zone:** *GMT.* **Emergency number:** *999.* **Did you know?** *In 1832 Scottish physician Neil Arnott invented the water bed.* **Football body:** *The Scottish Football Association, Hampden Park, Glasgow, G42 9AY; tel: +44 141 616 6000, fax: +44 141 616 6001, email: info@scottishfa.co.uk, website: www.scottishfa.co.uk. Founded 1873. Affiliated: 1910.*

Below: No trip to Scotland is complete without sampling its whisky.

A tale of two clubs

Bill Shankly laid the foundations for Liverpool to become England's most successful team, Sir Matt Busby built Manchester United into arguably the world's most famous club and Jock Stein engineered Britain's first European Cup triumph with Celtic. Scotland has provided some of the game's greatest managers, with United's Sir Alex Ferguson continuing the trend in modern times, but the country's playing talent has dried up.

Where the Scotland team were superior to England in the 1970s, these days they have fallen far behind. The two nations' Euro 2008 qualifying failures meant Scotland were missing from a fifth consecutive major tournament, while it was only England's first such absence since 1994. Then again, this disparity perhaps should be expected given Scotland's five million population is one-tenth of England's.

The two countries were pioneers, meeting in the world's first international match in 1872 and forming the first two national leagues, England in 1888 and their neighbours two years later. Even in the early days, two clubs stood out in Scotland and their dominance remains. Rangers have a world-record 51 domestic league titles, while Celtic are fourth on that global list with 42.

While these clubs have reached the Uefa Cup final recently – Celtic lost to Porto in 2003 and Rangers to Zenit St Petersburg in 2008 – they lag behind the English elite financially, leading the pair to covet places in the more lucrative Premier League to the south. Fifa have rejected the idea, though, so Scotland's two-horse race will run and run.

Above: Scottish fans urge their nation on **Below:** *Scottish fans are called the Tartan Army.*

GLASGOW

Europe's tough City of Culture

Universally known as a rough, tough city, this is not the place to be wearing football colours, most certainly not a Rangers or Celtic shirt if you have bought one for a souvenir. It's a friendly place, make no mistake, but football shirts are best avoided. In fact there are a lot of bars that won't even let you in if you are wearing one.

Built on the River Clyde in central Scotland, Glasgow is an important industrial and cultural centre (it was the European City of Culture in 1990) and is the country's largest city, with a population of around 650,000, although the greater urban area is well over a million. Sauchiehall Street is the main, and most well-known strip in Glasgow for business, shopping and nightlife. The 2.5 km (1.5 mile) street runs from the Buchanan Galleries, the city's large shopping complex at its eastern end, passing near the Charing Cross (Glasgow) rail station before crossing the M8 motorway, and ending eventually at the Kelvingrove Park, which adjoins the University of Glasgow. The Buchanan Galleries is situated near the heart of the city and is one of the UK's largest retail centres, housing most of the top outlets.

The 84-hectare Kelvingrove Park is situated in the city's West End and is popular with walkers, joggers and skaters all looking for an escape from the bustle of the city centre. It is home to the Kelvingrove Art Gallery and Museum, an ornate red sandstone building which houses one of the continents most impressive art collections.

Ibrox Stadium, home of Rangers, is just south of here, over the river in Govan district, while Celtic Park is much further to the east.

Below: *The stately Kelvingrove Park is perfect for an escape from the bustle of the city.*

3 THINGS YOU MUST DO...
(Apart from the football)

1 AUCHENTOSHAN WHISKY DISTILLERY

Tour the Auchentoshan Distillery (tel: +44 1389 878 561) to learn more about the country's national drink, and taste a few whiskies. Open: Mon–Sat 10.00–17.00, Sun 12.00–17.00. Price: adults £4.50. To get there: by car on the Great Western Road (A82) or by train to Kilpatrick.

2 CLYDE AUDITORIUM

There is some impressive architecture in Glasgow but the stand-out is the Armadillo, as the Clyde Auditorium (Finnieston Street, tel: +44 8700 404000 for box office) is known locally. Designed by Sir Norman Foster, it has drawn comparisons with the Sydney Opera House.

3 HAMPDEN PARK STADIUM

This 52,000-seater stadium (tel: +44 141 616 6139) is home to the Scottish national side and amateurs Queen's Park (tel: +44 141 632 1275). Open: tours daily 11.00, 12.30, 14.00 and 15.00 (15.30 Apr–Oct). Price: stadium and museum tour, adults £9, under 16s £4.50. To get there: buses 31, 37 and 75, or railway to Kings Park or Mount Florida.

GLASGOW

- 1. Auchentoshan Whisky Distillery
- Firhill (Partick Thistle)
- Ibrox (Rangers)
- 2. Clyde Auditorium
- Celtic Park (Celtic)
- 3. Hampden Park Stadium

A8, A80, M73, M8, A761, A737, M77, A749, M74, A725

N Not to scale

BARS > CLUBS > RESTAURANTS

Bars > One of the most famous bars in the city is the **Horse Shoe Bar** (17 Drury Lane, tel: +44 141 229 5711), with… a huge horseshoe-shaped bar. It's said to be the largest continuous bar in Britain. Nearby is the spacious **All Bar One** (56–72 St Vincent Street, tel: +44 141 229 6060).

Clubs > **The Tunnel** (84 Mitchell Street, tel: +44 141 204 1000) has attracted top DJs like Pete Tong, Judge Jules and Paul Oakenfold and hosted a party for 50 Cent since opening in 1990. Its different rooms offer everything from club anthems to commercial R&B and hip-hop.

Restaurants > One of the city's oldest and smartest restaurants is the **Rogano** (11 Exchange Place, tel: +44 141 248 4055). In a city awash with Indian restaurants, one with a good reputation is the **Shish Mahal** (60–68 Park Road, tel: +44 141 334 7899).

Below: Shopping in central Glasgow.

Weather	Low (°C)	High
January	0	6
February	1	6
March	2	8
April	3	10
May	6	15
June	8	17
July	11	18
August	10	18
September	8	15
October	6	12
November	2	8
December	1	6

CELTIC

Above: Cheering on the Bhoys of Celtic.

Triumphs and turbulence

TEN YEAR EURO RECORD		
Season	Competition	Finished
1998–99	Champs League	2nd qual rd
	Uefa Cup	Last 32
1999–00	Uefa Cup	2nd round
2000–01	Uefa Cup	2nd round
2001–02	Champs League	Group*
	Uefa Cup	Last 32
2002–03	Champs League	3rd qual rd
	Uefa Cup	Final
2003–04	Champs League	Group
	Uefa Cup	QF
2004–05	Champs League	Group
2005–06	Champs League	2nd qual rd
2006–07	Champs League	Last 16
2007–08	Champs League	Last 16

*1st of two group stages

What do Alan Shearer, Roy Keane, Ryan Giggs, Tony Adams, Bobby Charlton and Bobby Moore have in common? Answer – their testimonial matches were all against Celtic. With a large and widespread fanbase, especially in England, the Glasgow club are watched in great numbers wherever they go, so are ideal opponents for such games.

Those supporters will travel far for their team, as 80,000 of them showed by following Celtic to the 2003 Uefa Cup final in Seville, even though most could not get a ticket for the game. Back at home, their normal Celtic Park attendance of 60,000 is sometimes more than the combined turn-out at every other Scottish league match over the same weekend.

Celtic's prominent role in testimonials is an echo of their beginnings, as they were formed by Catholic priests in 1887 to play games that would generate funds for the poor. They quickly developed into a formidable team, winning 15 league titles by 1919, most of them under Willie Maley, the club's first manager.

The club had declined when their next great manager arrived in 1965, Jock Stein quickly engineering their first title in 11 years and extending the sequence to nine in a row. The high point was reached in 1967 when Celtic became Britain's first European champions, beating Inter Milan 2–1 with a team all born within 50 km (31 miles) of Celtic Park.

Celtic also reached the 1970 final, losing to Feyenoord, but they generally underperformed in Europe until their march to Seville in 2003. Since then they have made great strides in the Champions League, but only through their efforts on home turf. At the end of 2008 they had managed only one point in 20 away games in the competition proper.

GREATEST PLAYERS

> **HENRIK LARSSON (1997–2004)**
The Swedish forward played a key role as Celtic re-established domestic dominance over Rangers this decade. He was the league's leading scorer in his final four seasons at the club.

> **JIMMY JOHNSTONE (1963–75)**
A brilliant dribbler, the winger was voted by Celtic fans as the club's greatest ever player. He played in their European Cup winning team in 1967 and during their nine successive title-winning seasons.

MATTER OF FACT

Name: The Celtic Football Club
Stadium: Celtic Park
(capacity 60,832)
Address: Celtic Park, G40 3RE
To get there: Buses 43, 61, 62. Train
on Argyle Line (station: Dalmarnock)
Telephone: +44 871 226 1888
Email: th@celticfc.com
Website: www.celticfc.net

Stadium tour (includes museum –
you cannot just visit the museum)
Open: Mon–Sun, 11.00, 12.00, 13.45
and 14.30 (except match days). Extra
tours on Sat: 09.30, 10.00 and 10.30
Price: £8.50
Contact: Tel: +44 141 551 4308 or
email: visitorexperience@celticfc.co.uk

Home	Away

Trophies

1	European Cup/Champions League
42	Scottish League
34	Scottish Cup
13	Scottish League Cup

MAIN RIVALS

Celtic face city rivals Rangers (see
pages 24–25) in the Old Firm match.
Celtic, followed largely by Catholics,
and Rangers, with predominantly
Protestant fans, have long been bitter
enemies. Partick Thistle (tel: +44 141
579 1971, www.ptfc.co.uk) play at
Firhill (80 Firhill Road, G20 7AL).

Above: Celtic's Marc Crosas
outjumps Dundee United's
Morgaro Gomis.

THOMPSON TRAGEDY

Known as the Prince of Goalkeepers,
John Thompson was already a
Scotland international at 22 when
he faced Rangers in September
1931. Attempting a typically brave
save at the feet of Sam English, he
was kicked in the head and died
from his injuries.

RANGERS

Above: *Rangers hold the world record for domestic league titles won.*

TEN YEAR EURO RECORD		
Season	Competition	Finished
1998–99	Uefa Cup	Last 16
1999–00	Champs League	Group*
	Uefa Cup	Last 32
2000–01	Champs League	Group*
	Uefa Cup	Last 32
2001–02	Champs League	3rd qual rd
	Uefa Cup	Last 16
2002–03	Uefa Cup	1st round
2003–04	Champs League	Group
2004–05	Champs League	3rd qual rd
	Uefa Cup	Group
2005–06	Champs League	Last 16
2006–07	Uefa Cup	Last 16
2007–08	Champs League	Group
	Uefa Cup	Final

*1st of two group stages

The trophy hoarders

It is February 2006 and Rangers are the Scottish champions and League Cup holders. Their manager, Alex McLeish, has secured those trophies having won a domestic treble two years earlier. A recent draw against Inter Milan means his club are the first from Scotland to progress beyond the Champions League group stage since the competition replaced the European Cup in 1992. What happens? He is sacked.

Rangers are no ordinary club: witness their world-record 51 domestic league titles, in addition to 57 triumphs in the two main cup competitions. Moreover, most of those trophies have been lifted with one hand behind their back. For about 70 years until the late 1980s, they did not sign high-profile Catholic players, a nod to their mainly Protestant support.

The club established themselves as an enduring force between the two world wars, winning 11 of 13 titles from 1923 under the management of disciplinarian Bill Struth, who also oversaw the first treble by a Scottish team in 1948–49.

Willie Waddell, a player under Struth, was manager during perhaps the club's worst and best moments. The first occurred in 1971 when 66 fans were crushed to death at a match against Celtic. The second happened the next year, Rangers beating Dynamo Moscow to win the European Cup Winners' Cup.

Two trebles were secured in the mid-1970s but a decline set in until Graeme Souness arrived in 1986. The player-manager arrived like a hurricane, earning a red card for fighting on his debut and ignoring tradition by signing Mo Johnston, a Catholic and former Celtic star. Souness also blew Celtic away, setting the team on course for nine consecutive titles, equalling the record sequence of Rangers' big rivals.

GREATEST PLAYERS

> **JOHN GREIG (1960–78)**
The captain of the triumphant 1972 European Cup Winners' Cup team, Greig made a record 755 club appearances. For a defender or midfielder, his goal tally of 120 was impressive.

> **BRIAN LAUDRUP (1994–98)**
The Danish forward, a regular goalscorer and outstanding creator, helped Rangers sweep aside all domestic opposition. He was twice the Scottish Football Writers' Player of the Year.

MATTER OF FACT

Name: Rangers Football Club
Stadium: Ibrox (capacity 51,082)
Address: 150 Edmiston Drive, G51 2XD
To get there: Metro (station: Ibrox)
Telephone: +44 871 702 1972
Email: webmail@rangers.co.uk
Website: www.rangers.premiumtv.co.uk

Stadium tour (includes museum)
Open: Fri 11.00, 12.30 and 14.30. Sun 10.30, 11.00, 12.30, 13.00, 14.30 and 15.00
Price: £7
Contact: Phone and email as above

Home	Away

Trophies

1	European Cup Winners' Cup
51	Scottish League (including one shared)
32	Scottish Cup
25	Scottish League Cup

MAIN RIVALS

Celtic (see pages 22–23) are by far their biggest rivals, the Glasgow pair having been overwhelmingly the most successful clubs in Scottish football. City neighbours Partick Thistle (tel: +44 141 579 1971, www.ptfc.co.uk) were in the Premier League early this decade. They play at Firhill (80 Firhill Road, G20 7AL).

Above: *Sasa Papac (right) celebrates with team-mate Kris Boyd.*

'RATS' RIOT IN BARCELONA

The European Cup Winners' Cup final win over Dynamo Moscow in Barcelona in 1972 was marred by the rioting of Rangers fans, leading to a one-year ban for the club from European competition. Manager Willie Waddell criticized the supporters for their "gutter-rat behaviour".

DENMARK

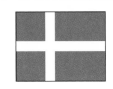

Capital: *Copenhagen.* **Language:** *Danish.* **Beer:** *Carlsberg, Tuborg.* **Food:** Frikadeller *(meatballs) with cabbage in white sauce, Danish pastries.* **National anthem:** *Der er et yndigt Land (There is a Lovely Land).* **Population:** *5,485,000.* **Time zone:** *GMT +1.* **Emergency number:** *112.* **Did you know?** *The Dannebrog, the country's national flag, is the oldest country flag still in use.* **Football body:** *Dansk Boldspil-Union, Allé 1, Brondby 2605; tel: +45 4326 2222, fax: +45 4326 2245, email: dbu@dbu.dk, website: www.dbu.dk. Founded 1889. Affiliated 1904.*

Below: Relaxed café culture in Copenhagen.

Better late than never

Denmark's leading players had expected to be on holiday in June 1992 while their coach, Richard Møller Nielsen, was planning to decorate his kitchen. Instead, they spent the month achieving the greatest feat in their country's footballing history. Summoned at short notice to replace war-torn Yugoslavia at Euro '92, they used their counter-attacking style to outlast their more talented opponents, including Germany in the final.

Yet Denmark arguably possessed a better side when coming up short in the previous decade. With Michael Laudrup and Preben Elkjær in attack, they reached the Euro '84 semi-finals, then beat West Germany and Uruguay 6–1 *en route* to the 1986 World Cup knock-out phase.

It was a case of making up for lost time. Having refused to pick their foreign-based professionals before the 1970s, and having also suffered from the absence of full-time players in the domestic league until that decade, Denmark's national team had long remained undistinguished. Their impressive modern-era record – for a nation of 5.5 million people – has also featured quarter-final appearances at the 1998 World Cup and Euro 2004, although their failure to qualify for the next two tournaments has been sobering.

The move to professionalism did little to help Denmark's clubs in European competition, however. None have contested a final, and the increasing tendency for the richer footballing nations to cream off the continental trophies means FC Copenhagen, Brøndby, Aalborg and the rest will struggle to break that duck.

Above: Streamers and cigarettes. *Below:* Frikadeller with cabbage and white sauce, anyone?

THE TEN YEAR GUIDE

Superliga

Season	Winner	Runner-up
1998–99	Aalborg	Brøndby
1999–00	Herfølge	Brøndby
2000–01	FC Copenhagen	Brøndby
2001–02	Brøndby	FC Copenhagen
2002–03	FC Copenhagen	Brøndby
2003–04	FC Copenhagen	Brøndby
2004–05	Brøndby	Copenhagen
2005–06	FC Copenhagen	Brøndby
2006–07	FC Copenhagen	Midtjylland
2007–08	Aalborg	Midtjylland

Landspokalturneringen

Season	Winner	Runner-up
1998–99	AB	Aalborg
1999–00	Viborg	Aalborg
2000–01	Silkeborg	AB
2001–02	Odense	FC Copenhagen
2002–03	Brøndby	Midtjylland
2003–04	FC Copenhagen	Aalborg
2004–05	Brøndby	Midtjylland
2005–06	Randers	Esbjerg
2006–07	Odense	FC Copenhagen
2007–08	Brøndby	Esbjerg

COPENHAGEN

The fairy tale city

Fairytale writer Hans Christian Andersen (and probably Carlsberg?) naturally dominate one's thoughts when Copenhagen is mentioned. *The Snow Queen*, *The Ugly Duckling*, *The Emperor's New Clothes* and *The Little Mermaid* remain popular to this day and the man is duly celebrated. It is the last of these stories that inspired a popular landmark and the city's main tourist attraction – the statue of the Little Mermaid was erected in the writer's honour in 1913. You will find it in the harbour, usually surrounded by a group of people; it is said that three out of every four people who come to the city visit the mermaid. Close by is the Amalienborg Palace if it's Danish royalty you are looking for, while just a few kilometres north is the home of FC Copenhagen.

The Copenhagen of today is a modern, thriving place. Look at any list of economic or social 'feel-good' indicators and Copenhagen will be near the top. In 2006 the country was named the happiest place in the world, and the city is consistently named in the top 20 when it comes to living standards. But be warned, it is also one of the world's most expensive cities. Modern and thriving comes at a price, and it'll come out of your pocket.

Copenhagen straddles the islands of Zealand and Amager and is linked to the Swedish city of Malmö by road and rail thanks to the Oresund Bridge (actually a bridge and a tunnel), which was completed in 2000.

There is evidence of people living here 6,000 years ago, probably thanks to good fishing initially, but the city charter was given to Copenhagen in 1254. The citizens had a wait of 551 years before H. C. Andersen came along and 593 years for Carlsberg.

Below: Although it has a historical past, Copenhagen is modern and thriving with spaces such as this new extension to the Royal Library on Copenhagen's waterfront.

3 THINGS YOU MUST DO...
(Apart from the football)

1 ORESUND BRIDGE
From the air this looks like a bridge that stops halfway and disappears into the sea. In some ways, it does. Leaving Malmö, the crossing is a winding 8 km (5 mile) bridge, when it reaches Pepparholmen, an artificially made island. From here it's a 4 km (2.5 mile) tunnel into Copenhagen.

2 CARLSBERG VISITORS' CENTRE
Probably the best thing to do in Copenhagen. The Visitors' Centre and Jacobsen Brewhouse (Gamle Carlsberg Vej 11, tel: +45 33 271 282). Open: Tues–Sun 10.00–16.00. Price: adults Kr50, ages 12–18 Kr35, children under 12 free entry. To get there: buses 18, 26.

3 VESTERBRO
Originally the city's red light district and meat-packing centre, today Vesterbro is the hippest attraction of Copenhagen with bars, shops, cafés and plenty of oh-so-cool people. The main street, and still shining its red lights, is Istedgade.

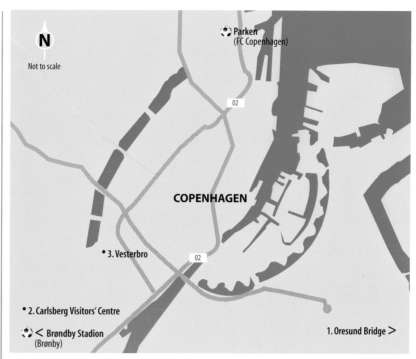

N
Not to scale

Parken
(FC Copenhagen)

02

COPENHAGEN

• 3. Vesterbro

02

• 2. Carlsberg Visitors' Centre

< Brøndby Stadion
(Brønby)

1. Oresund Bridge >

BARS > CLUBS > RESTAURANTS

Bars > Beautiful people, great mojitos, slick décor and sexy staff at **Café Ketchup** (Pilestræde 19, tel: +45 33 323 030). Another popular pre-club venue, and frankly it's worth a visit for its name alone, is **Pussy Galore's Flying Circus** (Sankt Hans Torv 30, tel: +45 35 245 300).

Clubs > **Rust** (Guldbergsgade 8, tel: +45 35 245 200) has been around since 1989 and is still pulling in near-on 700 people to their three floors. **Vega** (Enghavevej 40, tel +45 33 257 011) has a nightclub and two concert halls for live music.

Restaurants > Try the famous Danish *smørrebrød* at the (almost) equally famous **Ida Davidsen Restaurant** (Store Kongensgade 70, tel: +45 33 913 655). It will have to be for lunch because the restaurant closes at 4pm. **Café Sorgenfri** (8 Brolæggerstræde, tel: +45 33 115 880) is open later.

Below: Pussy Galore's Flying Circus has minimalistic decoration.

Weather	Low (°C)	High
January	-1	2
February	-2	2
March	0	5
April	2	9
May	7	15
June	11	18
July	12	20
August	12	21
September	10	16
October	7	11
November	2	6
December	0	2

FC COPENHAGEN

Above: FC Copenhagen players celebrate victory over Manchester United in the Champions League in 2006.

TEN YEAR EURO RECORD

Season	Competition	Finished
1998–99	C Winners' Cup	2nd round
1999–00	Intertoto Cup	2nd round
2000–01	DNQ	
2001–02	Champs League	3rd qual rd
	Uefa Cup	Last 32
2002–03	Uefa Cup	1st round
2003–04	Champs League	3rd qual rd
	Uefa Cup	2nd round
2004–05	Champs League	2nd qual rd
2005–06	Uefa Cup	1st round
2006–07	Champs League	Group
2007–08	Champs League	3rd qual rd
	Uefa Cup	Group

A capital feast

Consider this recipe for success. Take a well-supported club with the greatest history and stadium in the country but lacking money and top-flight status. Mix in a top-division neighbouring club with fine players but few fans. Sprinkle with the cash of a wealthy local businessman and serve just after the creation of the first wholly professional league.

This mouth-watering dish is FC Copenhagen, who were founded with a merger in 1992 and won the Danish league in their first season. After a subsequent lull, they had taken their championship haul to six by 2008, one behind B1903, one of the clubs from which they arose. The other of those clubs, KB, remain record champions with 15, but it may not be long before the latter's mark is challenged.

KB had twice tried and failed to adopt professionalism in the 1980s but possessed the freshly redeveloped Parken stadium, the plush base for the national team. For their part, B1903 could offer a decent team who had beaten Bayern Munich 6–2 the previous season, so FC Copenhagen took the bulk of them along with their coach, Benny Johansen. Moreover B1903 had an entrepreneur on hand, Alex Friedmann, anxious for a more attractive venture in which to invest.

Copenhagen are either a modern phenomenon or an institution with long traditions. Those who consider them to be a continuation of KB focus on the latter's formation in 1876 as the first club created in Europe outside the British Isles.

The new club became Denmark's best-supported team in the 1990s, but the turning point came with a Stock Exchange flotation in 1997, which allowed them to buy their Parken stadium and thus earn revenue from its many other uses.

GREATEST PLAYERS

> **SIBUSISO ZUMA (2000–05)**
The striker won three titles at the club, scoring with a scissor-kick from the edge of the penalty area in the win over Brondby that clinched the league in 2000–01.

> **CHRISTIAN POULSEN (2000–02)**
The combative midfielder made his debut aged 20 and helped Copenhagen win the title in his first season. His fine form earned a €7 million move to Schalke 04.

MATER OF FACT
Name: Football Club København
Stadium: Parken (capacity 41,000 when rebuilding completed)
Address: Oester Allé 50, 2100
To get there: Buses 1A, 3, 14, 15, 18, 184, 185, 150S. S-train from central station to Østerport station.
Telephone: +45 35 43 74 00
Email: info@fck.dk
Website: www.fck.dk

Stadium tour
Contact the club for details

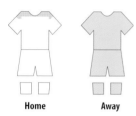

Home   **Away**

Trophies
6   Danish League
3   Danish Cup

Main rivals
Brøndby (tel: +45 4363 0810, www.brondby.com) are great foes who play on the outskirts of Copenhagen at Brøndby Stadion (Brøndby Stadion 30, 2605). The pair contest the New Firm derby.

Above: FC Copenhagen fans have had plenty to cheer about in recent years.

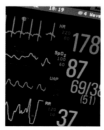

DAY OF NEAR-TRAGEDY
When Copenhagen's Ståle Solbakken collapsed during a training session in 2001, his heart stopped for several minutes before he was revived *en route* to hospital in an ambulance. He recovered fully and spoke of his desire to play again, but eventually took medical advice and retired.

ENGLAND

THE
3
MINUTE
GUIDE

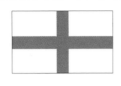

Capital: *London.* **Language:** *English.* **Beer:** *John Smith's, Old Speckled Hen.* **Food:** *Fish and chips, curry.* **National anthem:** *God Save the Queen.* **Population:** *60,944,000.* **Time zone:** *GMT.* **Emergency Number:** *999.* **Did you know?** *No word in the English language rhymes with orange or silver.* **Football body:** *The Football Association Ltd, 25 Soho Square, London W1D 4FA; tel: +44 20 7745 4545, fax: +44 20 7745 4546, email: communique@thefa.com, website: www.thefa.com. Founded 1863. Affiliated 1905.*

Below: Bold contemporary architecture often mixes with traditional styles in England.

Better late than never

Is this the best or the worst of times for the English game? The standard of football suggests the former interpretation; the predictability points to the latter.

The Premier League has become Europe's strongest league through lucrative television rights contracts, clever marketing, worldwide interest and huge numbers of spectators. This superiority was illustrated when England supplied three of the Champions League semi-finalists in 2007 and 2008. The latter season provided the ultimate show of strength. Manchester United beat Chelsea in the final after the other two representatives, Arsenal and Liverpool, only exited the competition via defeat by Chelsea.

However, while those four clubs fly the flag abroad, they leave their hapless rivals waving the white flag at home. Fortified by regular Champions League income, the quartet constituted the Premier League's top four for the third successive season in 2007–08, yet no four teams had managed this feat even twice in a row until the turn of the millennium. The days are over when English fans could laugh at other, stagnant European leagues with their Big Twos, Threes and Fours.

The England team have also been afflicted by predictability, namely the certainty that they will fail to reach a final on foreign land. The nation that first brought structure to the game has managed to reach only one major final, which came when they lifted the 1966 World Cup in London. No wonder England are keen to host the tournament again.

Above: Three Lions on their chest. *Below:* Trooping the Colour celebrates the Queen's birthday.

THE TEN YEAR GUIDE

Premier League

Season	Winner	Runner-up
1998–99	Manchester United	Arsenal
1999–00	Manchester United	Arsenal
2000–01	Manchester United	Arsenal
2001–02	Arsenal	Liverpool
2002–03	Manchester United	Arsenal
2003–04	Arsenal	Chelsea
2004–05	Chelsea	Arsenal
2005–06	Chelsea	Manchester United
2006–07	Manchester United	Chelsea
2007–08	Manchester United	Chelsea

FA Cup

Season	Winner	Runner-up
1998–99	Manchester United	Newcastle United
1999–00	Chelsea	Aston Villa
2000–01	Liverpool	Arsenal
2001–02	Arsenal	Chelsea
2002–03	Arsenal	Southampton
2003–04	Manchester United	Millwall
2004–05	Arsenal	Manchester United
2005–06	Liverpool	West Ham United
2006–07	Chelsea	Manchester United
2007–08	Portsmouth	Cardiff City

LONDON

Football, royalty and chatty taxi drivers

Travel on London's famous Underground on a weekend or weekday evening and it will be rare if you don't come across a group of (mostly) men travelling to or from a game of football and singing out of tune. With 13 professional clubs, numerous non-league clubs, plus England internationals at Wembley, it's unlikely you'll go short of your football fix in one of the world's great capitals.

With more tourist books on London than other cities have attractions, if you struggle for something to do while you are here then you are probably still in bed. Pubs? On every street corner. History? Buckingham Palace, the Houses of Parliament, the whole city. Theatre? Head to the West End. Museums, clubs, fashion, royalty, parks and football, this is a city that can offer it all. You want a chat with a Londoner? Get in a taxi. Drivers are paid to take you where you are going and give you their views on everything from politics to the national obsession, the weather. Fancy a kickaround? Put on your sports shoes and head to a park where you will find any number of casual games to get you puffing.

People have lived along this part of the River Thames, where London is situated, for thousands of years, and today more than 7.5 million people call it home. Famously the city grew as a collection of villages simply merged together, which is why you will find pockets of neighborhood life like other great old cities such as New York and Paris.

Among the city's clubs you will find Arsenal and Tottenham to the north (along with Wembley Stadium), Chelsea and Fulham to the south-west and West Ham to the east, not far from the 2012 Olympic Stadium.

Below: A view from the Houses of Parliament towards Big Ben, the River Thames and the London Eye.

3 THINGS YOU MUST DO...
(Apart from the football)

1 WEMBLEY STADIUM

The new 90,000 seater Wembley Stadium (No.1 Olympic Way, Wembley, tel: +44 844 800 2755) is the England national team home. Open: tours daily 09.30–16.30. Price: adults £15, children £8. To get there: tube to Wembley Park Station or Wembley Central, or rail to Wembley Stadium or Wembley Central.

2 INDIAN FOOD

Hot, spicy, mild, expensive, cheap, smart, down-at-heel – the country's favourite food comes in all guises, with over 2,000 Indian restaurants in the city. You'll find a 'curry house' on virtually every street. Try Brick Lane, which has a concentration of them that will astound. To get there: tube to Aldgate East.

3 GREYHOUND RACING

Not as glorious as it was in its heyday, but dog racing is still a great night out. Wimbledon Greyhound Stadium (Plough Lane, tel: +44 870 840 8905). Open: Tues, Fri, Sat, racing from 19.30. Price: adults £5, juniors 12–17 £2.50. To get there: rail to Haydons Road or tube to Wimbledon or Tooting Broadway.

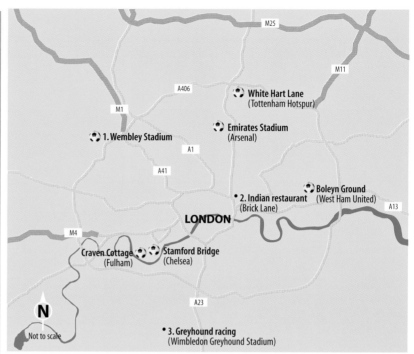

M25
M11
A406
M1
A1
A41
M4

White Hart Lane (Tottenham Hotspur)
Emirates Stadium (Arsenal)
1. Wembley Stadium
Boleyn Ground (West Ham United)
2. Indian restaurant (Brick Lane)
A13
LONDON
Craven Cottage (Fulham)
Stamford Bridge (Chelsea)
A23

N
Not to scale

3. Greyhound racing (Wimbledon Greyhound Stadium)

BARS > CLUBS > RESTAURANTS

Bars > For champagne and people-watching head to **Claridge's Bar** (Brook Street, Mayfair, tel: +44 20 7629 8860). **Cheers** (72 Regent Street, tel: + 44 20 7494 3322) offers a more laid-back vibe.

Clubs > For a stylish night in the heart of the city try **Chinawhite** (6 Air Street, Soho, tel: +44 20 7343 0040). And if you can get through the door then **Mahiki** (1 Dover Street, Mayfair, tel: + 44 20 7493 9529) is where you can mix with celebrities and royalty on two floors. More relaxed and always busy with a diverse crowd is **Tiger Tiger** (29 Haymarket, tel: +44 20 7930 1885).

Restaurants > Verraswamy (99 Regent Street, tel: +44 20 7734 1401) is pricey, but said to be the country's oldest Indian restaurant. Or for pricey celebrity food, try Jamie Oliver's **Fifteen** (15 Westland Place, tel: +44 871 330 1515).

Below: You'll find champagne cool at Claridges

Weather	Low (ºC)	High
January	1	6
February	1	7
March	2	9
April	3	12
May	7	17
June	10	18
July	11	21
August	11	22
September	8	18
October	6	15
November	3	10
December	2	7

ARSENAL

Above: Arsenal's Thierry Henry (left) and Robert Pires after winning the Premiership in 2004.

TEN YEAR EURO RECORD		
Season	Competition	Finished
1998–99	Champs League	Group
1999–00	Champs League	Group*
	Uefa Cup	Final
2000–01	Champs League	QF
2001–02	Champs League	Group**
2002–03	Champs League	Group**
2003–04	Champs League	QF
2004–05	Champs League	Last 16
2005–06	Champs League	Final
2006–07	Champs League	Last 16
2007–08	Champs League	QF

*1st of two group stages
**2nd of two group stages

From villains to heroes

To their detractors, some great Arsenal sides were lucky (1930s) or boring (half a century later), but the latest batch of trophy-winners have enjoyed adulation from neutrals. The club that was a byword for tradition, steadiness and even sterility have been given an exhilarating makeover by Arsène Wenger.

By influencing English football, the French manager took the innovative path of Herbert Chapman, who transformed a trophyless club into a world-famous one. Appointed in 1925, he changed training methods, advocated numbers on players' shirts and added an extra centre back to combat the new offside rule.

That tactical switch – widely copied – prompted cries of "Lucky Arsenal" as they thrived while sitting back, seemingly outplayed yet securing victories on the counter-attack. To prove it was no fluke, they won five league titles in the 1930s.

Chants of "Boring, boring Arsenal" during George Graham's spell as manager were closer to the mark, although they supplied English league football's most dramatic moment, when Michael Thomas's goal in the final seconds against Liverpool in 1989 pipped their opponents to the title on goals scored. Graham, part of the Arsenal team that won the League and Cup Double in 1971, collected another title in 1991 before the decline that led to Wenger's arrival in 1996.

The new manager, whose scientific approach to training and diet was copied by other clubs, secured a top-two finish in each of his first eight full seasons. They won the double in 1998 and 2002.

But further modernization awaited this pillar of the English game. In 2006 Arsenal's slick football moved to the impressive new Emirates Stadium. The 60,000 fans who attend certainly think they are lucky.

GREATEST PLAYERS

> THIERRY HENRY (1999–2007)
The French striker was arguably the finest player in the English league for two or three seasons, and a familiar figure at the top of the goalscoring and assists chart.

> ALEX JAMES (1929–37)
Just 5ft 5in tall, James was a brilliant passer who specialized in launching Arsenal's famous counter-attacks. The Scottish inside forward was the key player in the great 1930s side.

MATTER OF FACT

Name: Arsenal Football Club
Stadium: Emirates Stadium
(capacity 60,361)
Address: Drayton Park, N5 1BU
To get there: Tube on Piccadilly Line
(station: Arsenal), Victoria Line (station: Finsbury Park). Buses 1, 4, 17, 19,
29, 30, 43, 91, 106, 153, 159, 210, 236,
253, 254, 259, 271, 277, 393, W3, W7.
Telephone: +44 20 7619 5000
Email: via www.arsenal.com/
the-club/contact-directory
Website: www.arsenal.com

Stadium tour (includes museum)
Open: Mon–Fri first 9.30, last 15.00,
Sat–Sun first 9.30, last 14.00
Price: £12 (£15 weekends in July and
August). Museum only: £6
Contact: Phone as above or via
https://bookings.arsenal.com

Home	Away

Trophies

1	European Cup Winners' Cup
1	Inter-Cities Fairs Cup/Uefa Cup
13	English League
10	FA Cup
2	League Cup

Main rivals

The biggest enemies are North London
neighbours Tottenham Hotspur (tel:
+44 844 499 5000, www.tottenham
hotspur.com) who play at White Hart
Lane (748 High Road, N17 0AP).
Chelsea (see pages 38–39) are the
strongest city rivals. West Ham United
(tel: +44 20 8548 2748, www.whufc.
com) play at Upton Park (Green Street,
E13 9AZ). Fulham (tel: +44 870 442
1222, www.fulhamfc.com) play at
Craven Cottage (Stevenage Road,
SW6 6HH).

Above: The Emirates Stadium.

HOORAY FOR HENRY

Arsenal have played top-flight football since 1919 but reached the elite
controversially after finishing only
fifth in the second division. Henry
Norris, (second from right), chairman,
persuaded the Football League to
promote Arsenal ahead of the clubs
who finished third and fourth.

CHELSEA

Above: *Chelsea fans prepare for more trophies.*

The Roman Empire

TEN YEAR EURO RECORD		
Season	Competition	Finished
1998–99	C Winners' Cup	SF
1999–00	Champs League	QF
2000–01	Uefa Cup	1st round
2001–02	Uefa Cup	2nd round
2002–03	Uefa Cup	1st round
2003–04	Champs League	SF
2004–05	Champs League	SF
2005–06	Champs League	Last 16
2006–07	Champs League	SF
2007–08	Champs League	Final

In Chukotka, eastern Russia, one man possessed incredible wealth. In Porto, northern Portugal, another man possessed incredible self-assurance and tactical acumen. When Chelsea paired Roman Abramovich and Jose Mourinho in 2004, a century-old club afflicted by chronic under-achievement suddenly tripled their championship haul in the next two years.

This odd couple – Abramovich rarely spoke in public, Mourinho barely stopping talking – proved an irresistible mix. Chelsea, whose sole league triumph had come in 1955, won the 2005 title with 95 points, the best top-flight campaign by any side since 1889, and easily retained their crown. A falling out between the two men led to the Portuguese's departure.

Yet some Chelsea fans have mixed feelings about this success, with Abramovich, an oil billionaire, having pumped around £600 million into the club to fund

transfer spending unprecedented in English football. Many yearn for the earthy days of the 1980s, when the team played in the second tier, but, then again, most supporters are just enjoying the ride.

Rivals have mocked Chelsea as a modern-day plastic club with no tradition, but their attendances have been among the country's top ten almost throughout their existence. Their lack of trophies – nothing until the 1970 FA Cup – despite such backing, gave comedians some cheap laughs. That reputation grew in the 1960s, an era when film stars turned up at Stamford Bridge to watch a flamboyant team, when style triumphed over substance. The pragmatic Mourinho switched those two elements around.

Then Mourinho left and Abramovich cut his spending but, well established in England's Big Four, they are unlikely to slip back into joke books for a while.

GREATEST PLAYERS

> **FRANK LAMPARD (2001–)**
Accused of benefiting from nepotism at West Ham United, where his father was assistant manager, Lampard, a goalscoring midfielder, has made a nonsense of those claims with consistent excellence.

> **JOHN TERRY (1998–)**
While Chelsea have scoured the world for the best players, club-reared Terry has provided an English thread through the past decade, brave and outstanding in central defence.

MATTER OF FACT
Name: Chelsea Football Club
Stadium: Stamford Bridge
(capacity 41,841)
Address: Fulham Road, SW6 1HS
To get there: Tube on District Line to
Fulham Broadway. Buses 14, 211, 414
Telephone: +44 20 7386 9373
Email: enquiries@chelseafc.com
Website: www.chelseafc.com

Stadium tour (includes museum)
Open: Mon–Sun (except match days
and days before Champions League
games) 11.00, 12.00, 13.00, 14.00 and
15.00. Museum: Mon–Sun
10.30–16.30
Price: £15; museum only £6
Contact: Phone as above or email:
tours@chelseafc.com

| **Home** | **Away** |

Trophies
2	European Cup Winners' Cup
3	English League
4	FA Cup
4	League Cup

Main rivals
Arsenal (see pages 36–37) are
Chelsea's strongest London opponents.
There is also an intense rivalry with
Tottenham Hotspur (tel: +44 844 499
5000, www.tottenhamhotspur.com),
who play at White Hart Lane (748 High
Road, N17 0AP), and with West Ham
United (tel: +44 20 8548 2748,
www.whufc.com), who play at Upton
Park (Green Street, E13 9AZ). Fulham
(tel: +44 870 442 1222, www.
fulhamfc.com), who play at Craven
Cottage (Stevenage Road, SW6 6HH),
are the nearest neighbours.

Above: Chelsea's Stamford Bridge.

KEN'S SHOCKING PLAN
In the mid-1980s, with Chelsea fans
among the worst offenders as hooliganism blighted English football,
chairman Ken Bates proposed to
keep them off the pitch by building
an electric fence around the perime-
ter. However, the local authorities
banned him from doing so.

LIVERPOOL

Dock city rivalry

This is a city dominated by the rivalry of its two great clubs – the blue of Everton and the red of Liverpool. The two stadiums, Goodison Park and Anfield, sit within sight of one another, separated only by the urban space of Stanley Park. They are a few kilometres inland from the city's famous docks and northeast from the city centre.

The centre is compact, with main hubs such as Lime Street and Central railway stations and the Clayton Square and St John's shopping centres all close together. The city has a reputation for its architecture and many of the significant buildings – the World Museum, the Walker Art Gallery, the central library and St Georges Hall – are clustered around here. The city's most famous building, though, is the Royal Liver Building and this can be found riverside looking out across the water to the Wirral.

This is also where you will find Albert Dock, perhaps the best known of all the docks in this port city. Now the most popular place for visitors to the city, the converted warehouses of Albert Dock house shops, restaurants, bars and a range of other attractions such as Tate Liverpool, the Maritime Museum, the International Slavery Museum, and in homage to the city's musical sons, The Beatles Story.

The Fab Four are, of course, the city legends, and Liverpool has a rich musical heritage, being the birthplace to, among others, Echo and the Bunnymen, Frankie Goes to Hollywood and Gerry and the Pacemakers, who immortalized the city's river with their hit 'Ferry Cross the Mersey'.

Below: Grand architecture sits comfortably with warehouses in Albert Dock.

3 THINGS YOU MUST DO...
(Apart from the football)

1 MERSEY FERRY
All together now, 'Ferry Cross the Mersey...' A great and inexpensive way to see the city is to hop on the ferry (tel: +44 151 639 0609). Open: Mon–Fri 07.20–19.15, Sat–Sun 09.05–19.10. Price: adults from £1.45 single, children from £1.15 single. To get there: to Pier Head, Merseyrail to James St Station.

2 ALBERT DOCK
Enough to keep you busy day and night, there are an endless supply of Liverpool's visitor attractions, eateries and bars at the dock (2 Edward Pavilion, tel: +44 151 708 7334). To get there: smart buses 1 and 4A.

3 THE CAVERN CLUB
The club (10 Mathew Street, tel: +44 151 236 1965) has hosted the Beatles, Hollies, Rolling Stones and Yardbirds among others. Open Mon–Tues 11.00–19.00, Wed 11.00–00.00, Thur 11.00–02.00, Fri–Sat 11.00–02.30, Sun 11.00–00.30. Price: free except Sat–Sun after 18.00 when it's £1. To get there: it's in the city centre.

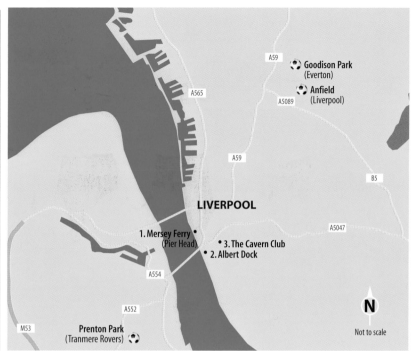

A59 · A565 · A5089 · Goodison Park (Everton) · Anfield (Liverpool) · A59 · B5

LIVERPOOL

1. Mersey Ferry (Pier Head) · 3. The Cavern Club · 2. Albert Dock · A5047 · A554 · A552 · M53 · Prenton Park (Tranmere Rovers)

N

Not to scale

BARS > CLUBS > RESTAURANTS
Bars > Get your Beatles fix to the full at **Rubber Soul** (2–8 Mathew Street, tel: +44 151 474 8845), the same street in which you will find the **Cavern Club** (*see* left). Or try **Flanagan's Apple** (18 Mathew Street, tel: +44 151 231 6821), an Irish bar in a city which truly can claim a heritage to the country it represents.

Clubs > The Krazy House (16 Wood St, tel: +44 151 708 5016) offers a diversity of music depending on the night of the week. Check to see if your particular brand of dancing juice is on offer.

Restaurants > Mayur (130 Duke Street, tel: +44 151 709 9955) offers Indian food in a designer setting. **Il Forno** (132 Duke Street, tel: +44 151 709 4002) is for lovers of Italian food in a slightly more informal setting.

Below: The Beatles and Liverpool go hand in hand.

Weather	Low (ºC)	High
January	2	6
February	2	6
March	3	9
April	4	11
May	8	15
June	10	17
July	12	20
August	13	19
September	10	16
October	7	12
November	4	9
December	2	7

LIVERPOOL

Above: *The Liverpool line-up of 2008–09 prepare for action.*

TEN YEAR EURO RECORD		
Season	Competition	Finished
1998–99	Uefa Cup	Last 16
1999–00	DNQ	
2000–01	Uefa Cup	Winners
2001–02	Champs League	QF
2002–03	Champs League	Group*
	Uefa Cup	QF
2003–04	Uefa Cup	Last 16
2004–05	Champs League	Winners
2005–06	Champs League	Last 16
2006–07	Champs League	Final
2007–08	Champs League	SF

*1st of two group stages

Triumph meets disaster

At the height of their triumph, Liverpool were taken to the depths of despair by tragedy. In an era when they enjoyed the most successful period of any English club both domestically (ten league titles in 15 years from 1976, better than Manchester United's ten in 16 from 1993) and in Europe (four times European champions in eight years from 1977), they were at the centre of the Heysel and Hillsborough disasters.

The fact that Liverpool progressed to those matches – the 1985 European Cup final against Juventus and a 1989 FA Cup semi-final against Nottingham Forest – underlined their pre-eminence, but the fixtures brought no celebrations. Their pursuit of successive European Cups became incidental given the death of 39 fans, mostly Italians, after a wall collapsed amid crowd trouble at Heysel Stadium. Then their attempt to become England's first team to win two League and Cup doubles was overshadowed when 96 of their fans were crushed to death at Hillsborough.

The two disasters arguably contributed to Liverpool's 1990s fall. Deprived of continental experience because of their six-year, post-Heysel ban they took until 2001 to win another European trophy, the second-rate Uefa Cup. As for Hillsborough, the tragedy affected manager Kenny Dalglish badly and probably contributed to his resignation in 1991. His replacement, Graeme Souness, oversaw a decline.

Liverpool did, though, win their long-awaited fifth European Cup in 2005, with Spanish manager Rafael Benítez guiding a team with only two Englishmen. That continued a tradition of sorts: the team's first league line-up in 1893 featured nine Scots. Then, in the 1960s, it was a Scot in the shape of Bill Shankly who set the club on the path to success.

GREATEST PLAYERS

> KENNY DALGLISH (1977–88)
Signed from Celtic as a replacement striker when Kevin Keegan left for Hamburg, Dalglish could see several moves ahead of many opponents. Formed a great partnership with prolific goal poacher Ian Rush.

> STEVEN GERRARD (1998–)
A swashbuckling midfielder, Gerrard has driven on Liverpool by example. His incredible energy and determination have led to countless crucial late goals, notably his long-distance equalizer in the dying moments of the 2006 FA Cup final victory over West Ham.

MATTER OF FACT
Name: Liverpool Football Club
Stadium: Anfield (capacity 45,276)
Address: Anfield Road, L4 0TH
To get there: Buses 14, 17, 19, 26, 27, 68, 168, 217
Telephone: +44 151 263 2361
Email: customerservices@ liverpoolfc.tv
Website: www.liverpoolfc.tv

Stadium tour (includes museum)
Open: Mon–Sun (except match days), 10.00, 11.00, 12.00, 13.00, 14.00 and 15.00. Museum: Mon–Sun, 10.00–17.00 (closes match days 30 mins before kick-off). Booking recommended
Price: £10; museum: £5
Contact: Tel: +44 151 260 6677

Home   **Away**

Trophies
5	European Cup/Champions League
3	Inter-Cities Fairs Cup/Uefa Cup
18	English League
7	FA Cup
7	League Cup

Main rivals
Everton (tel: +44 871 663 1878, www.evertonfc.com) are the neighbours across Stanley Park. They play at Goodison Park (Goodison Road, L4 4EL). Tranmere Rovers (tel: +44 871 221 2001, www.tranmererovers.co.uk), Merseyside's other league club, play at Prenton Park (Prenton Road West, Birkenhead, CH42 9PY). Liverpool's biggest enemies are Manchester United (see pages 46–47).

MAKING THE WRONG HEADLINES
Liverpool manager Graeme Souness underwent a triple heart bypass in 1992, and gave an exclusive inter-view to *The Sun* newspaper. This infuriated the many Liverpool supporters who had accused the paper of unfairly criticizing fans' behaviour during the Hillsborough disaster.

Above: The Kop, the famous stand for Liverpool's most fervent fans.

MANCHESTER

Let the music play

Today, sport and music run deep in the veins of this city, which originally built itself on the industrial strength of cotton and textiles. Manchester United and Manchester City are the city's football clubs, and there are many more within just a few kilometres. The 2002 Commonwealth Games were held here and helped boost the city's already impressive sporting facilities, with the National Squash Centre, Manchester Velodrome, Manchester Aquatics Centre and, most significantly, the City of Manchester Stadium, now the home of City.

But it is music that has given Manchester its verve. The Stone Roses, Inspiral Carpets, Simply Red, The Happy Mondays, and the less happy The Smiths were just some of the bands that formed the backbone of the city's line-up as Manchester stamped its mark on the UK's indie music scene in the 1980s. Before them was the punk of the Buzzcocks, Joy Division (and New Order) and in the 1960s Herman's Hermits and The Hollies. Take That and Oasis emerged in the 1990s. Legendary music venue the Haçienda was central to all this (it also drove the acid house and rave scene), and today venues like the huge Manchester Arena, Academy and Apollo continue the proud music tradition.

In the city centre near Victoria railway station is the Arndale Centre, Europe's biggest shopping centre with more than 220 shops. Originally built in the 1970s, it has been redeveloped extensively after 1996 when the city centre was the target of a bombing by the IRA.

Manchester United's home, Old Trafford, is about 5 km (3 miles) southwest of the centre.

Below: The Pop Café, the perfect symbol for a city that thrives on its music.

3 THINGS YOU MUST DO...
(Apart from the football)

1 URBIS
Urbis (Cathedral Gardens, tel: +44 161 605 8200) is a centrally located venue that has constantly changing exhibitions, events and tours that celebrate city life. Open: daily 10.00–18.00. Prices: vary. To get there: it's next to Victoria railway station.

2 CITY OF MANCHESTER STADIUM
The 48,000-seater stadium (SportCity, tel: +44 870 062 1894 for bookings) was built for the 2002 Commonwealth Games and is now the home of Manchester City. The regular tour lasts 60 minutes and ends with the club museum, although there is a 20 minute 'Walk of Pride' tour if you are in a rush.

3 COMEDY STORE
It's a nightclub, theatre, bar and restaurant, but go to the Comedy Store (1a–3a Deansgate Locks, tel: +44 161 839 9595) for the laughs. Open: Wed–Sun, comedy starts at 20.00. Prices: from £9.50. To get there: metrolink to Gmex.

MANCHESTER
- 1. Urbis
- 2. City of Manchester Stadium (Manchester City)
- 3. Comedy Store

Old Trafford (Manchester United)

N

Not to scale

BARS > CLUBS > RESTAURANTS

Bars > Looking for the best cocktails in the city? Then head to **Socio Rehab** (100–102 High Street, tel: +44 161 832 4529). **Marble Beer House** (57 Manchester Road, tel: +44 161 881 9206) is about beer, not cocktails. Situated about a 25-minute walk from Old Trafford, this is the perfect spot to start your pre-match drinks and has beer from its own microbrewery.

Clubs > Circle Club (Barton Arcade, tel: +44 161 839 9767). If you can get 'on the list' you will find a super cool club. Otherwise try **The Music Box** (65 Oxford Street, tel: +44 161 236 9971).

Restaurants > Rub shoulders with the rich and famous while eating great seafood in fantastically opulent surroundings in the city centre's **Ithaca** (36 John Dalton Street, tel: +44 870 740 4000). **The Gaucho Grill** (2a St Mary's Street, tel: +44 161 833 4333) is a top Argentinean steakhouse.

Below: Space-age fun at Manchester airport.

Weather	Low (ºC)	High
January	1	6
February	1	6
March	2	8
April	4	11
May	7	15
June	10	17
July	13	19
August	12	20
September	10	16
October	7	13
November	4	9
December	2	7

MANCHESTER UNITED

Above: Manchester United fans in Red Square, Moscow, during the 2008 Uefa Champions League.

TEN YEAR EURO RECORD		
Season	Competition	Finished
1998–99	Champs League	Winners
1999–00	Champs League	QF
2000–01	Champs League	QF
2001–02	Champs League	SF
2002–03	Champs League	QF
2003–04	Champs League	Last 16
2004–05	Champs League	Last 16
2005–06	Champs League	Group
2006–07	Champs League	SF
2007–08	Champs League	Winners

The business of winning

It was all coming together for Manchester United in 1992, a quarter-century since they were last champions. As football embraced commerce, such as the sale of replica shirts, the club were tapping into arguably the world's largest fanbase. And as the new Premier League kicked off, fuelled by satellite television's huge investment, England's higher-ranked teams could now earn fortunes in prize money.

United began a dash for cash and trophies, winning the new league's first title in 1993 and taking their tally to ten by 2008, all secured under Sir Alex Ferguson's management. While the Scot utilized the fine crop of early 1990s club trainees, he also used the club's vast wealth in the transfer market. The success tempts 76,000 fans to home games, a quarter more than any other English club, consolidating income.

Not that the finances and fanbase should detract from the feats of Ferguson, who has turned an under-achieving club into European champions twice, the first in 1999 as part of a treble that also featured the League and FA Cup.

He was not the first Scottish manager to transform United. Inheriting an ailing club in 1945, Sir Matt Busby established a philosophy of attacking football that remains today, creating the youthful Busby Babes team, who threatened to conquer Europe. After that dream was destroyed when eight of them died in a plane crash in Munich in 1958, Busby built another great side, this one lifting the European Cup in 1968.

United's glorious history and lucrative present persuaded the American Glazer family to buy them in 2005, saddling the club with a £666 million debt. Back-to-back titles followed, but a nagging nervousness afflicts fans over the takeover.

GREATEST PLAYERS

> **GEORGE BEST (1963–74)**
The Northern Ireland forward is considered by many to have been the greatest British player ever. Brave, skilful and impudent, he was European Footballer of the Year in 1968.

> **ERIC CANTONA (1992–97)**
Signed from Leeds United for just £1 million, the French forward inspired four league titles in his five seasons at the club and galvanized the young players with his diligent training.

MATTER OF FACT

Name: Manchester United Football Club

Stadium: Old Trafford (capacity 76,022)

Address: Sir Matt Busby Way, Old Trafford, M16 0RA

To get there: Metrolink tram in direction of Altrincham (station: Old Trafford). Train from mainline stations (station: Manchester United FC Halt). Buses 17, 114, 115, 252, 253, 254, 255, 256, 257, 263, 264

Telephone: +44 161 868 8000

Email: enquiries@manutd.co.uk

Website: www.manutd.com

Stadium tour (includes museum)
Open: Mon–Sun, 09.40–16.30.
Museum: Mon–Sun, 09.30–17.00
Price: £11.74; museum: £8.32
Contact: Phone as above, or email tours@manutd.co.uk

Home	Away

Trophies

3	European Cup/Champions League
1	European Cup Winners' Cup
17	English League
11	FA Cup
2	League Cup

Main rivals

Liverpool (see pages 42–43) and Manchester City (tel: +44 870 062 1894, www.mcfc.co.uk), who play at the City of Manchester Stadium (SportCity, M11 3FF). Open: tours Mon–Sat at 10.30, 14.00 and 15.15, Sun and holidays 11.45 and 13.45. Museum Mon–Sat 9.30–16.30, Sun and holidays 11.00–15.00. Price: adults £9.50, concessions £6. To get there: buses 53, 54, 185, 186, 216, 217, 230, 231, 232, 233, 234, 235, 236, 237, X36 and X37.

Above: Manchester United's Wayne Rooney celebrates after scoring.

PLAYERS LEFT IN A FIX

With United in danger of relegation from the top division in 1915, three of their players conspired with four Liverpool players to fix the result of a match between the teams. United duly won 2–0 but the players were caught and all banned for life.

BELGIUM

THE

3

MINUTE GUIDE

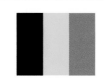

Capital: *Brussels.* **Languages:** *French, Flemish, some German.* **Beer:** *Trappist, Lambic, Stella Artois.* **Food:** *Mussels and frites, waffles.* **National anthem:** *La Brabançonne (The Song of Brabant).* **Population:** *10,404,000.* **Time zone:** *GMT +1.* **Emergency Number:** *112.* **Did you know?** *The world's first printed weekly newspaper was published in Antwerp.* **Football body:** *Union Royale Belge des Sociétés de Football-Association145, Avenue Houba de Strooper Bruxelles 1020; tel: +32 24 77 1211, fax: +32 24 78 2391, email: urbsfa.kbvb@footbel.com, website: www.footbel.com. Founded 1895. Affiliated 1904.*

Below: The next best thing to football — Belgian beer! And there's plenty.

When Belgians were famous

Aside from raising its head between the mid-1970s and late 1980s, Belgian football has largely stayed hidden away from the spotlight. For that brief period, though, the country made a major impression on the global game, for better or for worse.

The country's adoption of full professionalism in 1972 sparked great successes. All four of Belgium's European club competition wins came between 1976 and 1988, their only European Cup (or Champions League) final appearance was made by Bruges in 1978, and the national team recorded their best achievements in the European championship (1980 final) and World Cup (1986 semi-finals).

The period contained many scandals, however. In 1982 Standard Liége plotted to bribe league opponents to smooth their preparations for a European final, and two years later Anderlecht paid a referee to let them reach a European final. Worst of all, the ill-equipped Heysel Stadium in Brussels witnessed the death of 39 spectators at the 1985 European Cup final between Liverpool and Juventus after a wall collapsed amid hooliganism.

Belgium's split between Flemish and French speakers is reflected in their football, with Flemish-area Bruges and Francophile Anderlecht from Brussels collecting about two-thirds of the country's post-war league titles. But the 1995 Bosman ruling gave players greater freedom and thus strengthened wealthier footballing nations, preventing Anderlecht, Bruges and their domestic rivals from recreating Belgium's golden period in Europe.

Above Parading and pomp in Belgium. *Below:* Ahhh. Manneken Pis in Brussels.

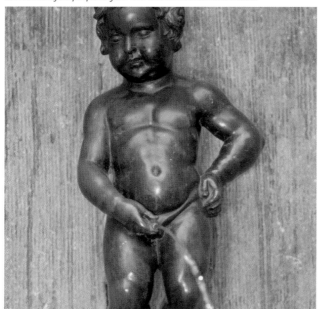

THE TEN YEAR GUIDE

Jupiler League

Season	Winner	Runner-up
1998–99	Genk	Bruges
1999–00	Anderlecht	Bruges
2000–01	Anderlecht	Bruges
2001–02	Genk	Bruges
2002–03	Bruges	Anderlecht
2003–04	Anderlecht	Bruges
2004–05	Bruges	Anderlecht
2005–06	Anderlecht	Standard Liège
2006–07	Anderlecht	Genk
2007–08	Standard Liège	Andlerlecht

Beker van België

Season	Winner	Runner-up
1998–99	Lierse	Standard Liége
1999–00	Genk	Standard Liége
2000–01	Westerlo	Lommel
2001–02	Bruges	Mouscron
2002–03	La Louvière	Sint-Truidense
2003–04	Bruges	Beveren
2004–05	Germinal Beerschot	Bruges
2005–06	Zulte-Waregem	Mouscron
2006–07	Bruges	Standard Liége
2007–08	Anderlecht	Gent

BRUSSELS

A naughty little boy and grey suits

Come on, be honest – you think of that little boy peeing when somebody mentions Brussels don't you? Nothing to be ashamed of, he's quite famous really. The wonderfully named Manneken Pis is simply a small bronze statue near the Main Square (Grand Place-Grote Markt), which shows a boy urinating, but he certainly brings in the crowds. Strangely, this irreverent symbol is at complete odds with the vision most people have of the city – as seat of the European Commission, Brussels has become a byword for grey suits and red tape. Poor old, boring Brussels.

Actually, as the capital of the country and meeting place of its two cultures you can get the best of what the Flemish and the French have to offer here. So it's beer galore – there are literally hundreds of smaller beers to try, as well as the giant Stella Artois – waffles, mussels, fries with mayonnaise and of course, the famous Belgian chocolates. Let's ignore the Brussels sprout shall we?

The Constant Vanden Stock, home of Anderlecht, is about 5 km (3 miles) to the east of the city centre.

Weather	Low (ºC)	High
January	1	5
February	0	5
March	3	9
April	4	12
May	8	17
June	11	19
July	13	22
August	12	22
September	11	18
October	8	15
November	3	8
December	1	6

Below: The Atomium, built in 1958 for the Brussels World's Fair.

3 THINGS YOU MUST DO...
(Apart from the football)

1 CANTILLON BREWERY-BRUSSELS GUEUZE MUSEUM
A tour of a traditional Belgian brewery, with a taste of the goods at the end. The brewery (56 rue Gheude, tel: +32 2 521 4928) makes, among others, the sour Gueuze-Lambic and the fruity Kriek beers. Open: Mon–Fri 08.30–17.00, Sat 10.00–17.00. Price: €5.

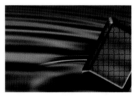

2 CHOCOLATES
Eat them, of course. Try Wittamer Café (13 Place du Grand Sablon, tel: +32 2 546 1111).

3 BELGIAN COMIC STRIP CENTRE
Any country that gave birth to Tintin must know its stuff about comic strips. The Centre (20 rue des Sables, tel: +32 2 219 1980). Open: museum Tues–Sun 10.00–18.00. Research centre Tue–Thur 12.00–17.00, Fri 12.00–18.00, Sat 10.00–18.00. Price: adult €7, children under 12 €3.

ANDERLECHT

Above: Anderlecht line up prior to a Champions League game at Constant Vanden Stock.

TEN YEAR RECORD

Season	Competition	Finished
1998–99	Uefa Cup	1st round
1999–00	Uefa Cup	2nd round
2000–01	Champs League	Group*
2001–02	Champs League	Group**
2002–03	Uefa Cup	Last 16
2003–04	Champs League	Group
2004–05	Champs League	Group
2005–06	Champs League	Group
2006–07	Champs League	Group
2007–08	Champs League	3rd qual rd
	Uefa Cup	Last 16

*2nd of two group stages
**1st of two group stages

Constant reminder of shame

Anderlecht's 29 league titles make them Belgium's most successful club, but they can surely claim another record: that of possessing the most unfortunately named stadium. Fully 25 years after he successfully bribed Spanish referee Emilio Guruceta to usher his team into the 1984 Uefa Cup final and a dozen years after he confessed to a court, Constant Vanden Stock's name still adorns the walls of the club's home.

Nottingham Forest, cheated in that semi-final by two widely ridiculed decisions, must be aghast that the late president is still celebrated. For good measure, Uefa decided that Anderlecht were also guilty of bribing referees a year earlier, when they also reached the Uefa Cup final.

Even so, Anderlecht owe a debt to Vanden Stock for building a grand arena fit for a team who have spent 45 successive seasons in European competition and have not finished outside the league's top six since World War Two. A club for all Belgium, their fans span the country, and they filled the entire national team for part of a match against Holland in 1964. They did not need Vanden Stock's corruption to achieve greatness.

MATTER OF FACT
Name: Royal Sporting Club Anderlecht
Stadium: Constant Vanden Stock (capacity 25,570)
Address: Avenue Théo Verbeecklaan 2, 1070
To get there: Metro from the main train station in the direction of Bizet (station Saint-Guidon)
Telephone: +32 2 522 1539
Email: secretariat@rsca.be
Website: www.rsca.be

Stadium tour (no museum, but trophies all around the stadium)
Open: Mon–Fri (except match days). Times to be agreed. Groups have to be a minimum of 25
Price: Depends on group size
Contact: Phone and email as above

Home   Away

Trophies

2	European Cup Winners' Cup
1	Inter-Cities Fairs Cup/Uefa Cup
29	Belgian League
9	Belgian Cup

Main rivals
The biggest rivals are Bruges (see page 53). FC Brussels (tel: +32 2 411 69 86, www.fc-brussels.be) are an offspring of 1975 title winners RWD Molenbeek and play at the Stade Edmond Machtens (Rue Charles Malis 61, 1080).

BRUGES

Discovering history and beer

Deep in the heart of Flanders, you'll travel a long way to find a more relaxed and attractive city than Bruges. This is a place where you can simply stroll aimlessly down cobbled alleyways and into squares ringed by medieval buildings. With intermittent stops to try a new Belgian beer, of course – it would be rude not to. Try a Trappist (if it's good enough for the monks...), a Lambic (wheat beer) or the best of the lot, a Duvel, which is a strong blonde ale.

Built originally on the cloth and wool trade, the Bruges of today has a population of a little more than 115,000. Not big by any city's standards, let alone the giants of the European football world.

This is a city for people who appreciate historic architecture, a diverse range of museums and festivals for everything from food to film and music. Culture and maintaining links with its historical past are high on the agenda for the city and the people of Bruges. That and enjoying a huge range of good-quality beers.

The Jan Breydal Stadium, which Club Brugge and Cercle Brugge share, is about 7 km (4 miles) southwest from the city centre.

Weather	Low (ºC)	High
January	2	4
February	1	3
March	3	7
April	6	10
May	9	15
June	12	17
July	14	18
August	15	20
September	12	17
October	10	14
November	6	8
December	5	7

Below: *Picturesque Bruges.*

3 THINGS YOU MUST DO...
(Apart from the football)

1 THE HALF MOON BREWERY

The De Halve Maan brewery (Walplein 26, tel: +32 50 332 697) can trace it roots as far back as 1564 so the beer must be pretty good. Open: Apr–Oct Sun–Fri 11.00–16.00 every hour, Sat 11.00–17.00 every hour. Nov–Mar Mon–Fri 11.00 and 15.00, Sat–Sun 11.00–16.00 every hour. Price: adults €5. To get there: it's in the centre.

2 DAMME

A small town with buildings dating back to medieval times. Take a 35 minute boat trip and enjoy a stroll around. Bruges berth is at Noorweegse Kaai 31 (tel: +32 9 233 8469). Departures: 1 Apr–15 Oct from Bruges at 10.00, 12.00, 14.00, 16.00 and 18.00. 16 Oct–30 Mar by request. Price: adult return €7.

3 DIAMOND MUSEUM

Diamantmuseum (Katelijnestraat 43, tel: +32 50 342 056). Open: daily 10.30–17.30 with a polishing demonstration at 12.15. Price: adults €6, children €6 (€9 for the demonstration and museum). To get there: it's in the centre.

BRUGES

Above: Bruges keeper Birger Jensen makes a one-handed save against Liverpool during the European Cup final at Wembley in 1978.

MATTER OF FACT
Name: Club Brugge KV
Stadium: Jan Breydel
(capacity 29,042)
Address: Olympialaan 74, 8200
To get there: Bus 5 from the main train station
Telephone: +32 50 40 21 35
Email: info@clubbrugge.be
Website: www.clubbrugge.be

Stadium tour
Contact club for details

Home   **Away**

Trophies
13   Belgian League
10   Belgian Cup

Main rivals
Fans in Flemish-speaking Bruges have a strong rivalry with Anderlecht (see page 51), based in French-speaking Brussels. The pair are Belgium's two most successful clubs. Cercle Bruges (tel: +32 50 38 91 93, www.cerclebrugge.be) share the Jan Breydel stadium with Bruges.

TEN YEAR RECORD

Season	Competition	Finished
1998–99	Champs League	2nd qual rd
	Uefa Cup	Last 16
1999–00	Uefa Cup	1st round
2000–01	Uefa Cup	Last 32
2001–02	Uefa Cup	Last 32
2002–03	Champs League	Group*
	Uefa Cup	Last 32
2003–04	Champs League	Group
	Uefa Cup	Last 16
2004–05	Champs League	3rd qual rd
	Uefa Cup	Group
2005–06	Champs League	Group
	Uefa Cup	Last 32
2006–07	Uefa Cup	Group
2007–08	Uefa Cup	1st round

*1st of two group stages

Small wave-makers

Bruges are a major force in Belgium but the club based in the Venice of the North made barely a ripple for their first 75 years. Formed in 1891, the canal city's leading side in modern times won just one trophy before the 1960s as neighbours Cercle Bruges held sway.

After lifting the first of ten Belgian Cups in 1968, they ended a 53-year wait for their second league title in 1973 and then appointed Austrian coach Ernst Happel to consolidate their gains. The next five years brought three more titles and two European finals, in the 1976 Uefa Cup and 1978 European Cup, both featuring narrow defeats by Liverpool. A move in 1975 to the new Olympiastadion (renamed Jan Breydel ahead of Euro 2000) reinforced the impression of a club on the march.

Happel's exit led to near-relegation in 1982 but they recovered and remain prominent domestically. Yet the days are long gone when Bruges almost became the smallest city to house the European champions. The club have never reached the Champions League knock-out stage.

LIÈGE

Wallonia's party central

Liège, situated in the east of Belgium, is the largest city in the French-speaking part of the country (Wallonia) with about 190,000 people calling it home. There is a large student population; in fact around one in five of Liège's inhabitants are studying there.

The most vibrant area is Le Carre ('The Square'), an area packed with bars, restaurants and cafés. It's more chilled in the day so you can sit and watch the world pass you by, but at night it comes to life, and fuelled by the large student population it's buzzing deep into the night and the next day. Look across the river and you will see the island of Outre Meuse, another area popular area among students, other locals and visitors alike.

The city is also big on events. Look out for the Liège–Bastogne–Liège cycle race (first raced in 1892) in late April, the *Jazz a Liège* in early May, the funfair during October and the St Nicholas Festival in December for wild student antics.

About 6 km (4 miles) along the river is Maurice Dufrasne, where Standard Liège are based.

Weather	Low (°C)	High
January	0	3
February	0	5
March	1	8
April	4	13
May	8	17
June	11	20
July	13	20
August	13	21
September	10	18
October	6	12
November	3	8
December	0	5

Below: *The city comes alive with colour in the summer.*

3 THINGS YOU MUST DO...
(Apart from the football)

1 CHÂTEAU DE JEHAY
A cool little 16th century castle (Rue de Parc 1, Amay, tel: +32 85 824 400). Open: Jun–Sept 11.00–18.00 on weekends, Jun Tues–Fri 14.00–17.00, July–Aug Tues–Fri 14.00–18.00, Sept Tues and Wed 14.00–17.00. Entry: adults €5. To get there: train to Amay then taxi. By car it's a 25 km (16 mile) drive southeast along the E25/E42.

2 MONTAGNE DE BUEREN
Liège is a hilly city so put your legs to good use and walk up the 373 steps of the Montagne de Bueren, which can only be described as a giant staircase. It was built in 1880 for the soldiers who were camped in the garrison at the top. To get there: it's a short (warm-up) walk from the heart of the city.

3 LIÈGE WAFFLES
You'll find these in the smaller shops and sold by street vendors as you stroll around. Not to be confused with the Belgian waffle, Liège's version is denser and the sugar is burned on to form a coating. They are served with cream and chocolate and sometimes fruit.

STANDARD LIÈGE

Above: Standard Liège in action.

MATTER OF FACT
Name: Royal Standard de Liège
Stadium: Maurice Dufrasne
(capacity 30,023)
Address: Rue de la Centrale 2, 4000
To get there: Bus on line 2, 3 and 27
Telephone: +32 4 254 4207
Email: direction@standard.be
Website: www.standard.be

Stadium tour
Open: Mon–Fri except match days if
there are sufficient numbers
Price: €3
Contact: Phone and email as above

Home	Away

Trophies
9	Belgian League
5	Belgian Cup

Main rivals
RFC Liège (www.rfcl.be), a second
division club in 2008–09, play at the
Stade de la rue Gilles Magnée. They
won five titles before Standard
achieved their first.

TEN YEAR RECORD
Season	Competition	Finished
1998–99	DNQ	
1999–00	DNQ	
2000–01	Intertoto Cup	SF*
2001–02	Uefa Cup	2nd round
2002–03	DNQ	
2003–04	DNQ	
2004–05	Uefa Cup	Group
2005–06	DNQ	
2006–07	Champs League	3rd qual rd
	Uefa Cup	1st round
2007–08	Uefa Cup	1st round

*One of six semi-finals

A big leap forward

When Standard Liège goalkeeper Rorys Aragon Espinoza marked their 2008 title by leaping into the River Meuse in front of 300 fans, it felt as if he was completing the cleansing of the club's soul. Having not been champions since 1983, a few months before coach Raymond Goethals and several players were banned for match-fixing, many considered they had served a quarter-century moral punishment.

They waited longer for their first league title. Formed in 1898, they only thrived when semi-professionalism arrived in the 1950s. Funded by local steelworks boss Paul Henrard, they achieved their debut title in 1958. Goethals added the 1982 and 1983 crowns, but the first of those came only after he had suggested bribing last-day league opponents Waterschei, allowing Standard to win the title and stay fit for their forth-coming European Cup Winners' Cup final, which they lost to Barcelona.

The league drought ended spectacularly in 2008 when Standard lost just one match all campaign. More joyous river plunges can be expected.

NETHERLANDS

<table>
<tr><td>

THE

3

MINUTE GUIDE

</td></tr>
</table>

Capital: *Amsterdam.* **Language:** *Dutch.* **Beer:** *Heineken, Grolsch, Amstel.* **Food:** *Cheese (Gouda, Edam).* **National Anthem:** *Het Wilhelmus (The William).* **Population:** *16,645,000.* **Time zone:** *GMT +1.* **Emergency Number:** *112.* **Did you know?** *Liftershaltes (formalized hitchhiking places) can be found dotted around the major cities.* **Football body:** *Koninklijke Nederlandse Voetbalbond Woudenbergseweg 56–58, PO Box 515, Am Zeist 3700; tel: +31 34 3499 201, fax: +31 34 3499 189, email: concern@knvb.nl, website: www.knvb.nl. Founded 1889. Affiliated 1904.*

Below: The Amsterdam Arena, home of Dutch giants Ajax.

High points for a Low Country

When Rinus Michels was appointed coach of Ajax in 1965, he delivered a brutally frank state-of-the-nation address. "Holland has no great clubs and has never had any," he said. Given that the national professional league was less than ten years old and no Dutch team had reached the final of a European competition at that point, it was hard to argue with him.

Yet the country would soon become a global force at club and country level and Michels' work earned him the award of Fifa coach of the century in 1999.

Using a system of total football and blessed with Johan Cruyff's talent, Michels guided Ajax away from relegation danger and turned them into European champions. Then, after Holland had qualified for the 1974 World Cup, he took charge and reached the final, in which they led hosts West Germany only to lose 2–1. Fourteen years later he guided the national team to their only major trophy to date, beating the Soviet Union in the European championship final.

Yet the national team have become Europe's most frequent glorious failures. They took hosts Argentina to extra time before losing the 1978 World Cup final, and three of their five semi-final defeats in the World Cup or European championship have come via a penalty shoot-out.

There is little strength in depth among league clubs. When PSV Eindhoven became champions for the fourth time in a row in 2008, it meant only once had the title not been won by PSV, Ajax or Feyenoord in 34 years.

Above: Skating on Holland's frozen rivers.　*Below:* The Dutch national team in 1934, before success.

AMSTERDAM

More than just tulips

Liberal is the word springing to the minds of most people. Amsterdam's forward-thinking attitude to prostitution and soft drugs has drawn a fascinated throng of tourists more used to the heavy-handed approaches of their own authorities. Of course, it's not the only place where you can see prostitutes openly working or even people enjoying a puff in a 'coffee shop' without the police marching in, but this city has become more synonymous than others for its tolerant attitude.

Probably unfairly, really, because the reality, as anyone who has visited Amsterdam knows, is that this is a city that is vibrant, varied and modern, as well as being laidback. It always features near the top of 'quality of life' indices, is home to some seriously big international companies, and let's not forget, is the city where Rembrandt spent most of his life.

The 'dam' in the city's name indicates the importance of water to the capital of Holland. With a population of around 750,000 the city is famously criss-crossed with canals, and, subsequently, lots of bridges.

So, where to start? Ah, that'll be the red light district will it? Basically, the area you'll be looking for is the side streets and canals close to Central Station. You'll know you 're there because you'll see women wearing underwear in the windows smiling at you as if you are the love of their life (if you're a man). And for a short time (for a fee) you can be. Most people, however, are just sex tourists in the voyeuristic way, and for them there are plenty of peep shows and sex shops.

Another forward-thinking institution is Ajax. You can find their stadium about 9 km (5.5 miles) south of the women in underwear.

Below: Beer is the staple drink in Amsterdam, with a huge variety of Dutch and foreign beers to choose from.

3 THINGS YOU MUST DO...
(Apart from the football)

1 THE SEX MUSEUM

Interesting. Sex Museum (Damrak 18, tel: +31 20 622 8376). Open: daily 09.30–23.30. Price: €3 (you must be over 16). To get there: follow the crowds. It's near Central Station.

2 THE HASH, MARIHUANA AND HEMP MUSEUM

Also interesting. The Hash, Marihuana and Hemp Museum (Oudezijdsachterburgwal 148, tel: +31 20 623 5961). Open: daily 10.00–22.00. Price: adults €5.70. To get there: it's a five-minute walk from Central Station.

3 WINDMILL

It might be wedged between the water and some high-rise buildings, but this is a windmill in Amsterdam. A real one. Near the centre: De Otter (Gillis van Ledenberchstraat 78). Apparently it even works sometimes. To get there: it's a 20 minute walk from Central Station. Tram 3 to Hugo de Grootplein. Buses 18, 80, 82, 352 to Gillis van Ledenberchstraat.

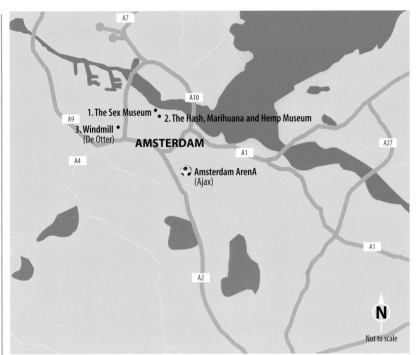

Map labels: A7, A10, A9, A4, A1, A27, A1, A2

1. The Sex Museum • • 2. The Hash, Marihuana and Hemp Museum
3. Windmill •
(De Otter)   **AMSTERDAM**

Amsterdam ArenA (Ajax)

N
Not to scale

BARS > CLUBS > RESTAURANTS

Bars > Sleek, designer bars are often more than happy just to live on their, well, design. **18Twintig** (Ferdinand Bolstraat 18–20, tel: +31 20 470 0651) is sleek and beautiful but it also has an interesting regular crowd, good cocktails and food. There's a fun retro feel to the **Chocolate Bar** (1e van der Helststraat 62a, tel: +31 20 675 767) where you can enjoy well-priced caprinhas and mojitos.
Clubs > Panama (Oostelijke Handelskade 4, tel: +32 20 311 8689 for restaurant and +32 20 311 8686 for nightclub) has been around since 2001 and offers a nice variation for a night out.
Restaurants > D' Vijff Vlieghen (Spuistraat 294–302, tel: +31 20 530 4060) is a city institution offering food dubbed New Dutch Cuisine. One of Holland's strongest influences has come from its former colony Indonesia. Try **Sama Sebo** (Pieter Cornelisz Hooftstraat 27, tel: +31 20 662 8146).

Below: Café culture in Amsterdam has been perfected.

Weather	Low (ºC)	High
January	1	5
February	1	5
March	2	8
April	4	11
May	7	16
June	11	18
July	12	21
August	12	21
September	10	17
October	8	13
November	3	8
December	2	6

AJAX

Above: The Amsterdam ArenA.

TEN YEAR RECORD

Season	Competition	Finished
1998–99	Champs League	Group
1999–00	Uefa Cup	Last 32
2000–01	Uefa Cup	2nd round
2001–02	Champs League	3rd qual rd
	Uefa Cup	2nd round
2002–03	Champs League	QF
2003–04	Champs League	Group
2004–05	Champs League	Group
	Uefa Cup	Last 32
2005–06	Champs League	Last 16
2006–07	Champs League	3rd qual rd
	Uefa Cup	Last 32
2007–08	Champs League	3rd qual rd
	Uefa Cup	1st round

Young, gifted and leaving

Ajax share with Marseille the distinction of clambering to the summit of Europe in the 1990s only to be pushed down again by lawyers before they could enjoy the view. But whereas the French club's fall was self-inflicted because of corruption that dragged key figures through the country's criminal courts, Ajax were an innocent party doomed by a verdict in the European Court of Justice.

Seven months after a youthful and largely home-grown Ajax side beat AC Milan to become 1995 European champions, the Bosman ruling covering the free movement of workers in Europe decreed that footballers could move clubs for no transfer fee when out of contract. For Ajax, who earned fortunes by selling players they had trained, it was a crushing blow.

The Amsterdam club had long been effectively a feeder club for Europe's elite, but now they would gain far less reward for their efforts. Almost their entire final-winning squad departed for little or nothing within three years, since when Ajax have not been a Champions League force.

Ajax rose to European heights after Rinus Michels arrived as coach in 1965 and introduced total football, where players changed positions freely during games. He inspired an era that brought three successive European Cups and six league titles, all in eight years.

Yet attendances at their De Meer stadium dipped to 8,000 even in those halcyon days, hence the need to sell players to survive. So some optimism can been taken from the near-50,000 average crowds in recent years at Amsterdam ArenA, which Ajax have occupied since 1996. But with little money on offer from local television contracts and the Bosman ruling still in effect, Europe's summit now seems unclimbable.

GREATEST PLAYERS

> **JOHAN CRUYFF (1964–73; 1981–83)**
Born a couple of hundred metres from Ajax's former De Meer stadium, the lithe Cruyff exhibited wonderful ball control and acceleration and was a keen tactician even as a player. European Footballer of the Year in 1971, 1973 and 1974, he left for Barcelona in 1973.

> **JOHAN NEESKENS (1970–74)**
Adept at full back and as an attacking central midfield player, Neeskens' versatility made him perfect for the total football strategy of Ajax. He joined Barcelona a year after Cruyff made the same move and played in the World Cup finals of 1974 and 1978.

MATTER OF FACT

Name: Amsterdamsche Football Club Ajax

Stadium: Amsterdam ArenA (capacity 51,628)

Address: Arena Boulevard 1, 1101 AX Amsterdam Zuidoost

To get there: Metro Line 54 (stop Strandvliet). Buses 29, 59, 60, 62, 137, 158, 174, 175 (stop Bijlmer)

Telephone: +31 20 311 1444

Email: info@ajax.nl

Website: www.ajax.nl

Stadium tour

Contact: Tel: +31 20 311 1336 (tour) or +31 20 311 1444 (museum)

Home	Away

Trophies

4	European Cup/ Champions League
1	European Cup Winners' Cup
1	Inter-Cities Fairs Cup/Uefa Cup
29	Dutch League
16	Dutch Cup

Main rivals

Ajax have no rivals in Amsterdam so Feyenoord (see page 65) are the targets of almost all the enmity held by their fans. Games between the two clubs are called De Klassieker and were once reasonably friendly affairs. But the hooliganism that has infected both clubs has created problems, most notoriously when the teams met in 1997 – a pre-arranged fight in a field resulted in the death of an Ajax fan. Such was the hostility between the clubs that Johan Cruyff is said to have moved to Feyenoord in 1983 as a way of gaining revenge on Ajax for refusing to offer him a new contract.

Above: Aston Villa's Carlos Cuéllar (standing) and Ajax's Klaas-Jan Huntelaar battle for the ball during a Uefa Cup match.

BARRED FROM EUROPE

During a Uefa Cup match in 1989–90, FK Austria goalkeeper Franz Wohlfahrt was struck by an iron bar thrown by an Ajax fan. The club were banned for a year from European competition and their captain Jan Wouters said: "I wanted to throw that bar straight back into the crowd."

EINDHOVEN

The city that Philips owns

The name Philips dominates Eindhoven, although it is no longer based in the city (the headquarters was moved to Amsterdam in 1997). Philips' complexes, research areas and parks are dotted endlessly around the city, while the Philips Stadion, home of PSV Eindhoven, is less than a kilometre from the heart of the city. Philips is also an official sponsor of the Fifa World Cup and has been for many years.

As with many cities, it is the market square (De Markt) that provides a focal point for its inhabitants, with its host of bars and cafés. A short walk from here (about 2 km/1.2 miles) is Stationsplein, near the central station, which also provides plenty of opportunities for eating, drinking and dancing. Stratumseind with its numerous bars, the old part of the town, De Bergen, and its lively street Kleine Berg, plus the busy and attractive square Wilhelminaplein, are nearby here. All these areas are situated around PSV's stadium.

Weather	Low (°C)	High
January	0	4
February	1	5
March	1	9
April	3	13
May	8	17
June	10	20
July	12	22
August	12	21
September	10	18
October	6	14
November	2	7
December	1	5

Below: Relaxing in one of Eindhoven's many outdoor cafés.

3 THINGS YOU MUST DO...
(Apart from the football)

1 THE DAF MUSEUM
Eindhoven's other big name. See cars and trucks dating back to 1928. DAF Museum (Tongelresestraat 27, tel: +31 40 244 4364). Open: Tues–Sun 10.00–17.00. Price: adults €7, children 5–15 €2.50, children under five free. To get there: a 15 minute walk from central station or bus 5.

2 EVOLUON
Amazing space ship-shaped venue (built by Philips) that used to be a museum but today is a conference centre. Evoluon (Noord Brabantlaan 1a, tel: +31 40 250 4666). To get there: a 15 minute walk from central station or buses 401 and 402.

3 STRATUMSEIND
This street is bar and café central so you won't go short of choices. To mix with the city's pretty people till the early hours head to Café Puur (Stratumseind 62).

PSV EINDHOVEN

Above: The first club logo designed in 1913.

MATTER OF FACT

Name: Philips Sport Vereniging
Stadium: Philips Stadion
(capacity 35,119)
Address: Frederiklaan 10a, 5616 NH
To get there: Train to main station
then 10 mins walk. Buses 401, 402
Telephone: +31 40 2505505
Email: fandesk@psv.nl
Website: www.psv.nl

Stadium tour
Open: Wed 14.30, Sat 13.00 (except
events or match days)
Price: €12.50. Must book at least one
week before. If a group booking, must
be for at least ten people. Book via
official website at: http://english.psv.
nl/web/show/id=57315
Contact: Tel: +31 40 2 505 505 (press
9) or email: guidedtour@psv.nl

Home	Away

Trophies
1	European Cup/ Champions League
1	Inter-Cities Fairs Cup/ Uefa Cup
21	Dutch League
8	Dutch Cup

Main rivals
FC Eindhoven (tel: +31 40 2112967,
www.fc-eindhoven.nl), who play at
the 4,600-capacity Jan Louwers
Stadium (Charles Roelslaan 1), face
PSV in the Lichtstad Derby (City of
Light Derby). Dutch champions in
1954, they have been in the second
division since 1977. PSV have
developed a big rivalry with Ajax
(see pages 60–61) as they are the
country's two most successful clubs.

TEN YEAR RECORD

Season	Competition	Finished
1998–99	Champs League	Group
1999–00	Champs League	Group*
2000–01	Champs League	Group*
	Uefa Cup	QF
2001–02	Champs League	Group*
	Uefa Cup	QF
2002–03	Champs League	Group*
2003–04	Champs League	Group
	Uefa Cup	QF
2004–05	Champs League	SF
2005–06	Champs League	Last 16
2006–07	Champs League	QF
2007–08	Champs League	Group
	Uefa Cup	QF

*1st of two group stages

Company sparks success

When Ronaldo left South America in 1994, he took the advice of fellow Brazil striker Romario (who spoke from experience) and made PSV Eindhoven his first European club rather than wait for a continental giant to approach him. Based in a city far smaller than Amsterdam and Rotterdam and playing in a stadium among tree-lined streets, the Boeren ('Farmers') offer a gentle introduction to European football. Both players benefited and subsequently thrived at Barcelona.

Yet the financial backing of local electronics giant Philips, who formed PSV in 1913, has brought huge success. Eindhoven is the smallest city to have provided the European champions and the club have won 21 Dutch league titles. The zenith came in 1988 when PSV won the domestic double and beat Benfica in the European Cup final.

Coach Guus Hiddink was significant in their success, leading them to European Cup glory and adding three more league titles on his 2002 return. With their electronics cash, PSV remain a tiny footballing power.

ROTTERDAM

The new Amsterdam

Rotterdam was dubbed the 'new Amsterdam' recently by a leading Dutch lifestyle and business magazine. While Amsterdam is being flooded by pot-smoking and prostitute-staring tourists, Rotterdam is trying to take over the stylish clubbing and restaurant scene.

To test how it is getting on in its quest, go for a big night out where you can choose to sample the host of clubs on Stadhuisplein (city hall square) or an evening of stylish people and stylish venues in the Meent area. Further south by the water is Oude Haven ('Old Harbour') where you can get your dose of pretty Rotterdam with its twinkling lights and cozy bars. The other popular area in the city is Eendrachtsplein, where you will find the artistic and musical crowd with a good number of bars and restaurants to keep you busy.

De Kuip, home to the city's famous club, Feyenoord, is 6 km (4 miles) to the south of the centre over the Nieuwe Maas river.

Weather	Low (°C)	High
January	1	5
February	0	5
March	2	8
April	3	11
May	7	16
June	10	17
July	13	20
August	12	21
September	10	17
October	8	14
November	4	9
December	2	6

Below: The party port city. **Bottom:** *The original harbour of Rotterdam is now surrounded by commerce.*

3 THINGS YOU MUST DO...
(Apart from the football)

1 WATT
Dance and save the planet. WATT (West Kruiskade 26-28, tel: +31 10 217 9190) is an environmentally sustainable club. Movement on the dance floor generates electricity and water is collected on the roof to flush the toilets. To get there: 5 minutes walk from central station or trams 21 or 23.

2 THE PORT
Huge and impressive, Rotterdam is Europe's largest port. Port of Rotterdam Authority (Wilhelminakade 909, tel: +31 10 252 1010). To get there: you can't miss it; look for the big ships.

3 KIJK-KUBUS
Imagine a giant twisting your apartment diagonally and sticking it onto a pole. That's Kijk-Kubus. Discover what it's like to live in a twisted cube. Kijk-Kubus show cube (Overblaak 70, tel: +31 10 414 2285). Open: daily 11.00—17.00. Price: adults €2.50, children €1.50. To get there: metro or tram 21 to station Blaak.

FEYENOORD

Above: Traditionally one of the Netherlands' Big Three, Feyenoord players train hard to keep it that way.

TEN YEAR RECORD

Season	Competition	Finished
1998–99	Uefa Cup	1st round
1999–00	Champs League	Group*
2000–01	Uefa Cup	Last 32
2001–02	Champs League	Group**
Uefa Cup	Winners	
2002–03	Champs League	Group**
2003–04	Uefa Cup	2nd round
2004–05	Uefa Cup	Last 32
2005–06	Uefa Cup	1st round
2006–07	Uefa Cup	Group
2007–08	DNQ	

*2nd of two group stages
**1st of two group stages

Three's a crowd

Surveys claim Feyenoord have the most fans in Holland; true or not, they must surely have the most frustrated fans. Not only have they lagged behind fellow Dutch Big Three members Ajax and PSV Eindhoven since their 1970 European Cup triumph, but many of their subsequent successes have been bittersweet.

The 1974 Uefa Cup final was overshadowed by Tottenham Hotspur supporters ripping out seats; the 1991 Dutch Cup final was tarnished because pitch invasions by Feyenoord fans led to an appeal by opponents Den Bosch (which eventually failed) for a replay; and their 1999 league title was soured when celebrating fans fought with police. Even the 1984 League and Cup double had the edge taken from it for some as it was inspired by Johan Cruyff, an icon of hated rivals Ajax.

No wonder their 2002 Uefa Cup final win over Borussia Dortmund on their own ground was greeted with delirium. Unless Feyenoord get their act together, those fans may be hearing the phrase Dutch Big Two soon.

MATTER OF FACT
Name: Feyenoord
Stadium: Stadion Feijenoord, or 'De Kuip' (capacity 51,177)
Address: Van Zandvlietplein 3, 3077 AA
To get there: *Maastaxi* (water taxi) from city centre (tel: +31 10 403 0303). Buses 49 (from main train station), 72, 75 (both from Zuidplein). Tram 23 (from main train station)
Telephone: +31 10 292 6874
Email: via gva@feyenoord.nl
Website: www.feyenoord.nl

Stadium tour
Open: Mon–Fri 12.30, Sat 10.30 and 12.30. Groups of five-plus (must reserve) Mon–Sat 10.30, 12.30, 14.30
Museum: Tues–Sat 10.00–16.30
Price: €11.50 (includes museum), €5 for museum only
Contact: Tel: +31 10 292 6822 or email: feyenoordtours@dekuip.nl

Home	Away

Trophies
1	European Cup/Champions League
2	Inter-Cities Fairs Cup/Uefa Cup
14	Dutch League
11	Dutch Cup

Main rivals
Biggest enemies by far are Ajax (see pages 60–61). Sparta Rotterdam (tel: +31 10 890 9210, www.sparta-rotterdam.nl) play at Het Kasteel (Spartapark Noord 1, 3027 VW). Excelsior (tel: +31 10 404 6041, www.sbvexcelsior.nl) play at Stadion Woudestein (Honingerdijk 110, 3062 NX).

GERMANY

| THE
3
MINUTE
GUIDE |  | **Capital:** *Berlin.* **Language:** *German.* **Beer:** *Take your pick, there are about 1,300 breweries in Germany.* **Food:** *Sausages,* sauerkraut, *potatoes, dumplings.* **National anthem:** *Das Deutschlandlied (The Song of Germany).* **Population:** *82,370,000.* **Time zone:** *GMT +1.* **Emergency number:** *Police 110 or 112, medical and fire 112.* **Did you know?** *Germany has around 5,000 different kinds of beer.* **Football body:** *Deutscher Fussball-Bund, Otto-Fleck-Schneise 6, Postfach 71 02 65, Frankfurt 60528; tel: +49 696 7880, fax: +49 696 788266, email: info@dfb.de, website: www.dfb.de. Founded 1900. Affiliated 1904.* |

Below: The exterior of the Allianz Arena in Munich.

The winning machine stutters

Are these halcyon or humbling days for German football? Its supporters could make a strong case for the former but its detractors could argue for the latter. While the game thrives on the domestic front, an increasingly weak threat is offered beyond the country's borders.

Blessed with a host of huge, gleaming stadiums built or improved for the 2006 World Cup, the Bundesliga attracts the planet's largest football crowds and routinely produces the most goals among Europe's major leagues. Yet, since 1997, the enormously successful national team has failed to win a tournament and only once – Bayern Munich's Champions League triumph in 2001 – has a German club prevailed in a European competition.

The football tourist will be more concerned with domestic fare and, in that respect, a treat awaits. From Bayern's 69,901-seat Allianz Arena to the 80,708-capacity Signal Iduna Park used by Borussia Dortmund, Germany's awesome collection of grounds is the envy of most of the world.

These German theatres have long staged great dramas. For each of the five seasons up to and including 2007–08 the Bundesliga boasted far more goals per game than its rival leagues in Spain, Italy, England and France, exceeding three per match both in 2003–04 and in the following campaign.

Exhilaration and tension have been commonplace, with the league title decided on the final day in five successive seasons from 1991 to 1995 and again on three consecutive occasions from 2000 to 2002, although Bayern have since developed a habit of wrapping things up early.

Above: The spectacular Allianz Arena in Munich. *Below:* German colours are flown.

THE TEN YEAR GUIDE

Bundesliga

Season	Winner	Runner-up
1998–99	Bayern Munich	Bayer Leverkusen
1999–00	Bayern Munich	Bayer Leverkusen
2000–01	Bayern Munich	Schalke
2001–02	Borussia Dortmund	Bayer Leverkusen
2002–03	Bayern Munich	Stuttgart
2003–04	Werder Bremen	Bayern Munich
2004–05	Bayern Munich	Schalke
2005–06	Bayern Munich	Werder Bremen
2006–07	Stuttgart	Schalke
2007–08	Bayern Munich	Werder Bremen

DFB-Pokal

Season	Winner	Runner-up
1998–99	Werder Bremen	Bayern Munich
1999–00	Bayern Munich	Werder Bremen
2000–01	Schalke	Union Berlin
2001–02	Schalke	Bayer Leverkusen
2002–03	Bayern Munich	Kaiserslautern
2003–04	Werder Bremen	Alemannia Aachen
2004–05	Bayern Munich	Schalke
2005–06	Bayern Munich	Eintracht Frankfurt
2006–07	Nuremburg	Stuttgart
2007–08	Bayern Munich	Borussia Dortmund

BREMEN

Let the music play

Schnoor, a quarter wedged between the River Weser and the canal that dates back to medieval times when the city needed such a thing for defences, is at the heart of the old town (Altstadt). It is an area of pretty cobbled streets and buildings and naturally attracts visitors looking to meander lazily along and explore the maze of alleys and the historic architecture and sample the shops, cafés and restaurants.

Another popular attraction in the old town is the market square (Markplatz), with its early 15th century Gothic town hall, listed as a World Heritage Site, towering proudly over it. While there you will also see the statue of Roland, the protector of the city, which dates back to 1404.

But much more fun, at least in the world of statues, is the Town Musicians. Inspired by the Brothers Grimm fairytale, the statue depicts a cockerel sitting on the back of a cat, who in turn is on the back of a dog, who itself is standing on a donkey.

The four animals are perched like this because they are performing for food. They are on their way to Bremen to become town musicians when they come across a house. Inside they see four thieves eating so they put on a performance in the hope of getting fed; instead they simply scare the thieves off with their noise. They pop inside and get comfortable but one of the men returns, only to be attacked viciously by our less-than-cuddly creatures. The thieves never return and the animals live happily ever after, never, in fact, even making it to Bremen. Except in statue form.

Weserstadion, Werder Bremen's home ground is about 3 km (2 miles) southeast along the river from the performing animals.

Below: The market square (Markplatz) in the old town of Bremen.

3 THINGS YOU MUST DO...
(Apart from the football)

1 BECK'S BREWERY
The tour is two and a half hours but just keep thinking of that tasting at the end. Beck's Brewery (Am Deich 18-19, tel: +49 421 50940). Tours: Thur–Sat 11.00, 12.30, 14.00, 15.30, 17.00 (no 11.00 tour Jan–Mar but an extra 09.30 tour on Sat Apr–Dec). Price: €8.50. To get there: buses 25, 26, 27, 62, 64 or trams 1,2, 3, 8 to Am Brill.

2 SCHLACHTE
Just a short walk from the city centre is the waterfront area with its host of bars, restaurants and throngs of people.

3 UNIVERSUM SCIENCE CENTRE
Science may have been dull at school but here they are big on interactive exhibitions not theory. The Universum Science Centre (Wiener Strasse 1a, tel: +49 421 33460) has three 'expeditions': mankind, earth, and the cosmos. Open: Mon–Fri 09.00–18.00, Sat–Sun and holidays 10.00–19.00. Price: adults €9.50–18.50, children €7–12.50. To get there: tram 6.

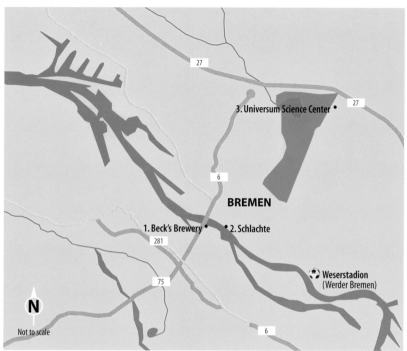

BARS > CLUBS > RESTAURANTS

Bars > Get your dose of Irish humour, beer and knick-knacks on the wall in a number of places. Choose from the **Irish Pub** (Stavendamm 18, tel: +49 421 321126), **Paddy's Pit** (Bahnhofsplatz 5–7, tel: +49 421 12310) or **Hegarty's** (Ostertorsteinweg 80, tel: +49 421 701297). You'll find something more Bremen than Dublin at **Paulaner's** (Schlachte 30, tel: +49 421 169 0691).

Clubs > Try the city centre's **Stubu Dancehouse** (Rembertiring 21, tel: +49 421 326 398), which has a relaxed vibe and music that will get you up and dancing pretty quickly. If the rock crowd and black clothes are your thing try **Aladin's Music Hall** (Hannoversche Str. 11, tel: +49 421 435 150).

Restaurants > An institution in the city is **Bremer Ratskeller** (Am Markt, tel: +49 421 321 676). Under the town hall, which dates back to 1405, it is said to be the country's oldest wine cellar.

Below: Stubu Dancehouse.

Weather	Low (ºC)	High
January	-1	3
February	-1	3
March	1	7
April	2	12
May	7	17
June	11	20
July	13	21
August	13	21
September	10	18
October	6	13
November	2	7
December	0	5

WERDER BREMEN

Above: *The Weserstadion, Bremen.*

Attacking crazy

TEN YEAR RECORD

Season	Competition	Finished
1998–99	Uefa Cup	Last 32
1999–00	Uefa Cup	QF
2000–01	Uefa Cup	Last 32
2001–02	Intertoto Cup	3rd round
2002–03	Uefa Cup	2nd round
2003–04	Intertoto Cup	SF*
2004–05	Champs League	Last 16
2005–06	Champs League	Last 16
2006–07	Champs League	Group
	Uefa Cup	SF
2007–08	Champs League	Group
Uefa Cup	Last 16	

*One of six semi-finals

While other clubs play out dramas behind the scenes, Bremen leave their theatre for the pitch. The off-field serenity resulting from the employment of two long-serving coaches has allowed Bremen to over-achieve during the past three decades, and they have thrilled neutrals in the process.

The team's attacking approach brought them an incredible average of 2.2 goals per game in the Bundesliga over five years from 2003. In 2006 they scored six goals three times in the space of five away league games, although the 7–2 Champions League defeat away to Lyon in 2005 gave less flattering testimony to their open style.

Bremen's craziness is long established. They lost the title on goal difference in 1983 and 1986, but in 1993 they pipped Bayern on the last day and the same year beat Anderlecht 5–3 in the Champions League despite them being 3–0 down with 25 minutes left.

The empire was built by Otto Rehhagel, who gained promotion and placed Bremen among the elite during his 14 years in charge from 1981, still the longest managerial reign at a German top-flight club. A string of players were inspired to commit to long-term careers under Rehhagel and he won two league titles and the 1992 European Cup Winners' Cup.

That longevity record was being challenged as Thomas Schaaf began his tenth season as Bremen coach in 2008–09 and the feeling of stability was reinforced by the fact that Schaaf played for 13 years under Rehhagel at the Weserstadion. The team have still only once failed to finish in the top half of the table since 1981. Consistent and understated, the club beside the Weser River continue to progress calmly – but with a large splash of colour.

GREATEST PLAYERS

> HORST-DIETER HÖTTGES (1964–78)

A hard-tackling full back, Höttges won the league title in his first season at the club and stayed put for another 13 seasons despite the team's lack of success. He won 66 caps for his country and played in the 1966 World Cup final.

> MARCO BODE (1989–2002)

A left-sided midfield player who could also play in attack, Bode was a key figure for 13 years as the club regularly challenged for the league title. His 40 appearances for Germany included the 1996 European championship final win over the Czech Republic.

MATTER OF FACT:

Name: Sportverein Werder Bremen
Stadium: Weserstadion
(capacity 42,354)
Address: Franz-Böhmert-Straße 1c,
28205
To get there: S-Bahn lines 2, 10
(station St Jürgen-Strasse), line 3
(station Weserstadion)
Telephone: +49 180 593 7337
Email: info@werder.de
Website: www.werder.de

Stadium tour
Open: Daily except match days –
times depend on demand. Museum:
every day, 10.00–18.00; closes one
hour before home games start
Price: €4 (museum €5)
Contact: As above

Home	Away

Trophies
1	European Cup Winners' Cup
4	German League
5	German Cup

Main rivals
Neighbours Hamburg have long been
the biggest rivals, dominating the
North Germany regional league and
continuing to outperform Bremen in
the Bundesliga initially. But since
Hamburg became European
champions in 1983 they have been
overshadowed by Werder. Bayern
Munich have also become big foes,
simply because they have regularly
been the greatest obstacle to Bremen
winning the league title, hence the
disquiet when coach Otto Rehhagel
left for Bayern in 1995.

WALKING INTO TROUBLE
When one of the goals collapsed
with the score 1–1 two minutes from
the end of Bremen's league game
against title-chasing Borussia
Monchengladbach in 1971, the latter
refused to wait for it to be fixed,
hoping a replay would be ordered.
But their walk-out led to the match
being awarded 2–0 to Bremen.

*Above: Andreas Reinke, Werder
Bremen goalkeeper in Champions
League action against Chelsea.*

DORTMUND

The industrial heart

Dortmund is an industrial city in Germany's famous Ruhr area and dates back to medieval times. Running from west to east right through the centre of the city is Westenhellweg becoming Ostenhellweg. The centre is neatly circled by a road that follows the site of the old city wall. You'll know you have reached it because all its guises include the suffix 'wall' (Südwall, Ostwall, Burgwall and so on).

An important city landmark is St Reinhold's Church in the old market square, and it is just one of a high concentration of churches in the centre. All around these, specifically along Westenhellweg, Kleppingstrasse and Bruckstrasse, is also a high number of shops, including many with luxury goods. But when you have had enough of culture and your shopping bags are full of designer names then look for a *Bierhausen* for a hearty sausage and beer.

Signal Iduna Park, home of Borussia Dortmund, is about 3 km (2 miles) south of the city centre.

Weather	Low (°C)	High
January	0	3
February	0	5
March	2	8
April	4	11
May	8	16
June	11	19
July	13	21
August	13	21
September	11	17
October	7	13
November	3	8
December	1	5

Below: *St Reinhold's Church rises above the old market square.*

3 THINGS YOU MUST DO...
(Apart from the football)

1 PFEFFERPOTTHAST AND BEER
Try the city's famous pepper beef stew with onions, washed down with the national drink. Dortmunder Helles is a local beer. Try Dimberger Glocke (Hohle Eiche 5, tel: +49 231 249 7490).

2 DORTMUND BREWERY MUSEUM
Dortmund is one of the world's great brewing centres and this museum is housed in the former machine house of the Hansa Brewery. Yes, there is a tasting. Brewery Museum (Steigerstrasse 16, tel: +49 231 84 0 0200). Price: adults €1.50. Open: Tues–Sun 10:00–17:00. To get there: subway U41 to Lortzingstr.

3 CASINO HOHENSYBURG
See the football, drink the beer, win at poker. Maybe. Casino Hohensyburg (Hohensyburgstr 200, tel: +49 231 77400. To get there: by car it's 13 km (8 miles) south of the city on the B54 or bus 444 from the city.

BORUSSIA DORTMUND

Above: The distinctive black and yellow of Borussia Dortmund.

MATTER OF FACT
Name: Ballspiel-Verein Borussia Dortmund
Stadium: Signal Iduna Park (capacity 80,552)
Address: Strobelallee 50, 44139
To get there: Metro from main station, lines U45, U46 (station: Westfalenstadion match days only, Westfalenhallen). From city centre, U42 (station: Theodor-Fliedner-Heim)
Telephone: +49 231 90 200
Email: verein@bvb.de
Website: www.bvb.de

Stadium tour (includes museum)
Open: Fri 16.00, Sat, Sun 14.00 (except match days). No booking needed for German tours; book for other languages. Expected times for new museum: Mon–Sun 10.00–18.00
Price: €6 (museum price to be decided)
Contact: Tel: +49 231 90 20 616 or email: info@stadion-live.de

Home	Away

Trophies
1	European Cup/ Champions League
1	European Cup Winners' Cup
6	German League
2	German Cup

Main rivals
Schalke (see page 81) and Dortmund are the Ruhr region's two biggest clubs and lock horns in the highly charged Revier derby. Dortmund took delight in beating their rivals in the penultimate game of 2006–07, effectively depriving them of the title, and a year later their fans celebrated the fact that Schalke had not won the league for 50 years. Schalke are from Gelsenkirchen, which is 30 minutes from Dortmund on line 2 of the S-Bahn train.

TEN YEAR RECORD
Season	Competition	Finished
1998–99	DNQ	
1999–00	Champs League	Group*
	Uefa Cup	Last 16
2000–01	DNQ	
2001–02	Champs League	Group*
	Uefa Cup	Final
2002–03	Champs League	Group**
2003–04	Champs League	3rd qual rd
	Uefa Cup	2nd round
2004–05	Intertoto Cup	3rd round
2005–06	Intertoto Cup	3rd round
2006–07	DNQ	
2007–08	DNQ	

* 1st of two group stages
** 2nd of two group stages

Masses face yellow peril

Having attracted the most Bundesliga spectators each season for the past decade and recorded an average attendance more than 10,000 higher than at any other European ground in 2003–04, Borussia Dortmund are renowned for the sea of yellow created by fans at their vibrant Signal Iduna Park stadium. Admirers call it the Opera House of German football but its huge redevelopment costs meant the fat lady almost sang as the club faced bankruptcy in 2005.

Dortmund's debt increased as big signings flopped and the Champions League group phase proved elusive; even proceeds from their 79,647 average turn-out in 2003–04 could not help. To recoup money, Dortmund cut wages and sold their ground before leasing it back.

This struggle contrasted with the wealth of the 1990s, when Matthias Sammer and four other German stars returned from Italy and the 1997 Champions League was won. After reaching the 1998 semi-finals, though, they were still waiting to reach the knock-out stage 11 years on.

LEVERKUSEN

Bayer's tapestry

Situated on the banks of the famous Rhine, Leverkusen is a relatively new city, being formed only in 1930 when several villages merged. Today it is home to about 160,000 people and is well situated for business, being close to Cologne and Dusseldorf (both these city's airports are close by). The chemical and pharmaceutical company, Bayer, has been integral in the growth of the Leverkusen since its arrival at the end of the 19th century and today employs about 65,000 people in the city.

Wiesdorf, an area near the river, is a popular area for its shopping arcades, and more shopping can be found further east in laid-back Schlebusch. A short distance to the north is Opladen district, also known for its shops, but more popular for its busy pub and restaurant scene and specifically, in August, the four-day Bierbörse (beer pub).

BayArena, where Bayer Leverkusen play their home matches is centrally located near the E35 and E37 roads.

Weather	Low (ºC)	High
January	1	4
February	1	5
March	2	10
April	5	14
May	8	18
June	12	21
July	13	23
August	13	23
September	11	19
October	7	15
November	4	8
December	2	5

Below: Small city, hardcore support. Leverkusen fans urge their team on.

1 OPLADEN
Stroll along Kölner Strasse and take your pick from the lively pubs and cafés. For a beer garden try Neustadt-Treff, Horst Beyer (Kölner Strasse 137, tel: +49 21 714 4472). To get there: train to Opladen.

2 THE BAYER CROSS
Erected in 1958, this 51 m (167 ft) diameter Bayer company logo is the biggest neon advertisement in the world. To get there: near the Wiesdorf district, you won't miss it.

3 THREE COUNTRIES IN A DAY
With Holland and Belgium so close it is easy to jump in the car and visit three countries in just a few hours. Got a bit more time on your hands? Make it five by adding Luxembourg and France.

BAYER LEVERKUSEN

MATTER OF FACT
Name: Bayer 04 Leverkusen Fussball
Stadium: BayArena (capacity 22,500)
Address: Bismarckstr 122 -124,
D-51371
To get there: Train (station:
Leverkusen-Mitte). Buses 203, 207, 222
Telephone: +49 214 86600
Email: info@bayer04.de
Website: www.bayer04.de

Stadium tour
Price: €5
Contact: Tel: +49 1805 040404 or
email: bayarenatour@bayer04.de

Home	Away

Trophies
1	Uefa Cup
1	German Cup

Main rivals
Leverkusen have a Rhineland rivalry
with Cologne (tel: +49 221 716 16300,
www.fc-koeln.de), who play only
11 km (7 miles) or so down the road at
the RheinEnergieStadion (Aachener
Straße 999, 50933). Leverkusen's
prominence in recent times despite
lacking Cologne's history and fanbase
has caused jealously among the latter's
fans, exacerbated by the feeling that
Leverkusen only thrive because of a
factory's money. Cologne fans suffered
in 2002 when they were relegated,
while Leverkusen had reached the
Champions League final.

Above: Bayer Leverkusen players line up against Liverpool before a Champions League match.

The perfect advert

One startling feature of the BayArena redevelopment plans caused a double take. Across the top of the stadium would be a luminous Bayer Cross company logo, 200 m (656 ft) in diameter and facing the sky – an irresistible aerial shot for TV directors. The Bayer pharmaceuticals firm created Bayer Leverkusen as a gift to their workers a century ago, but the club is now a global billboard that benefits the company.

"Our football team is an important flagship at home and abroad," says company chairman Werner Wenning. But although his firm's backing in recent decades has strengthened a club with few fans, the final step to greatness has proved elusive. Leverkusen have the third best overall German League record in the past 25 years yet await their first title.

Some mock them as an artificial club that lacks passionate support, a view encouraged when average attendances dipped below 10,000 in the 1980s. But empty seats at the BayArena are rare and the increase to 30,000-plus seats can lift the team – and company – another notch.

TEN YEAR RECORD

Season	Competition	Finished
1998–99	Uefa Cup	Last 32
1999–00	Champs League	Group*
	Uefa Cup	Last 32
2000–01	Champs League	Group*
	Uefa Cup	Last 32
2001–02	Champs League	Final
2002–03	Champs League	Group**
2003–04	DNQ	
2004–05	Champs League	Last 16
2005–06	Uefa Cup	1st round
2006–07	Uefa Cup	QF
2007–08	Uefa Cup	QF

* 1st of two group stages
** 2nd of two group stages

MUNICH

A glass always full

The Beer Festival. Come on, that's what you're after isn't it? If you're looking for one football match and one month to coincide then it has to be October (and September, actually). The world-famous Oktoberfest is the city's beer festival held over a 16-day period from the end of September into October and attracts over six million visitors.

But worry not, the beer flows freely throughout the year in the Bavarian capital. If there is one place where you have to visit a beer garden or hall then it has to be Munich. Sit at one of the large trestle tables, order a large beer and *Riesenbrezn* (giant pretzel) then simply watch the locals and enjoy the tradition. Then order another beer, of course.

Most visitors to Munich first head to Karlplatz or Marienplatz and then wander the streets that link and surround them. The main road that runs around this area (known as the Altstadtring) follows the line of the old city wall, parts of which can still be seen today.

Karlplatz (also called Stachus) was laid out in 1791 and has become one of the busiest squares in Europe, as it lies at the entrance to the city centre and the pedestrianized shopping area. Marienplatz is at the heart of the city and was used for markets and tournaments dating back to medieval times. Here you can see the new town hall, the old town hall, Mariensäule, the column that went up in 1638 to commemorate the end of the Swedish invasion, and the Glockenspiel, where you can see dancing mechanical figures.

Bayern Munich's home, the futuristic Allianz Arena, is about 11 km (7 miles) north of the city centre.

Below: No queueing for a drink here: Munich's famous Oktoberfest.

3 THINGS YOU MUST DO...
(Apart from the football)

1 HAIDHAUSEN
The nightlife centre of Munich with its host of bars, restaurants and clubs. Just take your pick. To get there: head to Ostbahnhof station.

2 HOFBRÄUHAUS BEER HALL
This famous beer hall (Am Platzl 9, tel: +49 89 221 676) has been around since 1644 for food, fun, and, er, beer. Open: daily 09.00–23.30. To get there: it's near Marienplatz.

3 BMW WELT
Housed in the prominent double cone building is the place to be if you are a fan and want to experience everything BMW (Am Olympiapark 1, tel: +49 180 211 8822). Open: daily 09.00–20.00. Price: free. To get there: subway U3 to Olympiazentrum.

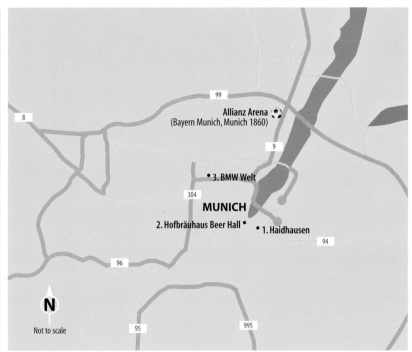

Allianz Arena
(Bayern Munich, Munich 1860)

3. BMW Welt

MUNICH

2. Hofbräuhaus Beer Hall
1. Haidhausen

N

Not to scale

BARS > CLUBS > RESTAURANTS

Bars > So you want cocktails and are prepared to pay the price? **Schumann's American Bar** (Odeonsplatz 6, tel: +49 89 229 060) is what you are looking for. You might even see the odd celebrity. And while we're at it let's go fully into stylish design. **Lenbach** (Ottostr 6, tel: +49 89 549 1300) has this in spades, plus good food, drink and the odd celebrity of its own.

Clubs > In the city's beating clubland, Haidhausen clubbers head to **Babylon 2** (Rosenheimerstr. 143, tel: +49 89 450 2660), the area's largest club with a choice of floors and music styles.

Restaurants > For some hearty Bavarian specialities on your plate to be enjoyed in a relaxed beer-drinking environment, head to **Augustiner** (Arnulfstr 52, tel: +49 89 594 393).

Below: *Marienplatz market and restaurants offer a traditional Munich experience.*

Weather	Low (°C)	High
January	-3	2
February	-3	3
March	0	8
April	2	11
May	6	17
June	10	20
July	12	22
August	12	22
September	8	18
October	4	12
November	0	6
December	-2	4

BAYERN MUNICH

Above: The Allianz Arena.

TEN YEAR RECORD

Season	Competition	Finished
1998–99	Champs League	Final
1999–00	Champs League	SF
2000–01	Champs League	Winners
2001–02	Champs League	QF
2002–03	Champs League	Group*
2003–04	Champs League	Last 16
2004–05	Champs League	QF
2005–06	Champs League	Last 16
2006–07	Champs League	QF
2007–08	Uefa Cup	SF

* 1st of two group stages

Devouring the opposition

Labelled the 'kitchen of gossip' by former captain Lothar Matthäus, Bayern Munich have served up a treat for newspapers. Claiming his players did not mind losing, general manager Uli Hoeness said: "Half an hour after the match they're playing cards and making big-shot comments. They eat their free scampi after the game, while I go home with indigestion watching them play like that." Goalkeeper Oliver Kahn retorted that Hoeness himself ate scampi and his "stupid populist talk isn't going to help us."

Club president Franz Beckenbauer declared after one defeat his players were "a disgrace" yet midfielder Stefan Effenberg, uncowed by his boss, replied that "Criticism is in order, but not if it is below the belt". Matthäus himself helped encourage the club's FC Hollywood nickname in the 1990s, notably through his enmity with team-mate Jürgen Klinsmann.

Perhaps Bayern pursue internal battles because few rivals give them a fight. They've won 14 of the past 24 Bundesliga titles and should stay on top, with their 2006–07 revenue of €223 million about €100 million more than the next biggest, Hamburg.

Munich 1860 were the city's sole Bundesliga pioneers in 1963 but Bayern soon flourished, winning three successive titles under coach Udo Lattek from 1972 and three European Cups from 1974. Their Magnificent Six of Beckenbauer, Hoeness, Sepp Maier, Paul Breitner, Hans-Georg Schwarzenbeck and Gerd Müller also inspired West Germany to become 1972 European champions and 1974 World champions.

Bayern's domestic dominance has helped ensure they have retained their huge nationwide support. They moved, in 2005, to the Allianz Arena, known by locals as the Rubber Dinghy, and sail on serenely.

GREATEST PLAYERS

> FRANZ BECKENBAUER (1964–77)
Voted his country's Footballer of the Year four times and Europe's best twice, Beckenbauer redefined the sweeper role, turning it into a position from which to make attacking bursts. He coached Bayern to the title in 1994, the year he became club president.

> GERD MÜLLER (1964–79)
Known as The Bomber, Müller was a short and stocky centre forward with an extraordinary eye for goal. He scored a record 365 Bundesliga goals, almost 100 more than the next best, and was the first German to be named as European Footballer of the Year in 1970.

MATTER OF FACT
Name: Fussball-Club Bayern Munchen
Stadium: Allianz Arena
(capacity 69,901)
Address: Werner-Heisenberg-Allee 25, 80939
To get there: S-Bahn to Marienplatz, then metro line U6 (station: Fröttmaning)
Telephone: +49 89 699 310
Email: webmaster@fcbayern.de
Website: www.fcbayern.de

Stadium tour (includes museum)
Open: Daily, except match days and event days, 10.00–19.00. Buy ticket at World of Brands on Level 3, or book (see below). Tour lasts 75 mins
Price: €10 (ages 4–12 €6.50)
Contact: Tel: +49 180 555 5101 or email: besucher@allianz-arena.de

Home	Away

Trophies
4	European Cup/Champions League
1	European Cup Winners' Cup
1	Inter-Cities Fairs Cup/Uefa Cup
21	German League
14	German Cup

Main rivals
Bayern's rivalry with city neighbours Munich 1860, their Allianz Arena tenants, has lessened since the latter were relegated from the Bundesliga in 2004. They previously co-habited at the Grünwalder Stadium from 1925 to 1972 and the Olympic Stadium for some periods from 1972 to 2005. Unterhaching, in far southern Munich, played in the Bundesliga from 1999 to 2001 but are now in the third division. Bayern also have a rivalry with Bavarian side Nuremberg, the fading giants, whose ninth and last league title came in 1968.

Above: Bayern's giant-flag man.

LIKE FATHER, LIKE SON
Karl-Heinz Wildmoser Jnr, head of the Allianz Arena stadium holding company, was jailed for four and half years for taking money from a building firm for giving information about the contract bidding process. His father, Karl-Heinz Wildmoser Snr, then president of Munich 1860, was charged but struck a plea bargain.

GELSENKIRCHEN

The coal miners

An industrial city in the North Rhine-Westphalia, Gelsenkirchen is probably best known by football fans for its inclusion as one of the 12 host cities for the 2006 World Cup, including the England v Portugal quarter-final.

On a more regular basis, the city famed for coal mining is home to Schalke 04. Their stadium, the Veltins-Arena, can be found 6 km (4 miles) north of the city centre near the A2 Autobahn.

The Schalke district, after which the team is named, is next to the Altstadt. It is here you will find many of the city's landmarks such as the Musiktheater, a modern glass-fronted building which hosts performances of Mozart, Bernstein and all things cultural, plus the drab looking Hans Sachs House (town hall), and the Bleckkirche, the city's oldest church, built in 1735. The Buer district, about 9 km (5.5 miles) north of Altstadt, is the place to head if you're looking for shopping and restaurants.

Weather	Low (°C)	High
January	0	3
February	1	5
March	2	8
April	4	11
May	8	16
June	12	19
July	13	21
August	13	21
September	11	17
October	7	13
November	3	8
December	1	5

Below: The closed entrance to an old coal mine, the industry the city is built on.

3 THINGS YOU MUST DO...
(Apart from the football)

1 MARKET HALL, BUER
For food and specialist shops try the Market Hall (Springeplatz, Buer). A popular watering hole in the hall is Kronski (tel: +49 209 702 2535). Open: bar Mon–Thur 12.00–01.00, Fri–Sat 12.00–04.00, Sun 15.00–01.00. To get there: Tram 301 to Buer Rathaus/Goldbergplatz.

2 SCHLOSS BERGE CASTLE
Either stay in the hotel or visit the restaurant. Dating back to 1284, the Schloss Berge (Adenauerallee 103, tel: +49 209 17740) is a castle, lake and park close to the football stadium. Open: the restaurant is open for breakfast, lunch and dinner. To get there: bus line 302 to Berger.

3 BRAUHAUS HIBERNIA
When in Germany... Visit this beer hall (Bahnhofsvorplatz 2, tel: +49 209 208 531) popular for its food, beer and occasional live music. Open: Sun–Thur 09.00–00.00, Fri–Sat 09.00–01.00. To get there: it's in the city centre. Tram 107 to Gelsenkirchen Hbf.

SCHALKE 04

Above: Schalke fans know all about disappointment.

MATTER OF FACT
Name: Fussball-Club Schalke 04
Stadium: Veltins-Arena
(capacity 61,673)
Address: Ernst-Kuzorra-Weg 1, 45891
To get there: Tram 302 (from the
city's railway station)
Telephone: +49 209 36180
Email: post@schalke04.de
Website: www.schalke04.de

Stadium tour (includes museum)
Opening hours: Tue–Fri tours at
12.00, 16.00, Sat–Sun tours at 11.00,
15.00. Not match days and event days
Museum: Tue–Fri 10.00–19.00,
Sat–Sun 10.00–17.00
Price: €8 (under-21s €4)
Museum: €4
Contact: Tel: +49 209 389 2900
(Tue–Fri, 09.00–18.00) or email:
tour@veltins-arena.de

| Home | Away |

Trophies
1	Inter-Cities Fairs Cup/Uefa Cup
7	German League
4	German Cup

Main rivals
Schalke contest the Revier derby with
bitter rivals Borussia Dortmund (see
page 73) – another club with
enormous support. Dortmund is
a 30 minute train ride away from
Gelsenkirchen on the S-Bahn line 2.
The Ruhr industrial region also houses
Bochum, Duisburg, Rot-Weiss
Oberhausen and Arminia Bielefeld.
Schalke have a strong rivalry with
Cologne, who are on the southern
tip of the Ruhr along with Borussia
Monchengladbach and
Bayer Leverkusen.

TEN YEAR RECORD

Season	Competition	Finished
1998–99	Uefa Cup	1st round
1999–00	DNQ	
2000–01	DNQ	
2001–02	Champs League	Group*
2002–03	Uefa Cup	Last 32
2003–04	Intertoto Cup	Winners**
	Uefa Cup	2nd round
2004–05	Intertoto Cup	Winners**
	Uefa Cup	Last 32
2005–06	Champs League	Group
	Uefa Cup	SF
2006–07	Uefa Cup	1st round
2007–08	Champs League	QF

* 1st of two group stages
** One of two winners

The nearly men

Parkstadion, 19 May 2001: thousands of fans flood the pitch as players swig beers in celebration. Schalke 04's home win against Unterhaching means their long title drought is over... or is it? The stadium screen switches to the match in Hamburg, where it was thought Bayern Munich had already lost. Bayern equalize with a 94th-minute free kick and, to the Parkstadion's horror, become champions instead.

Years later Schalke captain Mike Büskens recalled: "I just have to live with it, to have been a champion of hearts but not a champion of the Bundesliga." The misery was shared. "The whole of Germany is crying with Schalke," said a newspaper headline.

The 60,000 who attend Schalke's home matches are accustomed to disappointment, the club having reached 50 years without a championship in 2008. Go further back and they won six titles in nine seasons from 1934. Now, with the investment of Russian gas company Gazprom since 2006, the club are dreaming of becoming champions again.

FRANCE

THE 3 MINUTE GUIDE

Capital: *Paris.* **Language:** *French.* **Beer:** *Kronenbourg 1664.* **Food:** Coq au vin, *baguettes, truffles, foie gras.* **National anthem:** *La Marseillaise (The Song of Marseille).* **Population:** *64,058,000.* **Time zone:** *GMT +1.* **Emergency number:** *Police 17, medical 15/18, fire 18.* **Did you know?** *The bikini was invented by French designers Jacques Heim and Louis Reard. Fine idea, boys.* **Football body:** *Federation Française de Football, 87 Boulevard de Grenelle, Paris 75738; tel: +33 1 4431 7300, fax: +33 1 4431 7373, email: webmaster@fff.fr, website: www.fff.fr. Founded 1919. Affiliated 1904.*

Below: Known for their culinary excellence, the French boast a host of world-renowned restaurants.

All hail the organizers

If England created the soul of world football, then France was responsible for the body. Travelling Englishmen spread the word by playing in various outposts of the globe, but it was the French who took stock and created order by formulating an international structure.

The French-named Fédération Internationale de Football Association (Fifa) was founded in Paris in 1904. And their principal competition, the World Cup, began in 1930 following the persistent lobbying of Frenchman Jules Rimet, the organization's longest-serving president, whose name was attached to the trophy until 1970.

Henri Delaunay, Rimet's compatriot, also helped bring about the World Cup but his more significant legacy was the European championship, his drive prompting the tournament's trophy to be named after him. At club level, *L'Equipe* newspaper editor Gabriel Hanot dreamed up the European Cup, which started in 1955–56, and devised the European Player of the Year award for good measure.

But while France had early power, the glory came late. Not until 1993 did the country win a European club trophy when Marseille became continental champions, and even then the shine was taken off the achievement because they bribed their opponents in the last domestic league match before the final.

As for the national team, they secured the European Championship in Paris in 1984 but it was not until the last World Cup of the century that they finally stood tall over the rest of the planet, again succeeding on home turf.

Above: Paris St-Germain supporters.   *Below:* Romance is France's national sport.

THE TEN YEAR GUIDE

Ligue 1

Season	Winner	Runner-up
1998–99	Bordeaux	Marseille
1999–00	Monaco	Paris Saint-Germain
2000–01	Nantes	Lyon
2001–02	Lyon	Lens
2002–03	Lyon	Monaco
2003–04	Lyon	Paris Saint-Germain
2004–05	Lyon	Lille
2005–06	Lyon	Bordeaux
2006–07	Lyon	Marseille
2007–08	Lyon	Bordeaux

Coupe de France

Season	Winner	Runner-up
1998–99	Nantes	Sedan
1999–00	Nantes	Calais
2000–01	Strasbourg	Amiens
2001–02	Lorient	Bastia
2002–03	Auxerre	Paris Saint-Germain
2003–04	Paris Saint-Germain	Châteauroux
2004–05	Auxerre	Sedan
2005–06	Paris Saint-Germain	Marseille
2006–07	Sochaux	Marseille
2007–08	Lyon	Paris Saint-Germain

PARIS

For the love of food and romance

As soon as you arrive in Paris for the first time you naturally crane your neck to see the famous Eiffel Tower. Keep your eyes looking towards the west part of the central area and you'll see it peeping through soon enough, even if it's not so huge that it dominates the skyline by size alone.

Not too far away is the historic Arc de Triomphe looking down along the famous boulevard, the Champs-Elysées. Like other major world cities such as London and New York, it's impossible to wander around Paris without stumbling across film set-favourite landmarks. One of the city's sporting landmarks, Parc des Princes, where Paris Saint-Germain play their home matches, is to the west of the city by the Boulevard

Périphérique, the freeway that rings the city centre.

There are two big reasons to come to Paris: romance and food. Which one costs you more is up to you, but combine the two to the maximum and it'll cost you a fortune. French food, is of course, renowned and if you disappear to the nearest international fast-food joint you are missing a major part of this city (not to mention upsetting the romance part). Even a mid-range restaurant, or a cheaper one tucked away if you can find someone with local knowledge, will give you a taste of what all the fuss is about, even if it's not truffles and caviar on your plate. And you can always wash it down with decent champagne, whatever your choice of food.

Below: The area surrounding the Eiffel Tower is popular for leisure activities.

3 THINGS YOU MUST DO...
(Apart from the football)

1 STADE DE FRANCE
The stadium (Rue Jules Rimet, tel: +33892 700 900) is home to the national rugby and football teams. Tours last 60 minutes. Open: daily 10.30, 12.00, 14.30, 16.30 except event days. Price: adults €12, concessions €8. To get there: train RER B to La Plaine – Stade de France. Metro line 13 to St Denis – Porte de Paris. Bus 256 or 302.

2 KNICKERS
Girls treat yourself, and boys get them for your girlfriend. The French do women's underwear better than anyone. Try Alice Cadolle (4 rue Cambon, tel: +33 1 4260 2807). To get there: subway M1 to Tuileries.

3 THE LOUVRE
If you love art, head for the Louvre (99 rue de Rivoli, tel: +33 1 4020 5050). There are over 300,000 works of art in one of the world's most celebrated collections. Open: Mon, Thur, Sat, Sun 09.00–18.00, Wed, Fri 09.00–21.45. Price: €9 for full day entry to permanent collections. To get there: subway M1 or M7 to Palais Royal – Musée du Louvre.

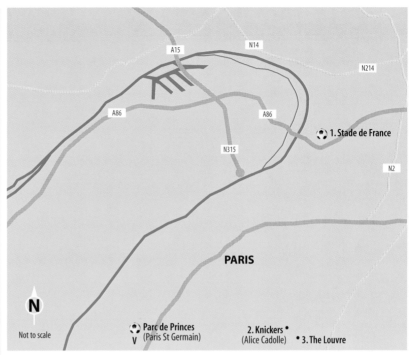

Map labels: N14, A15, N214, A86, A86, N315, N2, **1. Stade de France**, **PARIS**, N, Not to scale, **Parc de Princes** (Paris St Germain), **2. Knickers** (Alice Cadolle), **3. The Louvre**

BARS > CLUBS > RESTAURANTS

Bars > If you're after cocktails and a popular piano bar in a venue that has been around for nearly 100 years, then settle into **Harry's New York Bar** (5 rue Danou, tel: +33 1 4261 7114).

Clubs > You've heard the hype and seen the film, now go and see the dancing girls for yourself. **Bal du Moulin Rouge** (Montmartre, 82 Boulevard de Clichy, tel: +33 1 5309 8282). Have dinner and a show or just the show. Needless to say, it's better to make a reservation in this legendary venue. And leave the football shirt at the hotel.

Restaurants > Your wallet is full to brimming and you are determined to experience the ultimate in French cuisine. It's got to be the famous **Alain Ducasse** at the Plaza Athénée (25 Avenue de Montaigne, tel: +33 1 5367 6500). Enjoy a drink in the hotel bar before settling down.

Below: *Find a venue to match the food.*

Weather	Low (ºC)	High
January	1	6
February	1	7
March	3	10
April	5	13
May	9	17
June	12	21
July	14	23
August	13	23
September	11	20
October	7	15
November	3	9
December	2	7

PARIS ST-GERMAIN

Above: Paris football supporters finally have a club worth supporting.

TEN YEAR RECORD

Season	Competition	Finished
1998–99	DNQ	
1999–00	DNQ	
2000–01	Champs League	Group*
2001–02	Intertoto Cup	Winners**
	Uefa Cup	Last 32
2002–03	Uefa Cup	Last 32
2003–04	DNQ	
2004–05	Champs League	Group
2005–06	DNQ	
2006–07	Uefa Cup	Last 16
2007–08	DNQ	

* 2nd group stage
** One of three winners

Eureka, at last

If most major European clubs have grown naturally from a tiny seed that took hold a century or so ago, Paris St-Germain are straight out of a latter-day science lab. Founded as recently as 1970, they are an artificial creation born of desperation to give one of Europe's biggest cities a decent club to support. While the similar-sized city of London routinely boasts five or six top-division sides, the French capital has struggled at times to maintain even one place among the elite.

Without a frontline local club after the mid-'60s demise of Racing Club de Paris, about 20,000 Parisian football fans donated funds to form Paris FC in 1969. They soon merged with second-division Saint-Germain-en-Laye, and Paris St-Germain came into existence. The new club then split into two, Paris FC and PSG; the latter, who were placed in the third division, immediately gained consecutive promotions to reach the top level and have stayed there ever since.

Yet PSG faced bankruptcy in the 1990–91 season and were only kept alive for even more unconventional reasons than those that led to their foundation. Canal Plus feared their French league viewing figures would fall if the 10 million or so people in the Paris area had no local team to support so they baled out the club with heavy investment.

The Canal Plus money helped turn PSG into France's leading club in the mid-1990s, with six successive top-three finishes and five consecutive European semi-finals. They have since tailed off into a mid-table side, but the fervour of the 40,000 people who habitually attend the Parc des Princes suggests Paris finally has a durable force.

GREATEST PLAYERS

> LUIS FERNÁNDEZ (1978–86)
Part of the great France midfield quartet that featured Michel Platini, Alain Giresse and Jean Tigana, Fernandez was a ball-winner who helped PSG win their first league title in 1986. As a coach, he guided them to the 1996 European Cup Winners' Cup when just 36.

> DAVID GINOLA (1991–95)
The winger was the only player to start all 38 games in the 1994 title-winning season. Possessing great balance and skill and strong with both feet, he provided much of the flair in a prosaic side, although his lack of commitment to defending meant opinions of him varied.

MATTER OF FACT

Name: Paris Saint-Germain Football Club

Stadium: Parc des Princes (capacity 49,000)

Address: 24 rue du Commandant Guilbaud, 75016

To get there: Metro Line 9 (station: Porte de Saint Cloud). Line 10 (station: Porte d'Auteuil). Buses 22, 32, 52, 62, 72, 123, 175, 189, 241, PC1

Telephone: +33 1 4743 7171 (in France phone 3275)

Email: psg@psg.fr

Website: www.psg.fr

Stadium tour

Open: New days and times in 2009 to be decided

Price: To be decided

Contact: Email: visiteduparcdes princes@psg.tm.fr

Home	Away

Trophies

1	European Cup Winners' Cup
2	French League
7	French Cup

Main rivals

Marseille (see pages 92–93) and PSG meet in Le Classique and form the strongest rivalry in France even though the Paris club are less than 40 years old. The enmity is partly fuelled by Marseille suspicions that the Paris-based authorities do not treat the second-city club well, notably during the Marseille match-fixing scandal. City neighbours Paris FC (tel: +33 1 4416 6000, www.paris-fc.com), who play at the 20,000-seat Stade Sébastien Charléty (99 Boulevard Kellermann, 75013), were integral in PSG's formative years (see main story) but now languish in the third division.

BAD MANNERS

PSG were initially banned from the 2008–09 League Cup – a decision overturned – after fans displayed an offensive banner during the previous season's final against northern club Lens. The message read: "Paedophiles, unemployed, inbreeding ... welcome to the north."

Above: Paris St-Germain's Sammy Traoré (left) battles for the ball with Derry City's Kevin McHugh during a Uefa Cup match.

BORDEAUX

Let the wine flow

Situated at the heart of the world-renowned French wine-growing region, Bordeaux is located in the southwest of the country on the River Garonne. The Bordeaux region produces about 700 million bottles of wine every year for distribution around the globe.

The city itself is home to around 230,000 people, and the historic part is on the UNESCO World Heritage List. The urban area straddles both the west and east banks of the Garonne, linked by four bridges. On the west side is shopper's heaven, Rue Sainte-Catherine, a pedestrianized street of more than a kilometre, which runs from south to north until it meets Place de Comedie where you will find the 18th century Grand Théâter. Place de la Bourse and many of the city's other examples of outstanding architecture are found within walking distance.

The Stade Chaban-Delmas, home of Bordeaux's football club, is about 3 km (2 miles) southwest of here.

Weather	Low (ºC)	High
January	2	9
February	4	11
March	4	13
April	6	16
May	9	19
June	12	22
July	15	26
August	15	26
September	12	23
October	8	17
November	5	13
December	3	10

Below: Visit France and sample wines from Bordeaux.

3 THINGS YOU MUST DO...
(Apart from the football)

1 WINE TASTINGS

From walking tours to day or longer tours, a wide variety are available. Plus tastings of Bordeaux wine, of course. The tourist office (12 cours 30 Juillet, tel: +33 5 5600 6600) organizes a daily two-hour city tour and a wine tasting can be added. Open: Mon–Sat 10.00, Sun 11.00. Price €11. To get there: Trams B or C to Quinconces.

2 VIEUX BORDEAUX

If you're in one of the world's great wine regions, you'll need some great food to go with it. Vieux Bordeaux (27 rue Buhan, tel: +33 5 5652 9436) offers a menu with plenty of local ingredients. Open: Mon–Fri 12.00–14.00 and 20.00–22.30, Sat 20.00–22.30. To get there: trams A to Sainte-Catherine or Place du Palais.

3 ESPLANADE DES QUINCONCES

You'll find many interesting squares in Bordeaux and at 126,000 sq m (1,344,420 sq ft), Esplanade des Quinconces is Europe's largest. This is also where you will see the imposing Monument to the Girondins, which honours the deputies of the French Revolution. To get there: trams B or C to Quinconces.

BORDEAUX

Above: *Celtic's Stephane Mahe (right) holds off Laurent Battles of Bordeaux during a pre-season friendly at Celtic Park.*

Kicking rugby into touch

Unaccustomed to having top-division opponents within 200 km (124 miles), Bordeaux have football to themselves in their corner of the southwest. But rugby's hefty presence means they must achieve greatness to grab the kind of spotlight that shone on the club when led by wealthy president Claude Bez in the 1980s.

Bez appointed as coach Aimé Jacquet, who signed Jean Tigana to join Alain Giresse, giving Bordeaux two sides of France's 'magic square' midfield (the others were Michel Platini and Luis Fernández). They helped bring two titles, two cups and two European semi-finals.

But Bez saddled the club with great debts trying to keep pace with the big-spending Bernard Tapie at Marseille, and he left in 1990, later to be convicted of fraud. Bordeaux's insolvency caused an enforced relegation in 1991, but they bounced back to reach the 1996 Uefa Cup final and snatch the 1999 league title with an 89th-minute winner on the final day away to Paris St-Germain. Rugby was finally in the shade.

TEN YEAR RECORD

Season	Competition	Finished
1998–99	Uefa Cup	QF
1999–00	Champs League	Group*
2000–01	Uefa Cup	Last 16
2001–02	Uefa Cup	Last 32
2002–03	Uefa Cup	Last 32
2003–04	Uefa Cup	QF
2004–05	DNQ	
2005–06	DNQ	
2006–07	Champs League	Group
	Uefa Cup	Last 32
2007–08	Uefa Cup	Last 32

* 2nd of two group stages

MATTER OF FACT

Name: Football Club des Girondins de Bordeaux
Stadium: Stade Chaban-Delmas (capacity 34,198)
Address: Avenue de Lescure, 33000
To get there: Tram A (stop: Stade Chaban-Delmas). Bus 9 (stop: Stade Chaban-Delmas)
Telephone: +33 8 9268 3433
Email: infofcgb@girondins.com
Website: www.girondins.com

Stadium tour

No tours available

Home   **Away**

Trophies

5	French League
3	French Cup

Main rivals

Bordeaux have no close neighbours of any significance – Toulouse are the nearest, just over 200 km (124 miles) away. But they have held a long-standing rivalry with Marseille (see pages 92–93), fuelled by several close battles for trophies, such as when Bordeaux won their 1986 Cup final meeting in extra time and also during the title races of 1987, 1990 and 1999. Their contests in the late 1980s were given an extra edge by the competition between the clubs' ambitious presidents, Claude Bez, of Bordeaux, and Marseille's Bernard Tapie.

LYON

The rivers of Lyon

With a population of 470,000 Lyon is the third largest city in France behind Paris and Marseille. It is situated in central-east France, a relatively short distance from Geneva, Switzerland. The two rivers, the Saône and Rhône, that wind their way through it from the north and west respectively before converging in the south, have moulded the city's development. It means you are never far from the waterside.

The old part of the town, Vieux Lyon, which dates back to medieval times, is to the west by the Saône. Rising from here is the hill district of Fourvière where you will find the imposing Basilica Notre-Dame de Fourvière, completed in 1896, and the 'rival' to the Eiffel Tower, the Tour Métallique de Fourvière. The main shopping area and railway station are to the east in the Part Dieu district.

Lyon's football stadium, Stade Gerland is 6 km (3.7 miles) to the south of the city centre.

Weather	Low (°C)	High
January	0	5
February	1	7
March	3	11
April	5	14
May	10	19
June	13	22
July	16	26
August	15	26
September	12	22
October	8	16
November	3	10
December	1	6

Below: Lyonnais flags on proud display during a Uefa Champions League game.

3 THINGS YOU MUST DO...
(Apart from the football)

1 NINKASI KAFÉ
Enjoy a DJ and local artists in this bar and restaurant (267 rue Marcel Merieux, tel: +33 4 7276 8900) which brews six of its own beers on site. Open: Mon–Sat 10.00–late, Sun 16.00–00.00. To get there: metro B to Stade de Gerland.

2 CENTRE D'HISTOIRE DE LA RÉSISTANCE
The Museum of the French Resistance (14 Avenue Berthelot, tel: +33 4 7872 2311) charts the rise of fascism through to the liberation of France and recognizes the people of the Resistance. Open: Wed–Sun 09.00–17:30. Price: €4. To get there: tram T2 to Jet d'Eau – Mendes France.

3 PARC DE LA TÊTE D'OR
A 117-hectare public park to the north of the city beside the Rhône, this comprises a series of walks and a large lake. There is also a small zoo, various sporting activities and the Interpol office. To get there: buses C1 stop in the park.

LYON

Above: Lyon have been blowing away the opposition in the new millennium.

MATTER OF FACT
Name: Olympique Lyonnais
Stadium: Stade Gerland
(capacity 40,494)
Address: 350 Avenue Jean Jaures,
69007
To get there: Metro line B (stop:
Stade de Gerland). Bus 96
Telephone: +33 562 4 26 29 67 00
Email: ol@olympiquelyonnais.com
Website: www.olweb.fr

Stadium tour
Contact club for details

Home   **Away**

Trophies

7	French League
4	French Cup

Main rivals

St Étienne (tel: +33 47 792 3170, www.asse.fr) are 60 km (37 miles) southwest of Lyon at the Stade Geoffroy Guichard (14 Rue Paul et Pierre Guichard, St Etienne 42028). Lyon supporters did not warm to Jacques Santini when he coached their team from 2000 to 2002 partly because, so the theory goes, he spent most of his playing career at St Etienne. The latter have won ten French league titles, achieved between 1957 and 1981, a record that Lyon were threatening to beat in one go in the early 21st century.

TEN YEAR RECORD

Season	Competition	Finished
1998–99	Uefa Cup	QF
1999–00	Champs League	3rd qual rd
	Uefa Cup	Last 32
2000–01	Champs League	Group*
2001–02	Champs League	Group**
	Uefa Cup	Last 16
2002–03	Champs League	Group**
	Uefa Cup	Last 32
2003–04	Champs League	QF
2004–05	Champs League	QF
2005–06	Champs League	QF
2006–07	Champs League	Last 16
2007–08	Champs League	Last 16

* 2nd of two group stages

** 1st of two group stages

History meets the present

Depending on your viewpoint, Lyon were formed in either 1899 or 1950 (Lyon Olympique Universitaire took the current name in 1950), a difference of 51 years. Given their history, another 51 years might as well be added. A 2001 book would have detected no major impact by them, but now they are one of France's great clubs.

Lyon have crammed almost all their success into the post-millennium period. Having become first-time champions in 2002, their run of consecutive titles was up to seven by 2008, three more than France's next best.

Seeds were sown in 1987, when Jean-Michel Aulas began ploughing money into the club. So demanding is the president – especially in the Champions League – that Alain Perrin was sacked after clinching a League and Cup double, and three others left after winning the title.

Aulas remains influential. In 2008 he threatened to resign if the local council kept delaying his plans for a 60,000-capacity stadium due to open in 2013. Two weeks later the plans were approved.

MARSEILLE

Way down south

Located on the south coast of France, this port city is the second largest in the country and has a population of over 820,000. Although not part of the French Riviera, the city and surrounds is everything the mind conjures up about the 'south of France'.

The picturesque Vieux Port ('Old Port') is dominated by its two forts, Fort Saint-Jean on the north side, which dates back to the 13th century, and Fort Saint-Nicholas on the south. Just to the north is the Panier, the old town, while peering down on the port from the hills to the south is the Notre Dame de la Garde, a highly ornate church whose interior decorators were big on mosaics and marble. Inside you will see many personal items offered under vow, including shirts from players and fans of the Marseille club. Stade Vélodrome, the club's stadium, is about 3 km (2 miles) to the south of the city centre.

From Vieux Port runs the city's main throughfare, Canebière. Travelling along the 1 km (0.6 mile) road you will come to Place du Général de Gaulle, the pedestrianized Rue St Ferreol and the city's main shopping centre, the Centre Bourse, before entering the Réformés area. Just south of here is Place Jean-Jaurès, which attracts a young and lively crowd and is perfect for a *pastis*. Although popular across France, this aniseed drink, which emerged when absinthe was banned, is synonymous with Marseille, and you'll see the short drink at café tables everywhere.

Below: A meal with a view across the port of Marseille.

3 THINGS YOU MUST DO...
(Apart from the football)

1 NOTRE DAME DE LA GARDE
Even if you are not into ornate churches with inlaid marble interiors, Notre Dame de la Garde (Montée de la Bonne Mère, tel: +33 4 9113 4080) is worth a visit because of the views it offers down onto the old port and across the city. Open: 07.00–19.00. Price: free. To get there: bus 60.

2 THE PANIER
The old town, first settled by the Greeks in 600BC, has many small streets, perfect for strolling along before enjoying a *pastis* with the locals. To get there: it's just north of Vieux Port.

3 NOALLIES
Head to the area around Noallies, with its many shops and markets, and you can sample the Algerian influence in Marseille. Hundreds of thousands of North Africans came to the country through the Marseille gateway from this former French colony and many have settled here. To get there: metro M2 to Noallies.

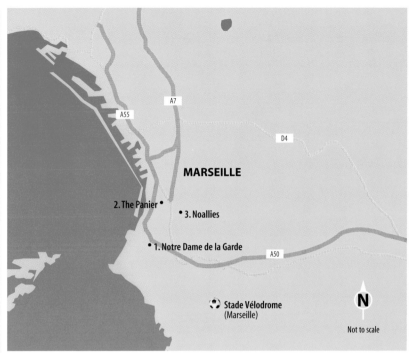

MARSEILLE

2. The Panier

3. Noallies

1. Notre Dame de la Garde

Stade Vélodrome (Marseille)

N

Not to scale

BARS > CLUBS > RESTAURANTS

Bars > Perfectly located with great views over the port, the **Le Bar du Sofitel Vieux Port** (36 Boulevard Charles, tel: +33 4 9115 5900) is in the Sofitel Hotel. Relax in one of the armchairs and order your cocktail of choice. **Le Guépard** (38A Place Thiars, tel: +33 4 9134 2371) is another great cocktail venue near the popular port area.

Clubs > If you don't want to go far when it's time to start dancing, you'll find the cavernous **Trolleybus** (24 Quai de Rive-Neuve, tel: +33 4 9154 3045) in the same area.

Restaurants > In Marseille it has to be *bouillabaisse*, the famous fish and vegetable stew. And for *bouillabaisse* it has to be the smart **La Miramar** (12 Quai la Port, tel: +33 4 9191 1040). For a taste of the city's North African influence try **Restaurant Le Souk** (98 Quai la Port, tel: +33 4 9191 2929).

Below: Bouillabaisse is a local speciality.

Weather	Low (°C)	High
January	2	10
February	3	11
March	5	14
April	8	17
May	12	21
June	16	25
July	18	27
August	18	28
September	15	25
October	12	20
November	6	14
December	3	11

MARSEILLE

Above: *Olympique Marseille's Habib Beye (left) tussles with Kevin Nolan of Bolton Wanderers.*

Seeking pride again after a fall

Season	Competition	Finished
1998–99	Uefa Cup	Final
1999–00	Champs League	Group*
2000–01	DNQ	
2001–02	DNQ	
2002–03	DNQ	
2003–04	Champs League	Group
	Uefa Cup	Final
2004–05	DNQ	
2005–06	Intertoto Cup	Winners**
	Uefa Cup	Last 16
2006–07	Intertoto Cup	Winners***
	Uefa Cup	1st round
2007–08	Champs League	Group
Uefa Cup	Last 16	

TEN YEAR RECORD

* 2nd group stage
** One of three winners
*** One of 11 winners

The bigger they come, the harder they fall, and no French club is bigger or has fallen harder than Marseille. In 1993, while confirming themselves as the country's greatest ever team, their world collapsed. By taking over a mid-table outfit and extravagantly funding an all-conquering side, president Bernard Tapie was true to the club's motto of *Droit au But* ('Straight to Goal'). But by choosing a dishonest path to glory, he instigated a decline they have yet to recover from. His own destiny became Straight to Jail.

Backed by the country's most vociferous fans, Marseille eclipsed St Etienne's record of four successive titles by triumphing in 1993, three days after they had secured their country's belated first European club trophy. But they had bribed three Valenciennes players – two successfully, the other was the whistle-blower – to go easy in a league match just before their

Champions League final against AC Milan. The trail led to Tapie, who spent eight months in prison.

The club were stripped of their 1993 French title, forcibly relegated at the end of 1993–94 and banned from defending their European crown. The financial muddle created by Tapie, whose corruption ran deeper than the Valenciennes affair, would eventually leave them bankrupt, so they were denied promotion despite finishing as second division champions in 1995. Rescued by a council loan, they returned a year later to the top flight but began the 2008–09 season still trying to claim the ninth league title that was briefly theirs in 1993.

Post-scandal, Marseille attract France's biggest attendances, their 52,601 average in 2007–08 beating all rivals by over 15,000, but no trophies followed for the club that flew too close to the Mediterranean sun.

GREATEST PLAYERS

> **JOSIP SKOBLAR (1966–67; 1969–75)**
Known to Marseille fans as Monsieur Goal, the Yugoslavian forward's phenomenal scoring record is shown neatly by the fact that his 100th league goal for the club came in his 100th match. He managed a French league record 44 goals in 1970–71.

> **JEAN-PIERRE PAPIN (1986–92)**
The diminutive striker with a powerful shot had such a reputation for acrobatic strikes from awkward positions that any such volleyed goal is still termed a *papinade* in France. The Frenchman was the league's leading goalscorer for five successive seasons from 1987–88.

MATTER OF FACT
Name: Olympique de Marseille
Stadium: Stade Vélodrome
(capacity 60,031)
Address: 3 Boulevard Michelet, 13008
To get there: Buses 19, 21, 21s, 21Jet,
22, 23, 41, 44, 45, 72 and 83 (stop:
Rond Point du Prado). Metro line 2
(station: Rond Point du Prado for the
stadium's Virage Sud or Tribune Jean
Bouin stands; station: Ste Marguerite
Dromel for the Virage Nord De Peretti
or Tribune Ganay stands)
Telephone: +33 491 76 56 09
Email: om@olympiquede
marseille.com
Website: www.om.net

Stadium tour
Open every two hours Mon–Fri
10.00–16.00 except match days
Price: €5
Contact: As above

Home   **Away**

Trophies
1	European Cup/Champions League
8	French League
10	French Cup

Main rivals
Matches against Paris St-Germain (see
pages 86–87) are intense and often
produce violence off the pitch. When
Marseille were banned from defending
their 1993 Champions League title
because of match-fixing, PSG, league
runners-up to Marseilles, declined to
replace them because, some suspect-
ed, they did not want to fan the flames
of hatred between the clubs any more.
The animosity is recent, as PSG were
only formed in 1970, whereas the
rivalry with St Etienne, which arose
because of the two clubs'
pre-eminence, dates further back.

CASH AND CARROTS
Christoph Robert was one of the
three Valenciennes players to whom
Marseille offered bribes to play badly
against them in 1993. He confessed
all after his arrest. Police duly visited
his aunt's garden in Périgueux,
where they found buried an
envelope containing 250,000 francs.

*Above: Olympique Marseille's
Hatem Ben Arfa skips over a tackle
by SK Brann's Kristjan Sigursson.*

SWITZERLAND

THE

3

MINUTE GUIDE

Capital: *Berne.* **Languages:** *French, German, Italian.* **Beer:** *Unser Bier.* **Food:** *Chocolate.* **National anthem:** *Schweizerpsalm (Swiss Psalm).* **Population:** *7,582,000.* **Time zone:** *GMT +1.* **Emergency numbers:** *Police 117, medical 144, fire 118.* **Did you know?** *Swiss chocolatier Daniel Peter invented milk chocolate.* **Football body:** *Schweizerischer Fussballverband Worbstrasse 48, Postfach Bern 3000; tel: +41 31 950 8111, fax: +41 31 950 8181, email: sfv.asf@football.ch, website: www.football.ch. Founded 1895. Affiliated 1904.*

Below: Switzerland is renowned for its natural beauty.

The administrators

They have long been at the heart of the game but, when the action starts, Switzerland are on the outside looking in. The organizing, staging and officiating of football is almost an art form in the country, but they have yet to master the ball.

Switzerland is home to Fifa (Zurich) – the Swiss are among the seven founder members – and Uefa (Nyon) and has hosted the World Cup (1954), European championship (jointly with Austria in 2008) and six European club finals. Their referees have taken charge of finals at the World Cup and European championship as well as five European Cup or Champions League finals. For good measure, Lausanne stages the Court of Arbitration for Sport, which devotes much time to football.

Yet the national team have never progressed beyond the quarter-finals of a major tournament, and exited at the group stage despite home advantage at Euro 2008. None of their clubs have reached a European club final. Hopes were raised when a drive to improve youth standards in the 1990s led to victory at the European Under-17 championship in 2002, but that potential has yet to be realized.

Swiss league football has an impressive past and a worrying present. While a national championship, initially with regional play-offs, has run since 1897, some clubs have proved less durable. Servette, Lausanne and Lugano, who have shared 27 league titles, have all gone bust this decade. At least they all showed typical Swiss organization by reforming swiftly as new clubs in lower divisions.

Above and below: The Swiss are great at hosting football events, but not winning them.

THE TEN YEAR GUIDE

Super League

Season	Winner	Runner-up
1998–99	Servette	Grasshopper
1999–00	St Gallen	Lausanne-Sports
2000–01	Grasshopper	Lugano
2001–02	Basle	Grasshopper
2002–03	Grasshopper	Basle
2003–04	Basle	Young Boys
2004–05	Basle	Thun
2005–06	Zürich	Basle
2006–07	Zürich	Basle
2007–08	Basle	Young Boys

Schweizer Cup

Season	Winner	Runner-up
1998–99	Lausanne-Sports	Grasshopper
1999–00	Zürich	Lausanne-Sports
2000–01	Servette	Yverdon-Sports
2001–02	Basle	Grasshopper
2002–03	Basle	Neuchâtel Xamax
2003–04	Wil	Grasshopper
2004–05	Zürich	Lucerne
2005–06	Sion	Young Boys
2006–07	Basle	Lucerne
2007–08	Basle	Bellinzona

BASLE

A truly European city

Basle is the archetypal modern European city. Although located in the southwest corner of Switzerland, it is on the doorstep of both France and Germany – so close, in fact, that it's easy to visit all three countries in just a short space of time. Its airport (EuroAirport Basel-Mulhouse-Freiberg) is not even in its own country, being entirely based just over the border in France.

Basle's location has helped it become a thriving base for the pharmaceutical industry and its position on the Rhine means it is the country's cargo port, feeding Rotterdam. Some 165,000 people call Basle home, a city that is split in two (Grossbasel and Kleinbasel) by the Rhine and joined by four bridges and a series of ferry boats. The old medieval town and St Jakob Park, home to FC Basle, can both be found in Grossbasel ('Great Basle') while Kleinbasel ('Little Basle') boasts most of the nightlife.

Weather	Low (ºC)	High
January	-1	3
February	-1	6
March	1	10
April	5	14
May	8	19
June	11	22
July	12	23
August	12	22
September	10	19
October	6	13
November	2	6
December	0	5

Below: Basle is divided in two and linked by ancient bridges.

3 THINGS YOU MUST DO...
(Apart from the football)

1 KARIKATUR AND CARTOON MUSEUM
A collection of more than 3,000 original drawings is on show at the museum (28 St Alban-Vorstadt, tel: +41 61 226 3360). Open: Wed–Sat 14.00–17.00, Sun 10.00–17.00. Price: adults CHF7, children CHF5. To get there: trams 1,2, 6, 8, 14, 15,16 to Kunstmuseum.

2 THE OLD TOWN
Head to Markplatz in Grossbasel and wander down as far as Barfüsserplatz and you will soon have your fill of quaint shops and chocolate. To get there: trams 2, 3, 6, 8, 14, 15, 16 to Markplatz.

3 BUY A WATCH
If there is one thing the Swiss know, it's how to make watches. You'll have no trouble finding everything your wrist desires. Try the centrally located Swatch (65 Freie Strasse, tel: +41 61 260 6565). To get there: trams 2,3, 6, 8, 14, 15, 16 to Barfüsserplatz.

FC BASLE

Above: Loyal fans watch players going through their paces at St Jakob Park.

MATTER OF FACT

Name: Fußball Club Basle 1893
Stadium: St Jakob Park
(capacity 42,500)
Address: Gellertstraße 235, 4052
To get there: Train from main SBB
station (station: St Jakob). Buses 36,
37. Tram 14
Telephone: +41 61 375 1010
Email: info@fcb.ch
Website: www.fcb.ch

Stadium tour
Contact club for details

Home	Away

Trophies
12	Swiss League
9	Swiss Cup

Main rivals
FC Concordia Basel (tel: +41 61 312
5454, www.congeli.ch) were in the
second tier in 2008–09. They play at
Stadion Rankhof.

TEN YEAR RECORD

Season	Competition	Finished
1998–99	DNQ	
1999–00	Intertoto Cup	3rd round
2000–01	Uefa Cup	2nd round
2001–02	Intertoto Cup	Final*
2002–03	Champs League	Group**
2003–04	Uefa Cup	2nd round
2004–05	Champs League	3rd qual rd
	Uefa Cup	Last 16
2005–06	Champs League	3rd qual rd
	Uefa Cup	QF
2006–07	Uefa Cup	Group
2007–08	Uefa Cup	Last 32

* One of three finals
** 2nd of two group stages

The Swiss Barcelona

Glancing at the logos of Basle and Barcelona prompts a double-take – they have an identical yellow football and feature the letters FCB. Throw in the red and blue shirts and it seems Joan Gamper had his captaincy of Basle in mind when founding Barcelona. The parallels have limits, though. The pair's first ever meeting in 2008 destroyed any Swiss delusions of grandeur, the Catalan visitors winning 5–0.

Basle are Switzerland's most successful post-millennium team, their 2008 domestic double producing their fourth league success in seven years. They are also the richest and best-supported club. In recent seasons their average attendance was three times higher than any rival.

Basle were late developers after forming in 1893, their first league title in 1953 coming 55 years after the first triumph of record champions Grasshopper. German coach Helmut Benthaus won seven league crowns in 14 years up to 1980 before a 21-year league title drought. Whisper it, but Barcelona have never endured such a lengthy barren run.

AUSTRIA

<table>
<tr><td>

THE

3

**MINUTE
GUIDE**

</td><td>

</td><td>

Capital: *Vienna.* **Language:** *German.* **Beer:** *Märzen.* **Food:** Wiener schnitzel, apfelstrudel.
National anthem: *Land der Berge, Land am Strome (Land of Mountains, Land on the River).*
Population: *8,206,000.* **Time zone:** *GMT +1.* **Emergency number:** *112.* **Did you know?**
Austria borders eight countries. **Football body:** *Österreichischer Fussball-BundErnst-Happel-
Stadion, Sektor A/F Meiereistrasse 7 Postfach 340 Wien 1021; tel: +43 1 727 180, fax: +43 1
728 1632, email: office@oefb.at, website: www.oefb.at. Founded 1904. Affiliated 1907.*

</td></tr>
</table>

Below: Vienna has a rich cultural legacy and is often called a 'living museum'.

Name of the game

To the uninitiated, the recent history of Austrian club football is a mystery on a par with Vienna-based film thriller *The Third Man*. The record books can only be comprehended with a huge knowledge of the frequent mergers, name changes and extinctions that have taken place.

Wacker Innsbruck were 1971 champions but their next four 1970s titles were as SSW Innsbruck after a merger. They re-adopted the Wacker Innsbruck name before new club Swarovski Tirol took their license and won the 1989 and 1990 titles. The club then changed to Tirol Innsbruck, who went bust in 2002 just after winning their third consecutive title. Wacker Tirol, the spiritual successors but a legally different club with no claim to the past honours, quickly rose to the top flight where they switched their name to – you've guessed it – Wacker Innsbruck.

To sum up, Wacker Innsbruck of 1971 and Wacker Innsbruck of 2008 are different clubs, but Wacker Innsbruck of 1971 and Swarovski Tirol of 1990 are the same. This is no isolated example – the advent of sponsors putting themselves in the club's name has added to the mix – and such confusing upheaval can only detract from the spectacle and hinder the establishment of fan loyalties.

The national team may hope fans are too busy working out which club is which to notice their struggles. They gained just one point when co-hosting Euro 2008 and still cringe at the memory of their defeat to the Faroe Islands in 1990. At least they are still named Austria.

Above: The Ernst Happel Stadion, Vienna, home of the national team. *Below:* Austrian colours.

THE TEN YEAR GUIDE

Bundesliga

Season	Winner	Runner-up
1998–99	Sturm Graz	Rapid Vienna
1999–00	FC Tirol Innsbruck	Sturm Graz
2000–01	FC Tirol Innsbruck	Rapid Vienna
2001–02	FC Tirol Innsbruck	Sturm Graz
2002–03	Austria Vienna	Grazer AK
2003–04	Grazer AK	Austria Vienna
2004–05	Rapid Vienna	Grazer AK
2005–06	Austria Vienna	Red Bull Salzburg*
2006–07	Red Bull Salzburg*	SV Ried
2007–08	Rapid Vienna	Red Bull Salzburg*

* SV Austria Salzburg became Red Bull Salzburg
** Only amateur clubs took part in Cup

ÖFB-Cup

Season	Winner	Runner-up
1998–99	Sturm Graz	LASK Linz
1999–00	Grazer AK	SV Austria Salzburg*
2000–01	FC Kärnten	FC Tirol Innsbruck
2001–02	Grazer AK	Sturm Graz
2002–03	Austria Vienna	FC Kärnten
2003–04	Grazer AK	Austria Vienna
2004–05	Austria Vienna	Rapid Vienna
2005–06	Austria Vienna	SV Mattersburg
2006–07	Austria Vienna	SV Mattersburg
2007–08	SV Horn**	SV Feldkirchen

VIENNA

Not a bad place to live, really

People live well in Vienna. At least according to *The Economist*, which consistently ranks the city near the top in its highest quality of life index covering everything from recreation to political stability. So what's all the fuss about?

Well, there's the musical heritage: both Mozart and Haydn spent large parts of their life living and working here. Johann Sebastian Strauss was born here. Oh, and Beethoven, Schubert and Brahms all have Vienna connections, too. The dancing: all-night Vienna balls and the Viennese Waltz. Good, hearty food: *wiener schnitzel* and *apfelstrudel*. The relaxed culture: get a caffeine fix in a Viennese café. Architecture: everything from grand palaces to a sweeping modern skyline. Plus they have their own vineyards, great beer, more parks than most cities can dream of, and the River Danube.

And then they had the player with possibly the greatest name of any footballer ever: Hans Krankl. *That's* why the 1.7 million people who live in Vienna are happy.

Weather	Low (°C)	High
January	-2	2
February	-1	3
March	1	9
April	5	13
May	9	19
June	12	22
July	14	24
August	15	24
September	11	20
October	6	13
November	1	6
December	-1	3

Below: A view of the formal gardens from the Austrian Gallery, which houses a fantastic collection of European art.

3 THINGS YOU MUST DO...
(Apart from the football)

1 COFFEE
The Viennese love coffee and their cafés. Café Frauenhuber (6 Himmelpfortgasse, tel: +43 1 512 432) has been around since 1788, so if anyone can get your coffee right, they will. Open: Mon–Sat 08.00–00.00, Sun 10.00–22.00. To get there: bus 3A to Plankengasse.

2 KUNSTHISTORISCHES MUSEUM
Quite simply one of the world's great art museums. The Museum of Modern Art (Maria Theresien-Platz, tel: +43 1 525 240). Open: Tue–Wed and Fri–Sun 10.00–18.00, Thu 10.00–21.00. Price: adults €10, reduced rate €7.50. To get there: subway U2 or buses N46, N49, 2A to Museumsquartier.

3 THE CITY CENTRE
Vienna has been called a 'living museum' and an 'open-air museum'. Tickets not required, so head to Stephansplatz to stroll around and enjoy. To get there: subway U1 or buses 1A, 2A, 3A to Stephansplatz.

RAPID VIENNA

Above: The Gerhard Hanappi Stadion.

MATTER OF FACT
Name: Sportklub Rapid Wien
Stadium: Gerhard Hanappi Stadion (capacity 17,500)
Address: Keisslergasse 6, A-1140
To get there: Buses 49, 52. U-Bahn line 4, or S-Bahn line 45 (station for both: Hütteldorf)
Telephone: +43 1 727430
Email: info@skrapid.com
Website: www.skrapid.at

Stadium tour
Contact club for details

Home	Away

Trophies
32 Austrian League
14 Austrian Cup

Main rivals
Long-term rivals Austria Vienna (tel: +43 1 6880150 380, www.fk-austria.at) play at Franz Horr Stadion (Matthias Sindelar-Tribüne, Fischhofgasse 14, A-1100).

TEN YEAR RECORD

Season	Competition	Finished
1998–99	Uefa Cup	1st round
1999–00	Champs League	3rd qual rd
	Uefa Cup	1st round
2000–01	Uefa Cup	2nd round
2001–02	Uefa Cup	2nd round
2002–03	DNQ	
2003–04	DNQ	
2004–05	Uefa Cup	1st round
2005–06	Champs League	Group
2006–07	DNQ	
2007–08	Intertoto Cup	Winners*
	Uefa Cup	1st round

* One of 11 winners

History's forgotten men

Had the European Cup been launched five years earlier, Rapid Vienna might now be regarded as one of the continent's greatest ever clubs. For a period in the early 1950s they were widely considered to be Europe's strongest team, but the absence of official competitions at that time means their pre-eminence is largely forgotten.

In friendlies they beat Arsenal 6–1 and ended the four-year unbeaten run of Ferenc Puskás's Honved. But their star had faded by the start of Uefa competition in 1955 and they have reached just two continental finals, finishing runners-up in the 1985 and 1996 Cup Winners' Cup.

Nevertheless, Rapid have enjoyed domestic glory aplenty. They have won by far the most league titles and received the acclaim of the country's largest fanbase. Even so, the club lack the wealth of many rivals and were run by a bank when their debts piled up in 1993–94. A historically deserved long run in the Champions League would certainly strengthen their hand.

ESTONIA

<table>
<tr><td>

THE

3

MINUTE

GUIDE

</td><td>

</td><td>

Capital: *Tallinn.* **Languages:** *Estonian and Russian.* **Beer:** *Saku.* **Food:** Leib *(black bread),* verivorst *(blood sausage).* **National anthem:** *Mu isamaa, mu õnn ja rõõm (My Fatherland, My Happiness and Joy).* **Population:** *1,308,000.* **Time zone:** *GMT +2.* **Emergency number:** *112 or police 110.* **Did you know?** *The fastest time recorded on the obstacle course of the World Wife Carrying Championships is by Estonians Margo Uusarj and Sandra Kullas.* **Football body:** *Estonian Football Association, A Le Coq Arena Asula, 4c Tallinn 11312; tel: +372 627 9960, fax: +372 627 9969, email: efa@jalgpall.ee, website: www.jalgpall.ee. Founded 1921. Affiliated 1923.*

</td></tr>
</table>

Below: Tallinn's old town.

Name of the game

Having been denied their own official league throughout the Soviet era, Estonian football fans might have shown more enthusiasm when a new national competition was launched in 1992. Fewer than 100 people watched Levadia Tallinn clinch the 2006 title with a home victory over Tammeka Tartu, a change of venue for the match to elsewhere in the capital seemingly requiring too much of a sacrifice for many supporters to make, despite the importance of the fixture.

Crowds have been so small that JK Nõmme Kalju's average league attendance of 329 in the 2008 season was the highest in the top division for three years. In 2005, FC Valga enticed an average of 41 people to their home games; unable to retain such popularity, they suffered a fall to 38 the following year. Perhaps these poor turn-outs should be expected, given the lack of quality in a league that regularly features several semi-professional teams.

A lack of attendance also marked the national team's most famous moment. Estonia refused to turn up for their World Cup qualifier at home to Scotland in 1996, protesting that they had been given insufficient notice to move the kick-off to earlier in the day, a switch ordered because the floodlights were sub-standard. The match was rearranged to be played in Monaco, where it finished 0–0, not that this affected the qualification prospects of a country who have yet to get close to winning a place at a major tournament. Just getting people through the turnstiles would be achievement enough.

Above: A bullish Estonian fan.   *Below:* he start of Estonia's famous annual Tartu Ski Marathon.

Meistriliiga

Season	Winner	Runner-up
1999	Levadia Tallinn*	Viljandi Tulevik
2000	Levadia Tallinn*	Flora Tallinn
2001	Flora Tallinn	TVMK Tallinn
2002	Flora Tallinn	Levadia Tallinn
2003	Flora Tallinn	TVMK Tallinn
2004	Levadia Tallinn	TVMK Tallinn
2005	TVMK Tallinn	Levadia Tallinn
2006	Levadia Tallinn	Narva Trans
2007	Levadia Tallinn	Flora Tallinn
2008	Levadia Tallinn	Flora Tallinn

** Then known as Levadia Tallinn

Eesti Karikas

Season	Winner	Runner-up
1998–99	Levadia Tallinn*	Viljandi Tulevik
1999–00	Levadia Tallinn*	Viljandi Tulevik
2000–01	Narva Trans	Flora Tallinn
2001–02	Levadia II Tallinn**	Levadia Tallinn*
2002–03	TVMK Tallinn	Flora Tallinn
2003–04	Levadia Tallinn	TVMK Tallinn
2004–05	Levadia Tallinn	TVMK Tallinn
2005–06	TVMK Tallinn	Flora Tallinn
2006–07	Levadia Tallinn	Narva Trans
2007–08	Flora Tallinn	Tammeka Tartu

TALLINN

Refreshed in the east

Few eastern European cities emerged from the Soviet era with a fresher reputation than Tallinn. Easy access through low-cost airlines, a picturesque city, friendly people, good nightlife and reasonable prices have all combined to pull in couples, families and groups of fun-seeking youngsters to make Tallinn one of the most talked-about places in Europe.

There are many attractions in the old town, parts of which date back to the 15th century, and it is compact enough to walk around. With its many busy bars and cafés, Raekoja Plats is a square that is popular among visitors and locals alike. This is also where you will find the town hall. Nearby is Viru Gate, entrance to the old town, the impressive Alexander Nevsky Cathedral and Toompea Castle, where the country's government sits.

A short distance to the east is the Kadriorg area, location of both Kadriorg Palace, the former palace of Peter the Great, and Kadrioru Staadion, home of the city's football club Levadia Tallin.

Weather	Low (°C)	High
January	-6	-2
February	-7	-2
March	-3	1
April	0	7
May	5	12
June	10	17
July	12	20
August	12	18
September	7	13
October	3	8
November	0	2
December	-4	0

Below: *The Tallinn skyline reveals a diversity of architectural styles.*

3 THINGS YOU MUST DO...
(Apart from the football)

1 MARINATED EEL
Marinated eel, blood sausage or tongue in horseradish sauce, anyone? Try Eesti Maja (1A Lauteri, tel: +372 6 455 252) for a friendly atmosphere in which to introduce your tastebuds to Estonian food. Open: daily 11.00–23.00. To get there: a short walk from the old town.

2 PIRITA
If the sun's shining (bright), Pirita's white, sandy beach is just 20 minutes away. There are also parklands for walks or the Pirita Top Spa Hotel (1 Regati pst, tel: +372 6 398 600). To get there: buses 1, 1A, 8, 34, or 38.

3 KADRIORG PALACE AND ART MUSEUM OF ESTONIA
The palace (37 Weizenbergi, tel: +372 6 066 400) is the ex-summer home of St Peter the Great, which he built for his empress Catherine. Now the Art Museum of Estonia. Open: May–Sept Tues–Sun 10.00–17.00, Oct–Apr Wed–Sun 10.00–17.00. Price: adults EEK80, concessions EEK40. To get there: tram 1, 3 to Kadriorg.

LEVADIA TALLINN

Above: Newcastle's Stephen Carr (right) jumps for the ball with Levadia Tallinn's Aleksandr Dmitrijev during a Uefa Cup match.

MATTER OF FACT

Name: Mittetulundusühing Spordiklubi Football Club Levadia Tallinn
Stadium: Kadrioru Staadion (capacity 4,750)
Address: Roheline aas 24, 10150
To get there: Ten minutes' walk from city centre, tram 1 or 3, or buses 31, 67 or 68
Telephone: +372 631 3017
Email: sport@levadia.ee
Website: www.fclevadia.ee

Stadium tour
No stadium tour but this is an open arena so fans can visit unaccompanied except on match days

Home   **Away**

Trophies
6   Estonian League
5   Estonian Cup

Main rivals
Flora Tallinn (tel: +372 627 9940, www.fcflora.ee) play at Le Coq Arena (Asula 4c, 11312). Levadia share the Kadrioru Staadion with TVMK Tallinn (tel: +372 626 1502, www.fctvmk.ee).

TEN YEAR EURO RECORD

Season	Competition	Finished
1998–99	DNQ	
1999–00	Uefa Cup	Qual rd
2000–01	Champs League	2nd qual rd
2001–02	Champs League	1st qual rd
2002–03	Intertoto Cup	2nd round
2003–04	Uefa Cup	1st qual rd
2004–05	Uefa Cup	2nd qual rd
2005–06	Champs League	1st qual rd
2006–07	Uefa Cup	1st round
2007–08	Champs League	2nd qual rd

Never a dull moment

Some clubs take their first steps tentatively, but Levadia Tallinn have travelled on a breathless journey since forming near the turn of the millennium. In their first ten years, they packed in a promotion, a merger, six league titles, four doubles, seven switches of manager, a name change and a stadium move.

They are considered to have been founded in 1998, when steel company OÜ Levadia invested heavily in second-division side Olümp Maardu, prompting a change of name to Levadia Maardu. After promotion, they joined with Tallinna Sadam and, still named Levadia Maardu, won the title in their first two top-flight campaigns.

In this decade, they moved 15 km (9 miles) from Maardu to Tallinn, took up residence at the Kadrioru Staadion and began calling themselves Levadia Tallinn. They got through several managers but Tarmo Rüütli stuck around for five years from 2003, overseeing the first two of three successive titles from 2006, averaging over three goals per league game.

RUSSIA

THE

3

MINUTE GUIDE

Capital: *Moscow.* **Language:** *Russian, but numerous other languages in use.* **Beer:** *Baltika.* **Food:** *Borscht (beetroot soup), beef stroganoff.* **National anthem:** *Gimn Rossiyskoy Federatsii (Hymn of the Russian Federation).* **Population:** *140,702,000.* **Time zone:** *GMT +2 to +12 (Moscow +3).* **Emergency number:** *112.* **Did you know?** *Russians drink on average 15 litres (3.3 gallons) of alcohol per year.* **Football body:** *Football Union of Russia, House of Football Ulitsa Narodnaya 7, Moscow 115 172; tel: +7 495 540 1300, fax: +7-495 540 1305, email: rfs@roc.ru, website: www.rfs.ru. Founded 1912. Affiliated 1912.*

Below: The Russian capital, Moscow.

A giant stirs

The world's biggest country is finally getting the hang of the planet's most popular game. It took 50 years of European club competition before CSKA Moscow broke Russia's duck by lifting the 2005 Uefa Cup and, to show it was no fluke, Zenit St Petersburg collected the same trophy three seasons later. The Soviet Union era had featured continental triumphs for Dynamo Kiev (Ukraine) and Dynamo Tbilisi (Georgia) but none for Russia's part of that country.

The Soviet break-up first hampered Russian football, but later invigorated it. At first the many clubs with affiliations to state organizations such as the army or KGB floundered without their traditional backing, but then the new private energy companies began investing in football. Oil money was behind CSKA and Zenit's European successes and, for that matter, helped Russia reach the Euro 2008 semi-finals, given that their coach Guus Hiddink's wages were being partly funded by the oligarch Roman Abramovich.

All but one of Russia's 23-man Euro 2008 squad were home-based, which shows the clubs are wealthy enough to keep their best talent. The improving health of the domestic league was emphasized when, after 11 successive titles for Moscow sides until 2006, there was variety as the next two were won by Zenit and the unfancied Rubin Kazan.

At least the Moscow teams had something to celebrate in 2008. The relegation of distant Luch-Energiya Vladivostok meant there would be no eight-and-a-half hour flight to a city with a seven-hour time difference. Russia is enormous and at last it is living up to its size.

Above: Flag carriers for Russia. *Below:* The Soviet break-up invigorated Russian football.

THE TEN YEAR GUIDE

* The league runs in calendar years, the cup from autumn to spring.

Premier League*

Season	Winner	Runner-up
1999	Spartak Moscow	Lokomotiv Moscow
2000	Spartak Moscow	Lokomotiv Moscow
2001	Spartak Moscow	Lokomotiv Moscow
2002	Lokomotiv Moscow	CSKA Moscow
2003	CSKA Moscow	Zenit St Petersburg
2004	Lokomotiv Moscow	CSKA Moscow
2005	CSKA Moscow	Spartak Moscow
2006	CSKA Moscow	Spartak Moscow
2007	Zenit St Petersburg	Spartak Moscow
2008	Rubin Kazan	CSKA Moscow

Russian Cup

Season	Winner	Runner-up
1998–99	Zenit St Petersburg	Dynamo Moscow
1999–00	Lokomotiv Moscow	CSKA Moscow
2000–01	Lokomotiv Moscow	Anzhi Makhachkala
2001–02	CSKA Moscow	Zenit St Petersburg
2002–03	Spartak Moscow	Rostov
2003–04	Terek Grozny	Krylia Sovetov Samara
2004–05	CSKA Moscow	Khimki
2005–06	CSKA Moscow	Spartak Moscow
2006–07	Lokomotiv Moscow	FC Moscow
2007–08	CSKA Moscow	Amkar Perm

MOSCOW

Vodka, culture and a difficult alphabet

The spirit of Moscow has changed beyond recognition since the Soviet era, thanks to the money of the so-called New Russians which has turned the place into the European city of conspicuous consumption, with luxury brand names the new symbols of success. But with the new money has come corruption, crime and relatively high prices. Add in the difficulty most visitors have with Cyrillic text and the fierce winter weather and you'll see this is not a city for the faint-hearted.

But this is one of the world's great historic cities, with a fine cultural heritage, outstanding architecture and a vibrant nightlife scene. Most of the after-hours action takes place along Tverskaya Street, (also well-known for its shopping) and, if you are looking to test your wallet, around the pedestrianized Menage Square and Red Square. And if you haven't had one to warm you up already, this will be the time to turn your thoughts to the national drink. The Russians' love of vodka stretches back years, although you will notice beer and other spirits being drunk with equal passion as the younger Russians move their minds Westwards.

Red Square is also the centre for the main attractions when the partying is over, with the Kremlin, Lenin's Tomb, St Basil's Cathedral, numerous other architectural gems and the nearby Moskva River and Ostankino Tower all clustered around here.

Dinamo Stadion, home of Dinamo Moscow is about 8 km (5 miles) northwest of the city, while Luzhniki, where Spartak Moscow play, is about 11 km (7 miles) to the southwest. CSKA Moscow are planning a move to a new stadium.

Below: Looking down on Moscow's famous Red Square.

3 THINGS YOU MUST DO...
(Apart from the football)

1 THE GREAT MOSCOW STATE CIRCUS

This famous circus (Prospekt Vernadskogo 7, tel: +7 495 930 0300) has been entertaining crowds with its world-famous show since it opened in 1971. The huge auditorium seats 3,400 people. To get there: subway to Universitet.

2 ST BASIL'S CATHEDRAL

Quite simply a fairytale building. The colourful pillars, towers and curves of St Basil's (Krasnaya pl, tel: +7 495 298 3304) right on Red Square has become a symbol of Russia. Open: daily 11.00–17.00 except Tues. To get there: subway to Ploshchad Revolyutsii.

3 THE COSMONAUTICS MUSEUM

The museum (Prospekt Mira 111, tel: +7 495 683 7914) celebrates the exploration of space and the days when Sputnik 1, the first satellite launched into space in 1957, was hi-tech. Open: 10.00–18.00 except Mon and last Fri of the month. To get there: subway to VDNKh.

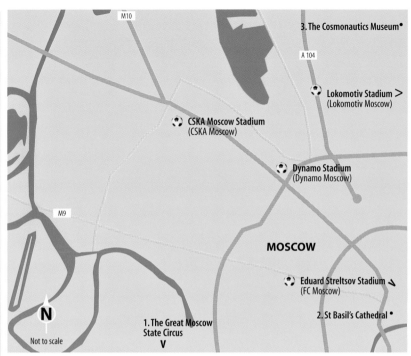

M10

3. The Cosmonautics Museum●

A 104

⚽ Lokomotiv Stadium >
(Lokomotiv Moscow)

⚽ CSKA Moscow Stadium
(CSKA Moscow)

⚽ Dynamo Stadium
(Dynamo Moscow)

M9

MOSCOW

⚽ Eduard Streltsov Stadium ↘
(FC Moscow)

2. St Basil's Cathedral ●

N
Not to scale

1. The Great Moscow State Circus
∨

BARS > CLUBS > RESTAURANTS

Bars > Legendary and wild, **The Hungry Duck** (Pushechnaya ul 9/6, tel: +7 495 923 6158) is a danc-ing-on-the-bar-why-have-those-people-taken-off-their-clothes place. And you'll find more of the same type of action at **Doug and Marty's Boar House** (ul Zemlyanoy val 26, tel: +7 495 917 9986). **Clubs > Cabaret** (Strastnoy bul 8a, tel: +7 495 789 8315) is a classy club with all the trappings in terms of décor and design plus some twinkly night views across the city. Glitzy to the extreme, **Jazztown** (Taganskaya pl 12, tel: +7 495 912 5726) has a restaurant, casino, and, of course, jazz. **Restaurants >** Worth a visit for its name alone is **Kitaysky Lyotchik Dzhao-Da** (Lubyansky proezd 25, tel: +7 495 623 2896). Enjoy the food then head to the club**.** For a taste of Russian cuisine, try **Godunov** (Teatralnaya Sq 5, tel: +7 495 298 5609).

Below: Moscow's nightlife has become legendary since the break-up of the Soviet Union.

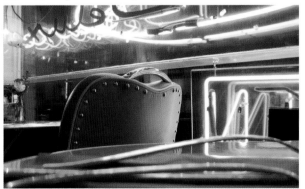

Weather	Low (°C)	High
January	-11	-6
February	-10	-4
March	-5	1
April	1	9
May	6	16
June	10	20
July	12	21
August	11	20
September	6	13
October	1	7
November	-4	0
December	-8	-3

CSKA MOSCOW

CLUB

Above: CSKA supporters.

MATTER OF FACT:
Name: PFC Central Sports Army
Club Moscow
Stadium: CSKA Moscow Stadium
(capacity 30,000)
Address: Peschanaya Street 3
Telephone: +7 495 612 0780
Email: cska@pfc-cska.com
Website: www.pfc-cska.com

Stadium tour
Open: To be decided (museum will be
near new stadium)
Contact: Phone and email as above

Home	Away

Trophies

1	Inter-Cities Fairs Cup/Uefa Cup
3	Russian League (plus 7 Soviet League)
4	Russian Cup (plus 5 Soviet Cup)

Main rivals
The biggest are Spartak Moscow (see page 113). Dynamo Moscow (tel: +7 495 612 71 72, www.fcdynamo.ru) play at Dynamo Stadium (Leningradsky pr 36, 125190). Lokomotiv Moscow (tel: +7 495 161 4283, http://eng.fcml.ru) are at Lokomotiv Stadium (Bolshaya Cherkizovskaya, 125 Ä, 107553). FC Moscow (tel: +7 495 544 4366, www.fcmoscow.ru/en) play at Eduard Streltsov Stadium (Maliy Tatarskiy side street 4a, 115184).

TEN YEAR EURO RECORD

Season	Competition	Finished
1998–99	DNQ	
1999–00	Champs League	2nd qual rd
2000–01	Uefa Cup	1st round
2001–02	DNQ	
2002–03	Uefa Cup	1st round
2003–04	Champs League	2nd qual rd
2004–05	Champs League	Group
	Uefa Cup	Winners
2005–06	Uefa Cup	Group
2006–07	Champs League	Group
	Uefa Cup	Last 32
2007–08	Champs League	Group

Happy travellers

As 2004–05 began, no Russian club had lifted a continental trophy and CSKA Moscow had not won a European tie in seven years. Yet, despite a hazardous route, the club won the Uefa Cup. They played two home matches in the competition in Krasnodar, 1,200 km (744 miles) from Moscow to escape the winter chill, and beat Sporting Lisbon in the final in their opponents' own stadium.

A League and Cup double that year confirmed the onset of CSKA's second great period. The first also featured tales of wanderings. Having won five in six titles up to 1951, the Army-backed club were the best represented side in the Soviet Union's Olympic team the next year, so defeat by Yugoslavia in a politically sensitive match prompted Stalin to disband CSKA for a while, obliging some players to uproot away from Moscow.

CSKA are consolidating their recent progress – achieved via the funding of Roman Abramovich's Sibneft oil company – by building a new stadium, not that they need home comforts to thrive.

SPARTAK MOSCOW

Above: Luzhniki, home of Spartak Moscow.

MATTER OF FACT
Name: FC Spartak Moscow
Stadium: Luzhniki (capacity 84,745)
Address: Luzhnetskaya naberezhnaya 24, 119048
To get there: Metro Line 1 (station: Sportivnaya)
Telephone: +7 495 646 1924
Email: info@spartak.com
Website: www.eng.spartak.com

Stadium tour
Contact club for details

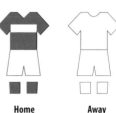

Home	Away

Trophies

9	Russian League (plus 12 Soviet League)
3	Russian Cup (plus 10 Soviet Cup)

Main rivals
The biggest now are CSKA Moscow (see page 112), but in Soviet times it was Dynamo Moscow (tel: +7 495 612 71 72, www.fcdynamo.ru), who play at Dynamo Stadium (Leningradsky pr 36, 125190). Lokomotiv Moscow (tel: +7 495 161 4283, http://eng,fcml.ru) are at Lokomotiv Stadium (Bolshaya Cherkizovskaya, 125 Å, 107553). FC Moscow (tel: +7 495 544 4366, www.fcmoscow.ru/en) play at Eduard Streltsov Stadium (Maliy Tatarskiy side street 4a, 115184).

TEN YEAR EURO RECORD

Season	Competition	Finished
1998–99	Champs League	Group
1999–00	Champs League	Group*
	Uefa Cup	Last 32
2000–01	Champs League	Group**
2001–02	Champs League	Group*
2002–03	Champs League	Group*
2003–04	Uefa Cup	Last 32
2004–05	Intertoto Cup	3rd round
2005–06	DNQ	
2006–07	Champs League	Group
	Uefa Cup	Last 32
2007–08	Champs League	3rd qual rd
	Uefa Cup	Last 32

* 1st of two group stages
** 2nd of two group stages

Hard labour pays off

Many football fans assume Oleg Romantsev is the most significant figure in Spartak Moscow's history. A former title-winning captain, his 13 years as coach (and sometimes club president) was the most successful era of any side in the Soviet or Russian leagues.

Yet Spartak's nine titles in ten seasons after the Soviet break-up in 1991 (Romantsev won eight) owed much to Nikolai Starostin, a former player, coach and president. A founder in 1922, he kept the club out of the authorities' hands, unlike Moscow rivals Dynamo (KGB-backed) and CSKA (army). Starostin was sent to a labour camp, effectively because the club outshone state-backed rivals, but his efforts meant that Spartak's reputation as a 'people's team' produced the country's largest fan base; also, state-supported sides suffered post-1991.

Spartak had endured a seven-year title drought by 2008 after Romantsev was sacked over a row with the president while oil money allowed rivals to catch up. Maybe a third inspirational figure will emerge.

ST PETERSBURG

The city with many names

Previously called Petrograd and Leningrad, St Petersburg is one of the continent's largest cities and is home to over five million people. It sits at the mouth of the Neva River on the Gulf of Finland and has been shaped by its waterways, with development along the shores of the Neva and on the many islands in its delta.

The central square in the city is the spacious Palace Square, where you will find the huge green and white Winter Palace, official residence of the Russian tsars between 1732 and 1917. It was in that year that the palace was stormed during the Russian Revolution, one of the events which led, ultimately, to the formation of the Soviet Union. Alongside is the city's main avenue, Nevsky Prospekt, and a wealth of St Petersburg's attractions, such as Kazan Cathedral, Gostiny Dvor, the Russian National Library, Grand Hotel Europe and Beloselsky-Belozersky Palace, can be seen along here as it heads eastwards.

Weather	Low (°C)	High
January	-9	-4
February	-8	-3
March	-4	1
April	0	7
May	6	15
June	11	18
July	13	21
August	12	18
September	7	13
October	2	7
November	-2	1
December	-6	-2

Below: The Winter Palace, former residence of the Russian tsars.

3 THINGS YOU MUST DO...
(Apart from the football)

1 ST PETERSBURG STATE CIRCUS
Not as famous as its Moscow contemporary, but the St Petersburg State Circus (nab reki Fontanki 3, tel: +7 812 314 8478) has been around since 1827. Open: shows usually daily at 11.30, 15.00, 19.00 but timetable varies. To get there: underground to Gostiny Dvor.

2 HERMITAGE MUSEUM
An amazing art collection of over three million exhibits put together over two and a half centuries (Palace Square 2, tel: +7 812 710 9079). Open: main complex Tues–Sat 10.30–18.00, Sun 10.30–17.00. Winter Palace Tues–Sat 10.30–17.00, Sun 10.30–16.00. Price: RUB350 to main complex. To get there: subway to Nevsky Pr.

3 GRAND HOTEL EUROPE
Enjoy the luxury surroundings that have been enjoyed by visitors as diverse as Peter Ilyich Tchaikovsky, Igor Stravinsky, H.G. Wells and Elton John. There are five restaurants, two cafés and a bar to choose from (Nevsky Prospekt, Mikhailovskaya Ulitsa 1/7, tel: +7 812 329 6000). To get there: subway to Nevsky Pr.

ZENIT ST PETERSBURG

Above: Zenit St Petersburg's captain Anatoliy Tymoschuk celebrates with the Uefa Super Cup after victory over Manchester United in 2008.

MATTER OF FACT
Name: FC Zenit St Petersburg
Stadium: Gazprom Arena
(capacity 62,000)
Address: Krestovskiy Island
To get there: Metro 4 to
Krestovskiy ostrov
Telephone: +7 812 315 6202
Email: dmc@fc-zenit.ru
Website: www.fc-zenit.ru

Stadium tour
To be confirmed

Home	Away

Trophies

1	Inter-Cities Fairs Cup/Uefa Cup
1	Russian League (plus 1 Soviet League)
1	Russian Cup (plus 1 Soviet Cup)

Main rivals
There are no other St Petersburg clubs in the top two divisions. Dynamo St Petersburg (tel: +7 812 232 1622, www.fc-dynamospb.ru) play at the third level at the Petrovsky Stadium (Petrovsky Island 2G, 197110).

TEN YEAR EURO RECORD

Season	Competition	Finished
1998–99	DNQ	
1999–00	Uefa Cup	1st round
2000–01	Intertoto Cup	Final*
2001–02	DNQ	
2002–03	Uefa Cup	1st round
2003–04	DNQ	
2004–05	Uefa Cup	Group
2005–06	Uefa Cup	QF
2006–07	DNQ	
2007–08	Uefa Cup	Winners

*One of three finals

City's new revolution

Showing he is not exactly Nostradamus, Zenit coach Vlastimil Petřĺela claimed his club would never become Russian champions because the authorities favoured Moscow teams and the capital's clubs were wealthier. Within two years Zenit were champions through the backing of the world's third largest company. Sadly for the Czech, energy giant Gazprom's involvement extended to sacking him and paying his replacement Dick Advocaat the largest coaching salary in the country's history.

As for favouritism towards opponents, Zenit stayed in the top division despite finishing bottom in 1967. The league was expanded from 19 to 20 teams amid claims the government did not want to dampen the city's 50th anniversary celebrations of the October Revolution.

Until recently, Zenit, the 2008 Uefa Cup winners, had given fans little cause for celebration, their 1984 Soviet championship proving their only league title before Gazprom powered them. The company are also funding a new 62,000-capacity stadium.

POLAND

THE

3

**MINUTE
GUIDE**

Capital: *Warsaw.* **Language:** *Polish.* **Beer:** *Specjal Jasny Pelny, Zywiec.* **Food:** Bigos *(stew),* kotlet schabowy *(breaded pork cutlet),* pierogo *(stuffed dumplings).* **National anthem:** *Mazurek Dabrowskiego (Dabrowski's Mazurka).* **Population:** *38,501,000.* **Time zone:** *GMT +1.* **Emergency number:** *112 997/112.* **Did you know?** *The second oldest rally in the world is the Rally of Poland.* **Football body:** *Polish Football Association, Miodowa 1 Warsaw, 00-080; tel: +48 22 551 2315, fax: +48 22 551 2240, email: pzpn@pzpn.pl, website: www.pzpn.pl. Founded 1919. Affiliated 1923.*

Below: Warsaw's Palace of Culture and Science, a skyscraper erected as a gift from the Soviet Union.

A host of troubles

By choosing Poland to co-host Euro 2012, Uefa lifted the sagging morale of the nation's footballing public. Two years earlier, in 2005, GKS Katowice owner Piotr Dziurowicz had shaken the game by claiming that "bribes for players and referees are normal in Polish football", adding that "trading in points is the only way to survive."

Dziurowicz spoke from experience, admitting he spent the equivalent of about €1.8 million in bribes for opponents and referees during the 1999–2000 season, when his club was promoted to the top flight. His revelations prompted investigations that have led to suspended prison sentences for several referees and Polish Football Federation officials as well as a series of enforced relegations, notably for Zaglebie Lubin in 2008, a year after they were champions.

It was not Poland's first such scandal. On the last day of the 1992–93 season, LKS Lodz and Legia Warsaw each recorded six-goal victories in their pursuit of the league title on goal difference, but both were found guilty of corruption in connection with those games, so the crown was awarded to third-placed Lech Poznan.

Poland were given joint hosting rights for Euro 2012 with Ukraine, and their national team will expect to impress after re-emerging recently from a dark period. Third-placed finishers at the 1974 and 1982 World Cups, they did not qualify for a major tournament in the 1990s but have featured at the past two World Cups and reached their first European championship in 2008. Their advances have helped to take minds off the troubles at home.

Above: Polish fans get in the mood for Euro 2012. *Below:* Polonia Warsaw, the capital's oldest club.

THE TEN YEAR GUIDE

Ekstraklasa

Season	Winner	Runner-up
1998–99	Wisla Kraków	Widzew Lódz
1999–00	Polonia Warsaw	Wisla Kraków
2000–01	Wisla Kraków	Pogon Szczecin
2001–02	Legia Warsaw	Wisla Kraków
2002–03	Wisla Kraków	Groclin
2003–04	Wisla Kraków	Legia Warsaw
2004–05	Wisla Kraków	Groclin
2005–06	Legia Warsaw	Wisla Kraków
2006–07	Zaglebie Lubin	GKS Belchatów
2007–08	Wisla Kraków	Legia Warsaw

Puchar Polski

Season	Winner	Runner-up
1998–99	Amica Wronki	GKS Belchatów
1999–00	Amica Wronki	Wisla Kraków
2000–01	Polonia Warsaw	Górnik Zabrze
2001–02	Wisla Kraków	Amica Wronki
2002–03	Wisla Kraków	Wisla Plock
2003–04	Lech Poznan	Legia Warsaw
2004–05	Groclin	Zaglebie Lubin
2005–06	Wisla Plock	Zaglebie Lubin
2006–07	Groclin	Korona Kielce
2007–08	Legia Warsaw	Wisla Kraków

KRAKOW

A city of squares

With its population of over 800,000, Krakow is a large industrial city in the southwest of Poland near to the borders of both Slovakia and the Czech Republic.

Stare Miasto is the old town, which is easy to identify because the line of the old city walls and moat has been replaced by gardens called the Planty. The old town, dating back to medieval times, is an area dominated by squares. The main square is Rynek Glowny, which is surrounded by a number of beautiful old buildings and a good choice of bars and restaurants.

Nearby are other squares, the adjoining Plac Mariacki, Maly Rynek, Plac sw Marii Magdaleny and Plac Szczepanski, to name just a few. Each has its own character, so stroll around and take your pick depending on whether you are looking for a bit of peace and quiet or a few Polish vodkas.

Stadion Wisly, home of Wisla Krakow, is a short distance northwest of all the Krakow squares.

Weather	Low (°C)	High
January	-5	0
February	-4	1
March	0	7
April	3	12
May	7	18
June	11	21
July	12	22
August	12	22
September	8	17
October	4	12
November	0	5
December	-3	2

Below: Just one of the many squares found in Krakow.

3 THINGS YOU MUST DO...
(Apart from the football)

1 BASILICA OF ST FRANCIS
In a city with a church on every corner, the one that can't be missed is the 13th century Basilica St Francis (Pl Wszystkich Âwi´tych 5, tel: +48 12 422 5376) with its legendary stained-glass windows by Stanislaw Wyspianski. Open: daily 06.00–20.00, but avoid visits during mass. Price: free. To get there: it's in the old town.

2 SALT MINE
Ever visited a salt mine? No, thought not. So here, only about 15 km (9 miles) from the city, is your chance to see one (ul Danilowicza 10, tel: +48 12 278 7302). Open 08.00–17.00. Tours at 10.00, 11.00, 11.30, 12.30, 13.45, 15.00, 16.00 and 17.00. Price: adults 64zl, children 49zl. To get there: train to Wieliczka.

3 FANTASY PARK
Good, unashamed fun without a church in sight. Ten-pin bowling, beers and other games to while away some time in the shopping centre. Fantasy Park (Aleja Pokoju 44, tel: +48 12 290 9515). To get there: tram 1, 14 or 22.

WISLA KRAKOW

Above: Tomas Jirsak, Wisla Kraków, in training.

MATTER OF FACT
Name: Wisla Kraków Spólka Akcyjna
Stadium: Stadion Wisly
(capacity 35,000)
Address: ul.Reymonta 22
To get there: Trams 15, 18 (stop:
Reymana), buses 103, 139, 144, 159,
173, 194 (stop: Kawiory)
Telephone: +48 12 630 7600
Email: sekretariat@wisla.krakow.pl
Website: www.wisla.krakow.pl

Stadium tour
Contact club for details

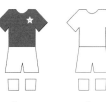

Home   **Away**

Trophies
11	Polish League
4	Polish Cup

Main rivals
City rivals Cracovia Kraków (tel: +48
12 427 3562, www.cracovia.pl) play at
the Stadion Marszalek Pilsudski
(Kaluzy 1, 30-111).

10-YEAR EURO RECORD

Season	Competition	Finished
1998-9	Uefa Cup	2nd round
1999-00	DNQ	
2000-1	Uefa Cup	2nd round
2001-2	Champs League	3rd qual rd
	Uefa Cup	2nd round
2002-3	Uefa Cup	Last 16
2003-4	Champs League	3rd qual rd
	Uefa Cup	2nd round
2004-5	Champs League	3rd qual rd
	Uefa Cup	1st round
2005-6	Champs League	3rd qual rd
	Uefa Cup	1st round
2006-7	Uefa Cup	Group
2007-8	DNQ	

Wired to success

When Maciej Skorza took over as Wisla Kraków coach in June 2007, he became the 20th occupant of the post since Boguslaw Cupial bought the club less than a decade earlier. Yes, despite the upheaval, the team have won more league titles during their billionaire owener's reign than in their previous 90 years.

Skorza guided Wisla to their sixth crown in ten years in 2007-08 to confirm their status as Poland's top club. It was their 11th title, three fewer than Ruch Chorzów and Górnik Zabrze, the joint record holders, neither of whom have added to their tally since the Iron Curtain fell.

Wisla's rise mirrors that of their owner, a paint store owner until he moved successfully into cable production. Such has been the club's pre-eminence with Cupial at the helm that they recorded a 73-game unbeaten home run in the league over five years until 2006. Their progress is also underlined by the refurbishment of their stadium, which is more than doubling capacity to around 34,000.

CZECH REPUBLIC

Capital: *Prague.* **Language:** *Czech.* **Beer:** *Pilsner Urquell, Budweiser Budvar.* **Food:** *Sviäková na smetane (slices of pork) with knedliky (dumplings).* **National anthem:** *Kde domov múj? (Where is My Home?).* **Population:** *10,221,000.* **Time zone:** *GMT +1.* **Emergency number:** *112.* **Did you know?** *People in the Czech Republic are the world's biggest beer drinkers per head of population.* **Football body:** *Football Association of Czech Republic, Diskarska 100, PO Box 11, Prague 16900; tel: +420 2 3302 9111, fax: +420 2 3335 3107, email: cmfs@fotbal.cz, website: www.fotbal.cz. Founded 1901. Affiliated 1907.*

Below: The castle in Prague, one of the landmarks of the capital.

Search for a new golden generation

The Czech Republic has had a topsy-turvy ride in world football, periods of 'Golden Generations' interspersed with long years in the nowhere leagues.

The country began life playing as Bohemia, but it was as the merged Czechoslovakia that they had arguably their greatest triumph when they won the 1976 European Championship. A 3–1 semi-final win over the Dutch put them in the final against West Germany, who amazingly actually lost a penalty shootout.

It was the Germans who again stood in their way after the recently partitioned Czech Republic had fought – with probably their most exciting-ever team featuring Pavel Nedved, Karel Poborsky and Patrick Berger – to the final of Euro '96. An Oliver Bierhoff golden goal ended the dream.

On the domestic front, the game is totally dominated by the capital's two clubs, Sparta Prague and Slavia Prague, who have, over the years, provided the backbone of the national side (though that trend has changed lately with the lure of bigger money abroad). Jan Koller, a Sparta man, is the nation's leading goalscorer with 55 goals and 90 caps, while Poborsky, a Slavia man, is the country's most capped player on 118 appearances. Each year the two Prague teams face a perennial battle for both the league and cup.

Sparta are way ahead with ten league titles (Slavia only have two) and wins in the last three cup finals, but a resurgent Slavia won the 2007–08 league with a team many expect to be the next golden generation.

Top: Czechs are the world's biggest beer drinkers. *Below: Czech fans dream of 1976-style success.*

THE TEN YEAR GUIDE

The Czech 1 Liga

Season	Winner	Runner-up
1998–99	Sparta Prague	Teplice
1999–00	Sparta Prague	Slavia Prague
2000–01	Sparta Prague	Slavia Prague
2001–02	Slovan Liberec	Sparta Prague
2002–03	Sparta Prague	Slavia Prague
2003–04	Baník Ostrava	Sparta Prague
2004–05	Sparta Prague	Slavia Prague
2005–06	Slovan Liberec	Mladá Boleslav
2006–07	Sparta Prague	Slavia Prague
2007–08	Slavia Prague	Sparta Prague

Czech Republic Football Cup

Season	Winner	Runner-up
1998–99	Slavia Prague	FC Slovan Liberec
1999–00	FC Slovan Liberec	Baník Ratískovice
2000–01	FK Viktoria Zizkov	Sparta Prague
2001–02	SK Slavia Prague	Sparta Prague
2002–03	FK Teplice	FC Jablonec
2003–04	Sparta Prague	FC Baník Ostrava
2004–05	FC Baník Ostrava	FC Slovácko
2005–06	Sparta Prague	Baník Ostrava
2006–07	Sparta Prague	FC Jablonec
2007–08	Sparta Prague	Slovan Liberec

PRAGUE

The popular party town

With its relaxed atmosphere, cultural attractions, good value, easy access from low-cost airlines, and good nightlife, tourism has boomed in Prague in recent years. It's the latter that has brought the younger crowds, particularly single-sex groups looking for fun, which in turn has spawned more clubs, bars and strip joints, and specialities such as 'steak and tits' where you get a meal and a strip show in one.

So Prague has become a historic, picturesque city by day and Europe's party central after dark. The Czechs are (in)famously the biggest beer drinkers in the world, consuming a whopping 150 litres and more (33 gallons) per head annually. Pilsner beer was invented here and the Czech Republic is home to well-known beers Pilsner Urquell, Budweiser Budvar and Staropramen. You will also find a well-priced range of dark lagers and wheat beers. It would be rude not to try them, don't you think?

At the heart of this city of over 1.2 million people is Wenceslas Square, with the beautifully symmetrical National Museum looking down on it. Founded in 1818, the museum is home to about 14 million exhibits. From here the new town, with the National Theatre, and the old medieval town, with its beautiful cobbled streets and fine architecture, can easily be explored on foot. Just over the River Vltava across the Charles Bridge is Prague Castle and the Lesser Town, with its own share of picturesque streets and churches.

The AXA Arena, the stadium of Sparta Prague is just 2 km (1 mile) north of the Old Town across the river.

Below: Even with Prague's reputation as a historical city, modernism has been allowed to squeeze in.

3 THINGS YOU MUST DO...
(Apart from the football)

1 MULLED WINE
A medieval city deserves a medieval drink to toast it. You'll find many street sellers around the busy tourist areas serving this spicy-sweet warm drink that you can enjoy on the street.

2 PUB CRAWL
Think of it as exploring a historic city with a guide. Prague Travel (Vinohradska 28, tel: +420 222 516 064) offers a three-hour tour with a meal and a beer at every bar visited. Meet: daily 18.00 at the Old Town Hall Old Astronomical Tower. Price: adults 450CZK. To get there: tram 17, 18 or metro A to Staromůstská.

3 CHARLES BRIDGE
The main link between the Old Town and the Lesser Town; work on this beautiful bridge was started in the 14th century. To get there: tram 17, 18 or metro A to Staromůstská.

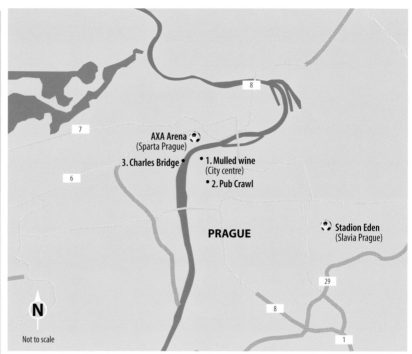

8

7

AXA Arena (Sparta Prague)

3. Charles Bridge • • 1. Mulled wine (City centre)

6

• 2. Pub Crawl

PRAGUE

Stadion Eden (Slavia Prague)

29

8

N

Not to scale

1

BARS > CLUBS > RESTAURANTS

Bars > In the new town you'll find **U Fleku Beer Hall Restaurant & Brewery** (Kremencova 11, tel: +420 2 2493 0019) a large Czech beer (and food) hall, complete with its own microbrewery and museum on-site. It's a fun place even if it is a bit touristy. For something completely different, head to the stylish and chilled **Radost FX** (Belehradska 12, tel: +42 2 2425 4776).

Clubs > Perfectly situated in Wenceslas Square, the **Duplex Dance Club** (Wenceslas Square 21, tel: +42 2 2423 2319) has multiple bars, good DJs, stylish décor and a cool crowd. **Futurum** (Praha 5 Zborovská 7, tel: +42 2 5732 8571) is the nightclub to visit if you're after live music

Restaurants > Try Czech food at **Novomestsky Pivovar** (Vodickova 20, tel: +42 2 2223 2448) or **Staromacek Restaurant** (Dlouha 4, tel: +420 2 2231 1366).

Below: Prague is not just about beer halls, potatoes and dumplings.

Weather	Low (ºC)	High
January	-4	1
February	-3	2
March	0	7
April	2	12
May	7	17
June	11	20
July	13	22
August	12	22
September	8	18
October	3	12
November	0	6
December	-2	2

SPARTA PRAGUE

Above: Republic of Ireland fans queue for tickets at the AXA Arena.

TEN YEAR RECORD

Season	Competition	Finished
1998–99	Champs League	Qual round
	Uefa Cup	1st round
1999–00	Champs League	Group**
2000–01	Champs League	Group*
2001–02	Champs League	Group**
2002–03	Uefa Cup	2nd round
2003–04	Champs League	Last 16
2004–05	Champs League	Group
2005–06	Champs League	Group
2006–07	Uefa Cup	Group
2007–08	Uefa Cup	Group

* 1st of two group stages
** 2nd of two group stages

The club that bounces back

The Velvet Revolution gave Czechoslovakia a smooth transition to democracy but threw Sparta Prague into rough waters. Having just won their fourth successive league title in 1990, a year when many of their players had inspired the national team to the World Cup quarter-finals, the team's leading talents were cherry-picked by richer western European clubs as borders opened up.

Severely weakened, Sparta stood sixth in the league table halfway through the next season, yet they recovered to become champions again, for good measure adding to that achievement by nearly reaching the European Cup final a year later. Backed by the Czech Republic's biggest fanbase, the club's ability to triumph over adversity has helped turn them into the country's most successful side.

Their resilience was demonstrated twice more later that decade. In 1994–95 they sacked coach Karol Dobias after two league games, played another seven under his temporary replacement Vladimír Borovicka, were guided by German Jürgen Sundermann for a few months, until he was dismissed after falling out with president Petr Mach, and were finally coached during the run-in by Josef Jarabinsky. Yet Sparta emerged from the upheaval as champions.

The following season the club almost went bust amid a financial crisis (see below right) but, after selling several players and ceding the 1996 title to Slavia Prague, they regrouped and won the next five titles.

One blot on their record came in 1975 when relegation meant they lost their status as the only team to have played in every Czechoslovakian top-flight season. Given their tendency to bounce back, it was no surprise that they returned at the first attempt.

GREATEST PLAYERS

> **PAVEL NEDVED (1992–96)**
A tireless midfielder with a quick turn of pace, Nedved almost single-handedly kept Sparta competitive as they faced financial turmoil and sold off players during the 1995–96 campaign.

> **TOMÁS ROSICKY (1998–2001)**
The creative midfielder was the inspirational force for Sparta when they made great strides in the Champions League around the turn of the millennium.

MATTER OF FACT
Name: AC Sparta Praha fotbal a.s.
Stadium: AXA Arena
(capacity 20,854)
Address: Milady Horákové 1066/98,
170 82
To get there: Metro on Line A (stop:
Hradčanská). Trams 25, 26
Telephone: +420 296 111 111
Email: football@sparta.cz
Website: www.sparta.cz

Stadium tour (includes Hall of Fame)
Open: Mon–Fri 10.00–12.00,
13.00–16.00, except match days.
Groups only. Tours in Czech only
Price: 30CZK
Contact: Tel: +420 296 111 400/402
or email: zcentrum@sparta.cz

Home	Away

Trophies
10 Czech League (plus 19
Czechoslovakian League)
5 Czech Cup (plus 8
Czechoslovakian Cup)

Main rivals
Slavia Prague (tel: +420 2330 817 53,
www.slavia.cz) play at the Stadion
Eden (Vladivostocká 1460/10, 100 10).

Above: *Arsenal's Mathieu Flamini beats Sparta Prague's Libor Dosek to the ball.*

RED FACES
An estimated €12 million in the red
and with several bad debts, Sparta
nearly went out of business in the
1995–96 season. Young president
Petr Mach was forced to sell the club
to a steelworks company that also
owned Slovakian side FC Kosice.

UKRAINE

THE 3 MINUTE GUIDE

Capital: *Kiev.* **Languages:** *Ukrainian and Russian, with numerous others in use.* **Beer:** *Obolon.* **Food:** Holubtsi *(stuffed cabbage rolls).* **National anthem:** *Shche ne vmerla Ukrainy (Ukraine's Glory Has Not Perished).* **Population:** *45,994,000.* **Time zone:** *GMT +2.* **Emergency number:** *police 02 or 102, medical 03 or 103, fire 01 or 101.* **Did you know?** *Chicken Kiev does not originate from the Ukraine. It was invented by a Frenchman.* **Football body:** *Football Federation of Ukraine Provulok Laboratornyi, 7-A PO Box 55, Kiev 01133, tel: +380 44 521 0521, fax: +380 44 521 0550, email: info@ffu.org.ua, website: www.ffu.org.ua. Founded 1991. Affiliated 1992.*

Below: Moscow's influence is evident in Kiev.

A giant stirs

The Soviet Union's squads at the 1986 and 1990 World Cups and Euro '88 featured a combined 37 Ukrainian selections to Russia's 17. To emphasize Ukraine's superiority over their neighbour, they recorded two European club triumphs to Russia's nil during the Soviet era. Yet when the USSR was dissolved in 1991, Fifa selected Russia as the official successor while Ukraine were not allowed to compete for the 1994 World Cup.

To add insult to injury, some leading Ukrainian players, such as Andrei Kanchelskis, opted to appear for Russia rather than wait until the Euro '96 qualifiers.

Ukraine endured further agony with defeats in three major tournament play-offs before finally reaching the 2006 World Cup, where they were quarter-finalists.

If the national team are finding their feet, the domestic league has its problems. Most European leagues are too predictable for their own good but Ukraine's is an extreme case, with Dynamo Kiev and Shakhtar Donetsk filling the top two places for 12 seasons in a row to 2007–08 and also monopolizing the domestic cup in that period. Not that this brings content for the pair, with Shakhtar coach Mircea Lucescu claiming in 2007 that his team would not win the league again (incorrect in the end) because referees favoured Kiev.

Such squabbling was forgotten when Ukraine won joint hosting rights for Euro 2012, although fears have been raised that they might lose the honour through lack of readiness. It would not be the first time the authorities had destroyed the country's footballing dream.

Above: Ukraine's international reputation grows.   *Below:* Kiev's Olympic Stadium, now being rebuilt.

THE TEN YEAR GUIDE

Premier League

Season	Winner	Runner-up
1998–99	Dynamo Kiev	Shakhtar Donetsk
1999–00	Dynamo Kiev	Shakhtar Donetsk
2000–01	Dynamo Kiev	Shakhtar Donetsk
2001–02	Shakhtar Donetsk	Dynamo Kiev
2002–03	Dynamo Kiev	Shakhtar Donetsk
2003–04	Dynamo Kiev	Shakhtar Donetsk
2004–05	Shakhtar Donetsk	Dynamo Kiev
2005–06	Shakhtar Donetsk	Dynamo Kiev
2006–07	Dynamo Kiev	Shakhtar Donetsk
2007–08	Shakhtar Donetsk	Dynamo Kiev

Ukrainian Cup

Season	Winner	Runner-up
1998–99	Dynamo Kiev	Karpaty Lviv
1999–00	Dynamo Kiev	Kryvbas Kryvyi Rih
2000–01	Shakhtar Donetsk	Arsenal Kiev
2001–02	Shakhtar Donetsk	Dynamo Kiev
2002–03	Dynamo Kiev	Shakhtar Donetsk
2003–04	Shakhtar Donetsk	Dnipro Dnipropetrovsk
2004–05	Dynamo Kiev	Shakhtar Donetsk
2005–06	Dynamo Kiev	Metalurh Zaporizhya
2006–07	Dynamo Kiev	Shakhtar Donetsk
2007–08	Shakhtar Donetsk	Dynamo Kiev

KIEV

Home for Euro 2012

Maidan Nezalezhnosti (Independence Square) is the heart of the city in geography and spirit. Located just south of the River Dnieper, it was here that the major demonstrations took place against the Soviet Union that led to Ukraine's independence in 1991. It was also the scene of the Orange Revolution, a protest against electoral fraud in 2004.

Just to the north of here is the city's large, picturesque parkland area, abutting the river. It is here you will find Lobanovs'kyi Dynamo Stadium, home to Dynamo Kiev. The Olympic Stadium, being rebuilt for Euro 2012, is to the southeast. Stretching from Independence Square is the city's main throughfare, the busy and popular Khreschatyk Street is where you will find the popular indoor market, the Besarabsky Market. Kiev is one of Europe's oldest cities, dating back as far as the fifth century, and has many sites of interest to visitors such as the Kiev Monastery of Caves, founded in the 11th century, as well as cultural attractions such as the Kiev Opera House and October Palace.

Weather	Low (°C)	High
January	-8	-2
February	-8	-1
March	-4	3
April	1	12
May	7	20
June	11	22
July	12	23
August	12	23
September	8	18
October	3	11
November	3	3
December	-1	0

Below: Independence Square, scene of many demonstrations, with the monument to female spirit Berehynia.

3 THINGS YOU MUST DO...
(Apart from the football)

1 KIEV PECHERSK LAVRA
The Monastery of Caves (25 Sichnevogo Povstannya st, tel: +380 44 254 2257) is a collection of architectural gems, historical sites and artefacts, and a complex of caves and passages. Open: daily 09.00–16.30. Price: free, although you are expected to buy a candle. To get there: metro to Arsenalna then trolleybus 38.

2 CHERNOBYL MUSEUM
The museum (1 Khoryvyj Pereulok Street, tel: +380 44 417 5427) charts the nuclear disaster that occurred in April 1986. Expect to see some gruesome photos. Open: Mon–Fri 10.00–18.00, Sat 10.00–17.00. To get there: metro to Kontraktova Ploscha.

3 OLIMPIYSKIY STADION
The 83,000-seater Olympic Stadium (vul Chervonoarmiyska 55, Ukrainian FA, tel: +380 44 521 0535) is home to the national team and is being rebuilt, as it is the planned venue for the 2012 European Championship final. To get there: metro to Respublikansky Stadion.

DYNAMO KIEV

Above: A statue of coach Valeri Lobanovsky in front of the stadium named after him.

TEN YEAR EURO RECORD

Season	Competition	Finished
1998–99	Champs League	SF
1999–00	Champs League	Group*
2000–01	Champs League	Group**
2001–02	Champs League	Garoup**
2002–03	Champs League	Group**
2003–04	Champs League	Group
2004–05	Champs League	Group
	Uefa Cup	Last 32
2005–06	Champs League	2nd qual rd
2006–07	Champs League	Group
2007–08	Champs League	Group

* 2nd of two group stages
** 1st of two group stages

An ace among coaches

When Dynamo Kiev coach Valeri Lobanovsky suffered a fatal stroke in May 2002, his team seemingly had their tenth consecutive Ukrainian title sown up. A month later, Shakhtar Donetsk had erased a four-point deficit and claimed the crown instead. Deprived of their colossus, it looked like they could not live without him.

Kiev have won further titles but are far from the European heights attained under Lobanovsky. After, as a striker, helping Kiev become the first non-Moscow Soviet title winners in 1961, he excelled in three spells as coach. The poker-faced trainer collected eight Soviet and five Ukrainian titles and two European Cup Winners' Cups, as well as making three European Cup semi-final appearances. For good measure he took 11 of his players to Euro '88 when doubling as USSR coach, reaching the final.

Such are expectations at the club, that Mikhail Fomenko's contract stated he would be sacked as coach if he didn't win the domestic double in 2002–03 (which he did). He could blame standards set by Lobanovsky.

MATTER OF FACT
Name: FC Dynamo Kyiv
Stadium: Valeri Lobanovsky Stadium (capacity 16,873)
Address: 3 Hrushevskyy st, 01001
To get there: Metro to Maydan Nezalezhnosti
Telephone: +380 44 536 0008
Email: alina@goal.com.ua
Website: www.fcdynamo.kiev.ua/en

Stadium tour
Contact: Museum tel: +380 44 278 4493

Home   **Away**

Trophies
2   European Cup Winners' Cup
12   Ukrainian League
      (plus 13 Soviet League)
9   Ukrainian Cup
      (plus 9 Soviet Cup)

Main rivals
Shakhtar (see page 131) have become the main foes. Arsenal Kiev (tel: +380 44 482 0504, www.arsenal-kiev.com.ua) currently play at the Valeri Lobanovsky Stadium as the Olympic Stadium (Vul Chervonoarmiyska 55) is being reconstructed for Euro 2012.

DONETSK

The far East

There are cities further east in Europe, but few of them have been such regular qualifiers in European competition thanks to Shakhtar's domination of the Ukraine league with Dynamo Kiev (they have finished in the top two from 1996–97 and 2007–08).

Donetsk is an important city in the region due to its coal and steel production, but there is no doubting the influence of Ukraine's richest man, Rinat Akhmetov, the man behind the investment in Shakhtar Donetsk, who are based in the city.

The downtown area is between Shcherbakov Park (where the Shakhtar Stadium is situated) and the River Kalmius. The 1,050 km (651 mile) River Donets, after which the city is named today, is some distance to the east, starting in Russia and flowing southeast through the Ukraine. Running through the centre, from south to north of Donetsk, is the main street, Artem Street, which is where you will find the Cathedral Transfiguration of Jesus, completely rebuilt between 1996 and 2006. Along this street or just off it are other important sites such as the Concert Hall, Lenin Square, the Opera and Ballet Theatre, and the Donetsk National University.

Weather	Low (°C)	High
January	-7	-2
February	-7	-1
March	-2	3
April	6	13
May	10	20
June	13	23
July	15	25
August	14	24
September	10	20
October	4	12
November	-1	3
December	-5	0

Below: The Orthodox Church is a central feature of Ukrainian culture.

3 THINGS YOU MUST DO...
(Apart from the football)

1 GET MARRIED!
You've seen the girls, now choose one as your bride... Like a lot of eastern Europe, there now seems to be an industry in marrying off the beautiful young ladies in Donetsk. So if you really don't like being alone at half-time and are wise to inter-net scams, then Google the appropriate words to find the love of your life.

2 SOLEDAR SALT MINE
A visit to a salt mine (1a Chkalov St, Soledar, tel: +38 62 744 4071) is appropriate as the club is called the Miners. Open: all year. To get there: Soledar is about 100 km (62 miles) north of Donetsk. Commuter train to Sol station. Or train to the nearest town, Artemovsk, then taxi or bus. Ask for the *shakhta* ('mine').

3 CATHEDRAL TRANSFIGURATION OF JESUS
The cathedral (129 Artem Street) was completed in 2006 after the city decided to rebuild it in 1996. It was originally founded in 1883 but was destroyed by the Soviets in 1933.

SHAKHTAR DONETSK

Above: *Matuzalem of Shakhtar Donetsk.*

Digging for victory

While Dynamo Kiev are associated with espionage, having been formed as the secret police's team, it is Shakhtar Donetsk who are known as the Moles. The nickname, however, merely reflects their founding in 1936 to represent the coal mining industry.

Shakhtar's initial name of Stakhanovets honoured local coal miner Oleksiy Stakhanovets, who, held up as a model Soviet worker for his prolific output, appeared on the front of *Time* magazine in 1935. Fast forward to 2008 and *Forbes* magazine featured another Shakhtar figure, club owner Rinat Akhmetov, as the world's 127th richest man. Such are the changes in Ukraine's political and economic climate.

The club had never won the Soviet or Ukrainian league when Akhmetov took charge in 1996, but he funded a star-filled team. Backed by the country's biggest attendances throughout this decade of around 20,000, they are big heroes in Donetsk. Big enough, perhaps, to appear on a magazine cover themselves.

MATTER OF FACT
Name: FC Shakhtar Donetsk
Stadium: Donbass Arena
(capacity 50,000)
Address: 15 Mira Av, 83015
Telephone: +38 62 387 0102
(Donbass Arena: +38 62 387 0227)
Email: feedback@shakhtar.com
Website: www.shakhtar.com

Stadium tour
Contact: Phone and email as above

Home	Away

Trophies
4	Ukrainian League
6	Ukrainian Cup
	(plus 4 Soviet Cup)

Main rivals
As perennial title rivals, Dynamo Kiev (see page 129) are the biggest enemies. Shakhtar contest the Donbass Derby against Metalurh Donetsk (tel: +380 62 385-0488, www.metallurg. donetsk.ua), who play at the Shakhtar Stadium (ul Kyubysheva 25-a).

TEN YEAR EURO RECORD		
Season	Competition	Finished
1998–99	Uefa Cup	2nd qual rd
1999–00	Uefa Cup	1st round
2000–01	Champs League	Group*
	Uefa Cup	Last 32
2001–02	Champs League	3rd qual rd
	Uefa Cup	1st round
2002–03	Champs League	3rd qual rd
	Uefa Cup	1st round
2003–04	Champs League	3rd qual rd
	Uefa Cup	1st round
2004–05	Champs League	Group
	Uefa Cup	Last 16
2005–06	Champs League	3rd qual rd
	Uefa Cup	Last 32
2006–07	Champs League	Group
	Uefa Cup	Last 16
2007–08	Uefa Cup	Group

* 1st of two group stages

HUNGARY

THE

3

MINUTE GUIDE

Capital: *Budapest.* **Language:** *Hungarian.* **Beer:** *Dreher Classic.* **Food:** *Goulash.* **National anthem:** *Himnusz: a Magyar nép Zivataros Századaiból (Anthem: from the Stormy Past of the Hungarian People).* **Population:** *9,931,000.* **Time zone:** *GMT +1.* **Emergency number:** *112.* **Did you know?** *The Rubik's Cube was invented by Hungarian Ernö Rubik in 1974.* **Football body:** *Hungarian Football Federation, Koerberek Tovaros Kanai ut, 314/24 Hrsz, Budapest 1112; tel: +36 1 577 9500, fax: +36 1 577 9503, email: mlsz@mlsz.hu, website: www.mlsz.hu. Founded 1901. Affiliated 1907.*

Below: The parliament buildings in Budapest.

Magnificent to moderate

The death in November 2006 of Ferenc Puskás, considered Hungary's greatest ever player, prompted recollections of the wonderful side he graced in the 1950s. A month before his passing, the long-struggling national team had lost to little Malta. The two events focused the country's attention on the two contrasting eras and reinforced the feeling of depression over the state of the game.

The Magnificent Magyars won the 1952 Olympic title and a year later inflicted England's first home loss to non-British Isles visitors, 6–3 at Wembley. When they beat the same opposition 7–1 in Budapest on the eve of the 1954 World Cup, which remains England's largest margin of defeat, they seemed on course to become world champions. But despite beating West Germany 8–3 in the group stage, they blew a two-goal lead against the Germans in the final to lose 3–2, their first defeat for four years.

If that result scarred the team, they were destroyed by the Hungarian Revolution of 1956, with Puskás, Sándor Kocsis and Zoltán Czibor all leaving the country and staying away for the rest of their careers. While the 10–1 win over El Salvador at the 1982 World Cup brought some joy, there has been little prospect of a return to the halcyon days. Hungary's inability to reach Euro 2008 was their eleventh successive failure to qualify for a major tournament.

At least the domestic league has been providing some long-awaited variety. While only three clubs outside of Budapest had won the title before 2000, Zalaegerszeg, Dunaferr and Debrecen had taken that figure to six by 2005.

Above: The ground of Szombathely Halada, Budapest. *Below:* Hungarian football fans light up.

THE TEN YEAR GUIDE

Nemzeti Bajnokság I

Season	Winner	Runner-up
1998–99	MTK Hungária	Ferencváros
1999–00	Dunaferr	MTK Hungária
2000–01	Ferencváros	Dunaferr
2001–02	Zalaegerszeg	Ferencváros
2002–03	MTK Hungária	Ferencváros
2003–04	Ferencváros	Újpest
2004–05	Debrecen	Ferencváros
2005–06	Debrecen	Újpest
2006–07	Debrecen	MTK Hungária
2007–08	MTK Hungária	Debrecen
		*As Videoton

Magyar Kupa

Season	Winner	Runner-up
1998–99	Debrecen	Tatabánya
1999–00	MTK Hungária	Vasas
2000–01	Debrecen	Fehérvár*
2001–02	Újpest	Haladás
2002–03	Ferencváros	Debrecen
2003–04	Ferencváros	Honvéd
2004–05	Matáv Sopron	Ferencváros
2005–06	Fehérvár	Vasas
2006–07	Honvéd	Debrecen
2007–08	Debrecen	Honvéd

BUDAPEST

A tale of two towns

Budapest, a city formed in 1873 when Buda and Pest, the two towns on opposite banks of the River Danube came together, has become one of the most visited places in Europe.

With its heritage and fine architecture, the city is ideal for strolling around. Popular attractions are the Buda Castle and the surrounding Castle Hill district, where you will find the Royal Palace, the national gallery and the city's most impressive church, Matthias Church. For relaxation, Budapest's many squares are full of cafés and restaurants spilling onto the street.

But much of the city's activity is tucked below the surface. The city has a lot of private parties in houses, gardens and apartments, as a surprising number of the nightlife hotspots close at midnight or before. Many bars, like the iconic Szimpla, are housed in abandoned buildings and specialize in not advertising and moving locations. It all adds up to a good test for visitors. MTK Hungaria's Hidegkuti Nandor Stadion is about 5 km (3 miles) east of the Danube.

Weather	Low (°C)	High
January	-3	2
February	-2	4
March	2	11
April	5	16
May	10	21
June	13	23
July	15	26
August	15	26
September	11	21
October	6	15
November	1	7
December	-2	3

Below: Medicinal baths have been popular for both leisure and health in Budapest for many years.

3 THINGS YOU MUST DO...
(Apart from the football)

1 RUDAS MEDICINAL BATHS AND SWIMMING POOL
One of the city's beloved Turkish Baths is Rudas (Döbrentei tér 9, tel: +36 1 356 1322). Open: steam bath Mon–Fri 06.00–20.00 (Tues women only), Sat–Sun 06.00–17.00 (both sexes), Fri–Sun 22.00– 04.00 (both sexes). Price: steam bath 2,000–2,400HUF. To get there: tram 18 or 19.

2 38
Drink, dance and eat on the 38 Ship (Petófi Bridge, Buda side, tel: +36 1 464 3940) on the River Danube. Open: Mon–Sat 11.00–04.00. To get there: tram 4 or 6.

3 SZIMPLA
The most well known of the city's underground pubs that open up in deserted buildings is Szimpla (VII Kertész u 48, tel: +36 1 321 5880). Open: daily 12.00–02.00. To get there: tram 4 or 6.

MTK HUNGARIA

Above: MTK Hungaria, now funded by music and diamonds.

MATTER OF FACT

Name: Magyar Testgyakorlók Köre Hungária FC
Stadium: Stadion Hidegkuti Nándor (capacity 12,740)
Address: Salgótarjáni út 12-14, 1087
To get there: Metro M2 to Stadionok then tram 1
Telephone: +36 1 333 8368
Email: info@mtkhungaria.hu
Website: www.mtkhungaria.hu

Stadium tour
Contact club for details

Home   **Away**

Trophies
23   Hungarian League
12   Hungarian Cup

Main rivals
Ferencváros (tel: +36 1 215 60 25, www.ftc.hu) were demoted to the second division in 2006 because of financial difficulties. They play at Stadion Albert Flórián (Üllöi út 129, 1091). Honved (tel: +36 1 357 6738, www.honvedfc.hu) play at Bozsik Stadion (Puskas Ferenc u 1-3, 1194). Újpest (tel: +36 1 231 0088, www.ujpestfc.hu) play at the Szusza Ferenc Stadion (Megyeri út 13, 1044).

TEN YEAR EURO RECORD

Season	Competition	Finished
1998–99	Euro C Winners' C	1st round
1999–00	Champs League	3rd qual rd
	Uefa Cup	2nd round
2000–01	Champs League	2nd qual rd
	Uefa Cup	2nd round
2001–02	DNQ	
2002–03	DNQ	
2003–04	Champs League	3rd qual rd
	Uefa Cup	1st round
2004–05	DNQ	
2005–06	DNQ	
2006–07	DNQ	
2007–08	Uefa Cup	1st qual rd

Hitting the high notes

For nearly 40 years MTK Hungaria fans had found little to sing about, until former rock star Gábor Várszegi bought the club in 1995. In that period the team had only added one league title to their previous tally of 18 but, just as Várszegi's fortunes had improved when he gave up music in Hungary to deal in diamonds in Los Angeles, MTK were transformed by his millions.

Várszegi's money funded almost a new team that won the championship two years after his arrival, and they added the 1999 title by a 19-point margin. When the club became 2008 champions, 17 squad members were former pupils at the youth academy set up by Várszegi.

Yet Várszegi suffered anti-Semitic abuse from rival teams' supporters, an echo of the troubled past of a club with strong Jewish roots. They won all ten league titles contested from 1913–14 onwards, but were disbanded by Hungary's pro-Nazi government during the Second World War. MTK re-formed but made little impression until Várszegi appeared.

DEBRECEN

Plain journey

L ocated in the east of the country near the Romanian and Ukrainian borders, Debrecen is the second largest city in Hungary after Budapest. Being built on the Great Plain of Hungary, it has no obvious geographical focal points enjoyed by many other cities, or even a high number of obvious visitor attractions.

You will soon know why this city of just over 200,000 was once the largest Calvinistic city on the continent. The centrepiece and icon of Debrecen is its most well known building, Nagytemplom ('Great Church'). Nearby is the popular Déri Museum. Just north of here is the main shopping area, the Debrecen Plaza, and further north still the city park, Nagyerdei. The large park is popular for walks and also features other attractions such as a small amusement park, skating rink and zoo. It is here you will also find Olah Gabor Stadion, home of Debrecen.

Weather	Low (°C)	High
January	-4	0
February	-1	3
March	2	10
April	5	15
May	10	20
June	13	23
July	15	25
August	14	25
September	12	21
October	6	15
November	1	7
December	-2	2

Below: Nagyerdei Park offers a day of fun.

3 THINGS YOU MUST DO...
(Apart from the football)

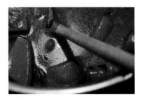

1 GOULASH
The famous spicy stew is Hungary's best known of all its hearty foods. For eastern European cuisine try the cellar restaurant Csokonai (Kossuth utca 21, tel: +36 52 410 802). To get there: tram 1.

2 DÉRI MUSEUM
The biggest museum in the city, Déri Museum (Déri Tér 1, tel: +36 52 322 207) has a wide-ranging collection including work by many Hungarian artists. Open: Tues–Sun, Apr–Oct 10.00–18.00, Nov–Mar 10.00–16.00. To get there: tram 1.

3 NAGYERDEI PARK
Choose from the zoo, the amusement park, or the skating rink at the city park (Fancsika, tel: +36 52 514 100). Or visit the Aquaticum with its pools, water park and restaurants. Open: 24 hours. Price: free. To get there: tram 1.

DEBRECEN

Above: Manchester United's Gary Neville (left) challenges Debrecen's Peter Halmosi.

MATTER OF FACT
Name: Debreceni Vasutas Sport Club
Stadium: Stadion Oláh Gábor Út
(capacity 9,640)
Address: Oláh Gábor u. 5, 4032
To get there: Tram 1
Telephone: +36 52 535 408
Email: dvscrt@dvsc.hu
Website: www.dvsc.hu

Stadium tour
Contact club for details

Home **Away**

Trophies
3	Hungarian League
3	Hungarian Cup

Main rivals
The club have no major city rivals.
Nyíregyháza Spartacus (tel: +36 42
500 171, www.szpari.hu) are about
50 km (31 miles) away and play at
Városi Stadion (Sóstói út 24/A, 4400).

TEN YEAR EURO RECORD		
Season	Competition	Finished
1998–99	Intertoto Cup	SF*
1999–00	Uefa Cup	1st round
2000–01	DNQ	
2001–02	Uefa Cup	1st round
2002–03	DNQ	
2003–04	Uefa Cup	Last 32
2004–05	Intertoto Cup	1st round
2005–06	Champs League	3rd qual rd
	Uefa Cup	1st round
2006–07	Champs League	2nd qual rd
2007–08	Champs League	2nd qual rd

* One of six semi-finals

No longer second rate

Until recently, the phrase 'first is first and second is nowhere' aptly described the footballing contributions of Hungary's largest two cities. While Budapest, the capital, dominated domestically for a century, the league title never went to Debrecen, the second largest city. Debrecen even spent a spell in the third division in the 1960s.

The change began when Debrecen won the 1999 and 2001 Hungarian Cups, their first major trophies. The latter year brought great fortune. They finished second bottom but were spared relegation because BKV Elöre declined their promotion slot on financial grounds, and they attracted huge investment from local businessman Gábor Szima.

A last-day defeat denied Debrecen the 2004 title but they broke their duck a year later, the first of three titles in a row, although Szima was a hard taskmaster. Coach Attila Supka won the first two of those crowns but was sacked early the next season after a Champions League qualifying round defeat.

CROATIA

THE

3

MINUTE GUIDE

Capital: *Zagreb.* **Language:** *Croatian.* **Beer:** *Olujsko, Pan.* **Food:** *Cevapcici (like a hamburger), paski sir (goat's cheese).* **National Anthem:** *Lijepa nasa domovino (Our Beautiful Homeland).* **Population:** *4,492,000.* **Time zone:** *GMT +1.* **Emergency number:** *Police 92, medical 94 or 112, fire 93 or 112.* **Did you know?** *The word 'cravat' originates from Croatian mercenaries who fought for France in the 17th century. It loosely means 'as worn by the Croats'.* **Football body:** *Croatian Football Federation, Rusanova 13, Zagreb 10 000; tel: +385 1 236 1555, fax: +385 1 244 1501, email: info@hns-cff.hr, website: www.hns-cff.hr. Founded 1912. Affiliated 1992.*

Below: *The old town of Dubrovnik.*

Rise and rise of Croatia

Of the new countries formed after the break-up of Yugoslavia, it is Croatia that has been far and away the most successful, finishing third at their very first World Cup in 1998 with the team that has come to be known as the Golden Generation.

The team was spearheaded by the masterful Davor Suker – who won the Golden Boot at France '98 with six goals in seven games – but it also featured such galactic names as Alen Boksic, Zvonimir Boban, Dario Simic (Croatia's most capped player) and Slaven Bilic. The team was, amazingly, undefeated in its first 36 home matches.

Croatia was first recognised by Fifa as an independent team in 1992, entering their rankings at 125th place. After a good run at their first tournament, losing to Germany in the quarterfinals of Euro '96, and then their France '98 exploits, they were catapulted to third in the world.

Croatian international success has been fed by two giant domestic clubs, Hadjuk Split and Dinamo Zagreb, who between them have won the Prva HNL league every year bar one since 1992. Hadjuk was started, like all the best football clubs, by students having a couple of beers in a bar, while Dinamo was formed by the merging of three Communist-era clubs. The clubs' fans (styled the Bad Blue Boys of Zagreb and the Torcida of Split) are renowned for their passion, and sometimes their excess of passion. They, and Croatian national fans, have often run into trouble with the authorities… perhaps not surprisingly, as the national team's nickname is *Vatreni* (the fiery ones).

Above: Croatia reached third in the world rankings. *Below:* The flags of Croatia and Varaždin region.

THE TEN YEAR GUIDE

Prva HNL League

Season	Winner	Runner-up
1998–99	Croatia Zagreb	Rijeka
1999–00	Dinamo Zagreb	Hajduk Split
2000–01	Hajduk Split	Dinamo Zagreb
2001–02	NK Zagreb	Hajduk Split
2002–03	Dinamo Zagreb	Hajduk Split
2003–04	Hajduk Split	Dinamo Zagreb
2004–05	Hajduk Split	Inter Zapresic
2005–06	Dinamo Zagreb	Rijeka
2006–07	Dinamo Zagreb	Hajduk Split
2007–08	Dinamo Zagreb	Slaven Belupo

The Croatian Cup

Season	Winner	Runner-up
1998–99	Osijek	Cibalia
1999–00	Hajduk Split	Dinamo Zagreb
2000–01	Dinamo Zagreb	Hajduk Split
2001–02	Dinamo Zagreb	Varteks
2002–03	Hajduk Split	Pula
2003–04	Dinamo Zagreb	Varteks
2004–05	Rijeka	Hajduk Split
2005–06	Rijeka	Varteks
2006–07	Dinamo Zagreb	Slaven Belupo
2007–08	Dinamo Zagreb	Hajduk Split

ZAGREB

Old city charms

Croatia's capital is located in the northwest of the country, close to the Slovenia border, and its medieval 'old city' charm means it is a popular tourist destination, especially among visitors from neighbouring countries.

Ban Josip Jelacic main square, just north of the main railway station, is at the heart of the city, and another important square, Trg Zrtava Fasizma ('Victims of Fascism') is close by. Just north of here is what is known as Gornji grad ('Upper Town'), the old, medieval part of the city, home to the presidential palace and many museums, while to the south towards the station and the River Sava is Donji grad ('Lower Town'), the area into which the city expanded later. It is in the Lower where most of the city life, including its bars and restaurants, can be found.

The Maksimir Stadium, home of Dinamo Zagreb is to the east of the city.

Weather	Low (°C)	High
January	-2	1
February	-1	3
March	2	10
April	7	13
May	12	19
June	15	22
July	16	24
August	15	23
September	12	20
October	7	13
November	3	7
December	0	4

Below: The skyline of Zagreb.

3 THINGS YOU MUST DO...
(Apart from the football)

1 MIMARA MUSEUM
The Museum (Roosevelt Square 5, tel: +385 1 482 8100) is a popular attraction in the city and houses over 3,700 works of art including work by Goya and Rembrandt. Open: Tues–Fri 10.00–18.00, Sat 10.00–13.00. To get there: it's close to the main railway station.

2 BAMBUS
A popular summer drink in Croatia is red wine with cola. Great to drink while watching the Zagreb world pass you by, or if you prefer a smarter set try Hemingway Bar (Tuskanac 1, tel: +385 1 485 4176).

3 RAÏNJIÇI
In a country that loves its grilled meats, *raïnjiçi* (shish kebab) is one of the most popular. Try the friendly and welcoming Kaptolska Klet (Kaptol 5, tel: +385 1 481 4838).

DINAMO ZAGREB

Above: Dinamo Zagreb fans display a message for the players.

MATTER OF FACT
Name: Nogometni klub
Dinamo Zagreb
Stadium: Maksimir Stadium
(capacity 37,168)
Address: 1289 Maximirska
Street, 10000
To get there: Trams 4, 7, 11, 12 (stop:
Maximir) and 1, 9, 17 (stop: Svetice)
Telephone: +385 1 2386 111
Email: dinamo@nk-dinamo.hr
Website: www.nk-dinamo.hr

Stadium tour
Contact club for details

Home	Away

Trophies

10	Croatian League (plus 4 Yugoslavian League)
9	Croatian Cup (plus 7 Yugoslavian Cup)

Main rivals
The principal foes are perennial title
rivals Hajduk Split. Neighbours NK
Zagreb (tel: + 385 1 366 8327,
www.nkzagreb.hr), play at Stadion
Kranjãevicéva (Kranjãevicéva 4,
10000).

TEN YEAR EURO RECORD

Season	Competition	Finished
1998–99	Champs League	Qual round
	Uefa Cup	1st round
1999–00	Champs League	Group**
2000–01	Champs League	Group*
2001–02	Champs League	Group**
2002–03	Uefa Cup	2nd round
2003–04	Champs League	Last 16
2004–05	Champs League	Group
2005–06	Champs League	Group
2006–07	Uefa Cup	Group
2007–08	Uefa Cup	Group

* 1st of two group stages
** 2nd of two group stages

Beauty and the presidential beast

Croatia coach Slaven Bilic was in a sarcastic mood as he spoke in 2008 about the Maksimir Stadium in Zagreb. "Visiting teams are overwhelmed by the beauty of the place," he said, mindful of what at the time was his country's 14-year unbeaten record at a ground where away sides had often folded in a hostile and ramshackle setting.

The stadium is also home to Dinamo Zagreb, but the nation's most popular club hardly needed such assistance from their surroundings in the 1990s because help was at hand from above. When Croatia president and Dinamo fan Franjo Tudman died in 2000, an investigation showed his government had waived taxes payable by the club of about €57 million (while also granting smaller favours to other clubs to keep them afloat).

Yet the club thrived before and after Tudman, winning the 1967 Fairs Cup and four league titles after he died. They will soon have to compete without another familiar helping hand, if indeed their run-down stadium unsettles opposing teams. The Maksimir is being refurbished.

SERBIA

THE **3** MINUTE GUIDE		**Capital:** *Belgrade.* **Language:** *Serbian.* **Food:** Rostilj *(grilled meat),* pljeskavica *(like a hamburger).* **Beer:** *Lav pivo, Jelen pivo.* **National anthem:** *Bože Pravde (God of Justice).* **Population:** *10,159,000.* **Time zone:** *GMT +1.* **Emergency number:** *112.* **Did you know?** *Serbia is one of the world's largest raspberry exporters.* **Football body:** *Football Association of Serbia, Terazije 35, PO Box 263, Belgrade 11000; tel: +381 11 323 4253, fax: +381 11 323 3433, email: fsj@beotel.yu, website: www.fss.org.yu. Founded 1919. Affiliated 1923.*

Below: Serbian hero Nikola Tesla, inventor and electrical engineer.

Breaking up is hard to do

The break-up of Yugoslavia has given Serbia the pleasure of having their own national team, but the political upheaval has been less kind to the club game. The country's teams have made little impression in Europe after their suspension from competition, while domestic league football has become a more tedious affair.

The United Nations sanctions prompted a three-year European ban on Serbian clubs until 1995 and, deprived of continental experience, a decent seeding position and many talented players who had moved abroad, it took a decade for any of them to last into the New Year in a Uefa competition (Partizan Belgrade did in the 2004–05 Uefa Cup).

The dissolution of Yugoslavia has left fans in Serbia with a predictable, annual two-horse race between Partizan and city rivals Red Star for the league title, now that powerful clubs such as Croatian pair Dinamo Zagreb and Hadjuk Split are not around to provide strong opposition. At least this situation satisfies the 80 per cent of the Serbian population who support one of those two Belgrade clubs.

Serbia has a strong footballing tradition, having staged eastern Europe's first European Cup final (in 1973) and European Championship final (1976), as well as producing the region's first European Cup finalists (Partizan were runners-up in 1966). Yugoslavia displayed their prowess by reaching the 1990 World Cup quarter-finals, since when Fifa have handed their official status first to a combined Serbia and Montenegro team and, in 2006, to Serbia alone. The struggle to recreate former glories has begun.

Above: Crvena Zvezda Stadion.   *Below:* Partizan Belgrade fans watch a defeat against Newcastle.

THE TEN YEAR GUIDE

* Montenegrin clubs took part until 2005–06

Superliga*

Season	Winner	Runner-up
1998–99	Partizan Belgrade	Obiliç
1999–00	Red Star Belgrade	Partizan Belgrade
2000–01	Red Star Belgrade	Partizan Belgrade
2001–02	Partizan Belgrade	Red Star Belgrade
2002–03	Partizan Belgrade	Red Star Belgrade
2003–04	Red Star Belgrade	Partizan Belgrade
2004–05	Partizan Belgrade	Red Star Belgrade
2005–06	Red Star Belgrade	Partizan Belgrade
2006–07	Red Star Belgrade	Partizan Belgrade
2007–08	Partizan Belgrade	Red Star Belgrade

The Cup of Serbia*

Season	Winner	Runner-up
1998–99	Red Star Belgrade	Partizan Belgrade
1999–00	Red Star Belgrade	Napredak Krusevac
2000–01	Partizan Belgrade	Red Star Belgrade
2001–02	Red Star Belgrade	Sartid Smederevo
2002–03	Sartid Smederevo	Red Star Belgrade
2003–04	Red Star Belgrade	Buduçnost Ban'ski Dvor
2004–05	Îeleznik Belgrade	Red Star Belgrade
2005–06	Red Star Belgrade	OFK Belgrade
2006–07	Red Star Belgrade	Vojvodina Novi Sad
2007–08	Partizan Belgrade	Zemun

BELGRADE

Where great rivers meet

Sitting at the confluence of the River Sava and the River Danube, Belgrade is the capital of Serbia, and was previously the capital of Yugoslavia.

Looking out on the two rivers from a rocky ridge on the east bank is the Belgrade Fortress and Kalemegdan, the manicured park and popular recreation area and residential area. This the oldest part of the city; in fact, this was the whole of the city when people lived behind ramparts. Nearby is the zoo, a number of museums and galleries, and Knez Mihailova Street, a shopping centre and pedestrian zone.

The city spreads out south from here to the two squares, the Terazije and Republic, that can be considered the heart of the city. Both were formed in the middle of the 19th century and Republic Square is the site of the National Theatre. The popular party area, the pretty Skadarlija district, is also nearby.

Belgrade has a large number of parks (all with plenty of monuments) and these, along with the islands dotted along the Danube and Sava, are heavily used for recreation. There are 16 islands in Belgrade, the most popular being Ada Ciganlija and Veliko ratno ostrvo, which attract large numbers of visitors for sport, bird-watching, picnics and swimming. The new Belgrade area and the old town of the Zemun district are located on the opposite bank of the river.

Stadion Partizana, home of Partizan Belgrade and Crvena Zvezda Stadion, where Red Star Belgrade play, are both further south of here.

Below: Being at the meeting point of two great rivers, water naturally plays a big part in daily life in Belgrade.

3 THINGS YOU MUST DO...
(Apart from the football)

1 BELGRADE FORTRESS AND KALEMEGDAN
Simply stroll around and enjoy the gardens, fortifications and great views out across the Sava and Danube.

2 NIKOLA TESLA MUSEUM
The museum (Krunska 51, tel: +381 11 24 33 886) houses a large collection of personal and work items and generally pays tribute to a Serbian hero, the electrical engineer and inventor Nikola Tesla. Open: Tues–Fri 10.00–18.00, Sat–Sun 10.00–13.00.

3 BALLOON ACROSS BELGRADE
See the historic city by air. Flights last 60–90 minutes and the basket can hold five people. Balloon Service (Salvadora Aljendea 5, tel: +381 62 252 067). Flights: daily, usually morning and evening. Price: €100 per person.

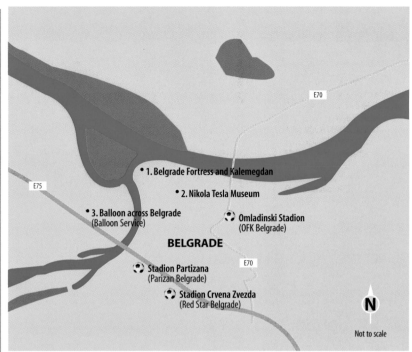

- 1. Belgrade Fortress and Kalemegdan
- 2. Nikola Tesla Museum
- 3. Balloon across Belgrade (Balloon Service)
- Omladinski Stadion (OFK Belgrade)

BELGRADE

- Stadion Partizana (Parizan Belgrade)
- Stadion Crvena Zvezda (Red Star Belgrade)

E70, E75

N

Not to scale

BARS > CLUBS > RESTAURANTS
Bars > Perfectly situated in the heart of the city, **Tribeca** (Knez Mihailova 50, tel: +381 11 328 5656) is a cool designer bar, with good food to go with it. Or try the buzz of **Bar Central** (Kralja Petra 59, tel: +381 11 262 6444).

Clubs > Blaywatch (Obala Dunava, tel: +381 11 319 1228) is the best known of a number of boats that line the bank of the river and form an important part of Belgrade's nightlife. They boast bars, a dancefloor and sexy people spread out across two levels. For alternatives simply stroll along the bank of the Danube and take your pick.

Restaurants > Enjoy fresh fish on the River Danube aboard **Yachting Club Kej** (Usce Street, tel: +381 64 825 1103) and view the sights of Kalemegdan, the island Veliko ratno ostrvo and Zemun.

Below: Relaxed Belgrade nightlife.

Weather	Low (ºC)	High
January	-2	3
February	-1	5
March	2	11
April	6	16
May	11	21
June	13	24
July	15	27
August	15	27
September	12	23
October	7	17
November	2	8
December	-1	5

RED STAR BELGRADE

Above: Red Star Belgrade's Goran Drulic (left) and Mihailo Pjanovic (right) celebrate after a goal by Milenko Acimovic (centre).

MATTER OF FACT
Name: Fudbalski klub Crvena Zvezda
Stadium: Stadion Crvena Zvezda
(capacity 54,000)
Address: Ljutice Bogdana 1a, 11000
To get there: Trams 2,7 or 9
Telephone: +381 11 367 2060
Email: office@fk-crvenazvezda.com
Website: www.crvenazvezdafk.com

Stadium tour (and museum)
Open: Museum Mon–Sat
10.00–14.00
Contact: Phone and email as above

Home   **Away**

Trophies
1   European Cup/
           Champions League
1   Serbian League (plus 19
           Yugoslavian League and 5 in
           Serbia/Montenegro era —
           1991-2006)
1   Serbian Cup (plus 12
           Yugoslavian Cup and 9 in
           Serbia/Montenegro era)

Main rivals
They contest the Eternal Derby with
great foes Partizan Belgrade (see
page 147). OFK Belgrade (tel: +381
11 3292 340, www.ofkbeograd.co.yu)
play at Omladinski Stadion (Mije
Kovaăeviça 10).

TEN YEAR EURO RECORD		
Season	Competition	Finished
1998–99	Uefa Cup	Last 32
1999–00	Uefa Cup	1st round
2000–01	Champs League	3rd qual rd
	Uefa Cup	2nd round
2001–02	Champs League	3rd qual rd
	Uefa Cup	1st round
2002–03	Uefa Cup	2nd round
2003–04	Uefa Cup	2nd round
2004–05	Champs League	3rd qual rd
	Uefa Cup	1st round
2005–06	Uefa Cup	Group
2006–07	Champs League	3rd qual rd
	Uefa Cup	1st round
2007–08	Champs League	3rd qual rd
	Uefa Cup	Group

Red Star lose shine

Red Star Belgrade's 1991 European Cup triumph was either well timed – or came at the worst moment. The former viewpoint is that the club became Yugoslavia's first continental champions just in time because the country soon dissolved. The other laments how civil war and Uefa destroyed their hopes of lasting dominance.

With conflict raging, Red Star staged European home games the next season in Hungary and Bulgaria, before United Nations sanctions led to a three-year Uefa ban. Seeking safer, more lucrative alternatives at clubs not barred from Europe, the Red Star XI that beat Marseille in the 1991 final had all joined foreign clubs within 18 months.

On Red Star's European re-admittance in 1995, the shrunken Yugoslavia's seeding started from scratch. So, despite winning the 1991 European Cup and just missing the next final, Red Star's 1995 league title merely brought a Uefa Cup berth. The country's top title winners have yet to taste the Champions League group stage.

PARTIZAN BELGRADE

Above: The Partizan Belgrade wall attempts to block a free kick during a match versus Lazio.

MATTER OF FACT
Name: Fudbalski klub Partizan
Stadium: Stadion Partizana
(capacity 32,710)
Address: Humska 1, 11000
To get there: Buses 40, 41, 94
Telephone: +381 11 3229 691
Email: football@partizan.rs
Website: www.partizan.rs

Stadium tour (includes museum)
Open: Mon–Fri 09.40–16.30;
museum: Mon–Fri 9.30–17.00
Price: Free
Contact: Tel: +381 11 3227 181 or
email: stadion@partizan.rs

Home **Away**

Trophies
1   Serbian League (plus 11 Yugoslavian League and 8 in Serbia/Montenegro era – 1991–06)
1   Serbian Cup (plus five Yugoslavian Cup and four in Serbia/Montenegro era)

Main rivals
The fixture against Red Star Belgrade (see page 146) is the country's biggest by far. OFK Belgrade (tel: +381 11 3292 340, www.ofkbeograd.co.yu) play at Omladinski Stadion (Mije Kovaăeviça 10).

TEN YEAR EURO RECORD

Season	Competition	Finished
1998–99	C Winners' Cup	2nd round
1999–00	Champs League	3rd qual rd
	Uefa Cup	1st round
2000–01	Uefa Cup	1st round
2001–02	Uefa Cup	1st round
2002–03	Champs League	3rd qual rd
	Uefa Cup	2nd round
2003–04	Champs League	Group
2004–05	Uefa Cup	Last 16
2005–06	Champs League	3rd qual rd
	Uefa Cup	1st round
2006–07	Uefa Cup	Group
2007–08	Uefa Cup	1st qual rd*

* Won tie but expelled after crowd trouble

Fighting for European comeback

Formed as the Army team in 1945, Partizan Belgrade had severed their military links within a decade or so but they retain unwanted associations with combat. When their violent fans halted a Uefa Cup match in Bosnia-Herzegovina in 2007–08, the club received their 25th hooliganism-related fine in 36 European games over five years, and those cumulative offences led to their expulsion from the competition.

Missiles struck the referee and German goalkeeper Oliver Kahn during a defeat by Bayern Munich, but disturbances have not always arisen from frustration over results. In 2004–05, a season when Partizan were crowned unbeaten Serbian champions, their derby with title rivals Red Star featured fighting and seat-throwing.

Partizan were Yugoslavia's first European Cup runners-up in 1966, recovering from 4–1 down after the the first leg to beat Sparta Prague *en route* to the final. Recently, though, they have struggled in Europe, and there is no sign of a comeback from that.

BULGARIA

THE

3

MINUTE GUIDE

Capital: *Sofia*. **Languages:** *Bulgarian and Turkish*. **Beer:** *Kamenitza, Pirinsko*. **Food:** Kebapcheta *(minced-meat rolls)*, kyufteta *(meatballs)*, shopska *(salad)*. **National anthem:** *Mila Rodino (Dear Motherland)*. **Population:** *7,263,000*. **Time zone:** *GMT +2*. **Emergency number:** *112*. **Did you know?** *When Bulgaria played Sweden in the 1994 World Cup, every player in the starting line-up had a surname ending with 'ov'.* **Football body:** *Bulgarian Football Union, 26 Tzar Ivan Assen II Str, Sofia 1124; tel: +359 2 942 6253, fax: +359 2 942 6200, email: fu@bfunion.bg, website: www.bfunion.bg. Founded 1923. Affiliated 1924.*

Below: The Rila Monastery, south of Sofia, is one of the country's biggest attractions.

Hristo and Hristo

You don't get far reading anything about Bulgarian football before you bump into the name Hristo Stoichkov. The prodigiously talented left winger, known as much for his aggressive temperament as his trademark ambitious shots at goal, was the inspiration behind Bulgaria's greatest moment in football, their defeat of Germany in the 1994 World Cup which put them in the semi-finals for the first and only time.

He won that tournament's Golden Boot award for the (joint) most goals, he scored against Germany, and scored in the subsequent semi-final loss to Italy. When he wasn't arguing with the referee he found time to score 35 other goals in 83 caps.

However, it was another Hristo, Hristo Bonev, the Bulgarian hero of the 1970s, who is the country's leading scorer, 47 from 96 caps.

Football was introduced to Bulgaria by Swiss gymnastic teachers, of all people, in 1893, but it wasn't until the World Cup of 1962 that they appeared on the world stage (they were knocked out in the first round of their first four World Cups).

Domestically, the scene is dominated by the Sofia teams, especially CSKA Sofia (CSKA stands for Central Sport Club of the Army). They have won the league 31 times but close behind are rivals Levski Sofia on 25. Levski have won the Cup 26 times compared with CSKA's 19 wins. No prizes for the name of the man with the record number of goals in a league season (38, for CSKA in 1989–90): one H. Stoichkov.

Above: Bulgaria's Zoran Iankovic (in red). *Below:* The Naftex Stadium in Burgas.

THE TEN YEAR GUIDE

Bulgarian A PFG league

Season	Winner	Runner-up
1999	Litex Lovech	Levski Sofia
2000	Levski Sofia	CSKA Sofia
2001	Levski Sofia	CSKA Sofia
2002	Levski Sofia	Litex Lovech
2003	CSKA Sofia	Levski Sofia
2004	Lokomotiv Plovdiv	Levski Sofia
2005	CSKA Sofia	Levski Sofia
2006	Levski Sofia	CSKA Sofia
2007	Levski Sofia	CSKA Sofia
2008	CSKA Sofia	Levski Sofia

Bulgarian Cup winners

Season	Winner	Runner-up
1999	CSKA Sofia	Litex Lovech
2000	Levski Sofia	Neftohimik Plovdiv
2001	Litex Lovech	Velbuzhd Kyustendil
2002	Levski Sofia	CSKA Sofia
2003	Levski Sofia	Litex Lovech
2004	Litex Lovech	CSKA Sofia
2005	Levski Sofia	CSKA Sofia
2006	CSKA Sofia	PFC Cherno More Varna
2007	Levski Sofia	Litex Lovech
2008	Litex Lovech	PFC Cherno More Varna

SOFIA

Churches and the party heart

The Bulgarian capital, one of the oldest in Europe, dating back some 7,000 years, is home to around 1.4 million people. Its long history means you won't be short of views of important religious sites as you enjoy the city, including the medieval Boyana Church, the Church of St George and the 19th century St Alexander Nevsky Cathedral, one of the world's largest Orthodox churches.

But away from its numerous churches, museums and other historical sites, Sofia has a reputation as a party city, with many people carousing late and often right through the night. Head to the long Vitosha Boulevard that is lined with numerous bars, cafés and nightspots and Ulitsa Rakovski, both popular streets for partygoers. Another 24-hour party area is Studentski grad by the university, to the south of the city centre, where you will naturally enough find large numbers of students and other young people.

There are a good selection of beers in Bulgaria, including Kamenitza, sponsors of the national football team, but for a real local taste try the popular Baltic drink *rakia*, a fruit brandy. *Rakia* can be made from many fruits, including apples, figs, pears and apricots, but one of the most common is the plum *rakia*, known as *sljivovica*. Be warned, it is related to the better-known grappa, which many people will know well from their morning headaches.

The Vasil Levski National Stadium and Bulgarski Armiya, home of CSKA Sofia are centrally located in Tsar Boris Park. Levski Sofia's Stadion Georgi Asparuv is to the east of the city.

Below: One of the oldest cities in Europe, Sofia has a high concentration of religious sites.

3 THINGS YOU MUST DO...
(Apart from the football)

1 NATIONAL MUSEUM OF HISTORY

Enter with an open mind and leave the museum (16 Vitoshko Lale str. tel: +359 2 955 42 80) knowing everything there is to know about Bulgaria and the Balkans. Open: Nov–Mar 09.00–17.30, Apr–Oct 09.30–18.00. Price: adults 10lv, children 3lv. To get there: trolley 2, buses 63 and 111, minibus 21.

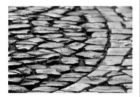

2 VITOSHA BOULEVARD

If a city likes to party 24 hours a day we really should support it, don't you think? Take your pick of the many bars and clubs along this popular road, sleep, and return for more the next day. To get there: trams 1 and 7.

3 CHANGING OF THE GUARD

Head to the president's office (pl Nezavisimost) for a bit of Bulgarian pomp as the soldiers march theatrically to their posts. When: on the hour. To get there: it's central.

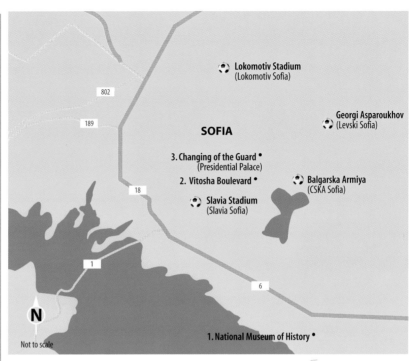

Lokomotiv Stadium (Lokomotiv Sofia)

802

189

SOFIA

Georgi Asparoukhov (Levski Sofia)

3. Changing of the Guard (Presidential Palace)

2. Vitosha Boulevard

18

Balgarska Armiya (CSKA Sofia)

Slavia Stadium (Slavia Sofia)

1

6

N

Not to scale

1. National Museum of History

BARS > CLUBS > RESTAURANTS

Bars > Want to splash out in opulent surroundings? Try the **Piano Bar** (100 James Bourchier Blvd, tel: +359 2 969 2222) in the Kempinski Hotel. For something more relaxed there is **Dondukov** (Kniaz Al Dondukov 14, tel: +359 886 439 050).

Clubs > If you can get past the doormen you will join models, wannabes and Sofia's money set jostling for attention at the slick **Club Chervilo** (9 Tzar Osvoboditel St, tel: +359 2 981 6633). Take your pick from one of the four rooms as you seek out attention.

Restaurants > Try traditional food in a restaurant designed to look like a traditional tavern (known as a *meyhane*): **Manastirska Magernitsa** (Han Asparuh Street 67, tel: +359 2 980 3883). And for more local fare with design to suit, try **Pri Yafata** (ul Solunska 28, tel: +359 2 980 1727).

Below: Colourful drinks – always dangerous in a city that parties hard like Sofia.

Weather	Low (°C)	High
January	-3	2
February	-2	4
March	1	9
April	5	14
May	9	18
June	12	22
July	14	25
August	13	25
September	11	22
October	6	16
November	1	7
December	-2	3

CSKA SOFIA

Above: CSKA Sofia's Valentin Iliev (centre) celebrates with team mates after scoring against Liverpool during a Champions League qualifying match at Anfield.

TEN YEAR EURO RECORD

Season	Competition	Finished
1998–99	Uefa Cup	2nd round
1999–00	Uefa Cup	1st round
2000–01	Uefa Cup	1st round
2001–02	Uefa Cup	2nd round
2002–03	Uefa Cup	1st round
2003–04	Champs League	3rd qual rd
	Uefa Cup	1st round
2004–05	Uefa Cup	1st round
2005–06	Champs League	3rd qual rd
	Uefa Cup	Group
2006–07	Uefa Cup	1st round
2007–08	Uefa Cup	1st round

Sofia, so good

In 2004–05, CSKA Sofia were three minutes from the first unbeaten Bulgarian top-flight campaign since the switch to a 30-game season in 1962, only to concede a late winning goal to Lokomotiv Plovdiv. A once-in-a-lifetime chance gone? Not for a club of CSKA's pedigree. Three years later they duly avoided a single defeat in collecting their 31st title, a remarkable tally given that it was only their 60th anniversary.

Yet 2008 was bittersweet for CSKA, who received a Champions League ban because of debts that included unpaid taxes, prompting several players to leave. Enforced demotion to Bulgaria's amateur ranks was threatened, but the country's football association eventually showed mercy.

CSKA know about upheaval. Formed as Septemvri pri CDV, with army connections, their name was changed repeatedly by the government for political ends. One constant, though, was their pre-eminence, with nine league titles in a row from 1954 and a European Cup semi-final in 1967. European advances are rare now, but domestic games are a different matter.

MATTER OF FACT

Name: PFS CSKA Sofia
Stadium: Balgarska Armiya (capacity 22,000)
Address: Sofia 1504, 3 Dragan Tsankov blvd
To get there: Trams 2, 12, 14, 19. Buses 76, 84
Telephone: +359 2 963 4279
Email: info@cska.bg
Website: http://cska.sportal.bg

Stadium tour

No tour available

Museum

Open: Weekdays 09.00–17.00; match days until two hours before kick-off
Price: Free
Contact: Phone and email above

Home   **Away**

Trophies

31 Bulgarian League
10 Bulgarian Cup

Main rivals

Levski Sofia (see page 153) are the greatest foes. Lokomotiv Sofia (tel: +359 2 837 8479, www.lokomotiv-sofia.bg) play at Lokomotiv Stadium (Bul Rozhen 23, 1220). Slavia Sofia (tel: +359 2 856 9197, www.pfcslavia.com) are based at Slavia Stadium (Ul Koloman 1, 1618).

LEVSKI SOFIA

Above: Levski Sofia's Stanimir Stoilov curls a free kick around the Chelsea wall.

MATTER OF FACT
Name: PFC Levski Sofia
Stadium: Georgi Asparoukhov
(capacity 29,200)
Address: 15 Lege St, 1000
To get there: Buses 78, 120. Tram 22
Telephone: +359 2 989 2156
Email: office@levski.bg
Website: www.levski.bg

Stadium tour
No official tour, but contact club to
arrange visit. No museum

Home	Away

Trophies

25	Bulgarian League
12	Bulgarian Cup

Main rivals
They meet CSKA Sofia (see page 152)
in the Eternal Derby. Lokomotiv Sofia
(tel: +359 2 837 8479, www.
lokomotivsofia.bg) play at Lokomotiv
Stadium (Bul Rozhen 23, 1220). See
Slavia Sofia (tel: +359 2 856 9197,
www.pfcslavia.com) at Slavia Stadium
(Ul Koloman 1, 1618).

TEN YEAR EURO RECORD		
Season	Competition	Finished
1998–99	Cup Winners Cup	1st round
1999–00	Uefa Cup	2nd round
2000–01	Champs League	2nd qual rd
2001–02	Champs League	3rd qual rd
	Uefa Cup	1st round
2002–03	Champs League	3rd qual rd
	Uefa Cup	2nd round
2003–04	Uefa Cup	3rd round
2004–05	Uefa Cup	1st round
2005–06	Uefa Cup	QF
2006–07	Champs League	Group
2007–08	Champs League	2nd qual rd

No longer feeling blue

With the 2005–06 title secured, Levski Sofia players entered the pitch for their final home game sporting blue hair and carrying 24 balloons – one for each league title. It may have seemed over the top but, having endured considerable government interference in their affairs during the Communist era, Levski could be forgiven for displaying some independence of spirit.

The authorities changed the club's name to the Soviet-style Dynamo for a while, imposed a merger and another name switch to Levski-Sofia, and affiliated the club with the Bulgarian Interior Ministry. In 1985, after the team's Cup final against CSKA Sofia, in which players fought, the government stripped Levski of the league title and disbanded the club, re-forming them as Vitosha (both decisions were reversed a few years later).

The Cup final took place amid suspicions that the authorities would try to help CSKA win, reflecting Levski's long-held belief – true or otherwise – that their bitter rivals received favours from above.

PORTUGAL

THE

3

MINUTE
GUIDE

Capital: *Lisbon.* **Language:** *Portuguese.* **Beer:** *Super Bock, Sagres Branca.* **Food:** Bacalhau *(cod)* sardinhas *(sardines),* espetada *(skewered beef).* **National anthem:** *A Portugesa (The Portuguese Song).* **Population:** *10,677,000.* **Time zone:** *GMT.* **Emergency Number:** *112.* **Did you know?** *The Vasco da Gama Bridge near Lisbon is the longest in Europe at 17.2 km (11 miles) in length.* **Football body:** *Federaçao Portuguesa de Futebol, Rue Alexandre Herculano, No 58 Apartado 24013 Lisbon 1250-012; tel: +351 21 325 2700, fax: +351 21 325 2780, email: secretario_geral@fpf.pt, website: www.fpf.pt. Founded 1914. Affiliated 1923.*

Below: The cock of Barcelos is a traditional symbol of Portugal.

Almost like watching Brazil

Most European leagues suffer from an over-concentration of talent among a few clubs, but Portugal's case is particularly bad. Since 1946 just once has the championship not been won by Benfica, Porto or Sporting Lisbon – Boavista triumphed in 2001 – and only seven runners-up spots have gone to outsiders.

Such predictability might end should the proposed Atlantic League ever come to fruition. Given Portuguese clubs' lack of revenue compared with those in the continent's wealthiest leagues, it is not surprising the country has been grouped with the Netherlands, Belgium and Scotland as a possible member of this international league at times.

During this period of domestic stagnation there has at least been plenty for the neutral Portuguese fan to enjoy internationally. Portugal's rise can be measured in their matches against England. They lost 10–0 at home in 1947 but have suffered only one defeat in their past 11 meetings, beating them in quarter-final penalty shoot-outs at Euro 2004 and the 2006 World Cup.

That was poor repayment to England for their contribution to Portuguese football; seven different English coaches have brought their expertise to win a combined 13 post-war league titles, the last two secured by Bobby Robson for Porto in 1995 and 1996.

The greatest influence nowadays is Brazil, whose players slip easily into a league where language is no barrier. Indeed the stylish Portugal national team have even been called the Brazilians of Europe. But where are the trophies?

Above: Benfica's Estádio du Luz in Lisbon. *Below:* Estádio Algarve in Faro was built for Euro 2004.

LISBON

Southern charm

Situated on the Atlantic Coast, Portugal's capital has a population of around 560,000, although the greater metropolitan area numbers about five times that. As a city that has been ruled or influenced during its history by, among others, Celts, Phoenicians, Romans, Vandals and other Germanic peoples, Moors and Christians, it is not surprising that it is littered with historical sites of interest.

There is the beautifully cloistered Jerónimos Monastery, which took 50 years to build from 1502, the Lisbon Cathedral, built on the site of the city's largest mosque when the Christians reconquered the city from the Moors in 1147 (and added to over the years), and the city's symbolic 16th century Belém Tower.

One of the city's biggest attractions, the Castle of São Jorge, looks down on the oldest part of the city, Alfama, which was the extent of the city during Moorish times. This is the area in which to simply stroll through crooked alleys enjoying the reflective Mediterranean light on red roofs and dazzling white walls.

Today the downtown area is Baixa, an elegant district built following the destruction of the 1755 Lisbon earthquake. Among its gridded streets are the well-known squares Praça do Comércio and the huge Praça da Figueira. But for shopping and nightlife head to the nearby Bairro Alto ('Upper Quarter'), the beating heart and the beating loudspeakers of Lisbon after dark.

To the north of the city is Sporting Lisbon's Estádio José Alvalade and Estádio de Lu of Benfica.

Below: The Monument to Discoveries with the 17.2 km (11 mile) Vasco da Gama bridge in the background.

3 THINGS YOU MUST DO...
(Apart from the football)

1 SANTA JUSTA'S ELEVATOR
For great views take this turn of the (last) century vertical elevator (Rua de Santa Justa, tel: +351 21 361 3054) from Baixa to Carmo Square a few metres up the hill. Open: 07.00–21.00. Price: €1.40 for a single. To get there: metro to Baixa/Chiado.

2 BAIRRO ALTO
Lisbon's party central. Bars, clubs, music and late nights. To get there: metro to Baixa/Chiado.

3 CHAIDO
Lisbon's trendy central. Bookshops, galleries and frothy coffees. To get there: metro to Baixa/Chiado

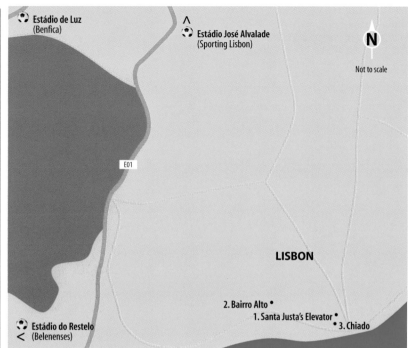

Estádio de Luz (Benfica)

Estádio José Alvalade (Sporting Lisbon)

N

Not to scale

E01

LISBON

Estádio do Restelo (Belenenses)

2. Bairro Alto •
1. Santa Justa's Elevator •
• 3. Chiado

BARS > CLUBS > RESTAURANTS

Bars > Find it and a good time could be yours at **Bar Incognito** (Rua Poliais de São Bento 37, tel: +351 21 390 8755). Music, drinks and a fun crowd. You want something altogether more cool? Then it's **Cinco Lounge** (Rua Ruben A Leitão 17-A, tel: +351 21 342 4033) for you, Mr/Ms Stylish Pants.

Clubs > People either love it (those who can get in) or hate it (those who can't). Try **Lux** (Avenida Infante D Henrique, tel: +351 21 882 0890) and make your own mind up. It's a late one whether you're there or not.

Restaurants > If you like traditional food served in a place that has a history, you'll go a long way to beat **Café Martinho da Arcada** (Praça do Comércio 3, tel: +351 21 887 9259). It's been serving the city since 1782. An alternative is **Alfaia** (Travessa da Queimada 18, tel: +351 21 346 1232).

Below: Lisbon's nightlife buzzes loudest and longest at Bairro Alto.

Weather	Low (°C)	High
January	7	13
February	9	15
March	9	16
April	11	19
May	12	21
June	15	25
July	16	26
August	17	28
September	16	26
October	13	21
November	10	17
December	8	14

BENFICA

Above: *Benfica are a Portugese institution, so winning is everything.*

TEN YEAR EURO RECORD		
Season	Competition	Finished
1998–99	Champs League	Group
1999–00	Uefa Cup	Last 32
2000–01	Uefa Cup	1st round
2001–02	DNQ	
2002–03	DNQ	
2003–04	Champs League	3rd qual rd
	Uefa Cup	Last 16
2004–05	Champs League	3rd qual rd
	Uefa Cup	Last 32
2005–06	Champs League	QF
2006–07	Champs League	QF
	Uefa Cup	QF
2007–08	Champs League	Group
	Uefa Cup	Last 16

Struggling to satisfy the majority

Tired of six million Portuguese breathing down his neck, Graeme Souness almost breathed a sigh of relief when dismissed as Benfica coach in 1999. "It's a national disaster if Benfica don't win the title because 60 per cent of the population support them," said the Scot, in which case the fans have endured almost unremitting disaster recently. After securing a record 30th league championship in 1994, they added just one in the next 14 years.

Souness went on:"The Portuguese people are wonderful until they go to watch Benfica play. Then they take their sensible heads off and all common sense goes out of the window." However, it was hard for the supporters to remain level-headed during the late 1990s presidential reign of Joao Vale e Azevedo, who pocketed part of a transfer fee – reportedly using it to buy himself a luxury yacht – for which he was jailed, and which left the club €98 million in debt.

Formed in 1908, the Eagles are accustomed to soaring above the rest of Portugal and even, briefly, did the same above Europe. Under Hungarian coach Béla Guttmann they ended Real Madrid's five-year run of success with thrilling victories in European Cup finals against Barcelona (3–2 in 1961) and Real (5–3 a year later). Their 130,000-capacity Stadium of Light – since rebuilt – was then the continent's largest ground.

Their recent decline included their first failures to qualify for European competition, for two years from 2001. The low period has featured over-spending, players' pay cheques bouncing on a couple of occasions and a huge turnover of coaches and players. It seems sensible heads are needed in the boardroom as well as in the stands.

GREATEST PLAYERS

> EUSÉBIO (1961–75)
Extremely quick, technically gifted and with a fierce shot, Eusébio was Portugal's leading player in the 1960s. Benfica's all-time leading goalscorer, he was European Footballer of the Year in 1965.

> RUI COSTA (1991–94; 2006–08)
An attacking midfield player, Rui Costa won nearly a century of Portugal caps. His two spells at Benfica sandwiched a 12-year stint in Italy with Fiorentina and AC Milan.

MATTER OF FACT
Name: Sport Lisboa e Benfica
Stadium: Estádio de Luz
(capacity 65,400)
Address: Av. General Norton
De Matos 1500
To get there: Metro on blue line
(station: Colegio Militar/Luz or Alto
dos Moinhos)
Telephone: +351 21 721 95 00
Email: serv.clientes@slbenfica.pt
Website: www.slbenfica.pt

Stadium tour (includes museum)
Open: 10.00, 11.00, 12.00, 14.30,
15.30, 16.30 (cannot visit
museum only)
Price: €10.
Contact: Tel: +351 21 721 95 20 or
email: visitasestadio@slbenfica.pt

Home	Away

Trophies

2	European Cup/ Champions League
31	Portuguese League
24	Portuguese Cup

Main rivals
Sporting Lisbon (see pages 160–161)
meet Benfica in O Classico, though
Porto are especially bitter enemies.
Belenenses (tel: +351 21 301 0461,
www.osbelenenses.com) are Lisbon's
third biggest club. They play at
Estádio do Restelo (Avenida
Restelo, 1449-015).

Above: A statue of Benfica's great
Eusébio outside the Estádio de Luz.

SOUNESS BARKS ANGRILY
Graeme Souness was suspended as
coach for allegedly pulling faces at
president Joao Vale e Azevedo
during a game. Souness rejected the
charge, claiming it was a means of
getting rid of him without paying a
departure settlement that had been
agreed: "It's an absolute disgrace. I've
been treated worse than a dog."

SPORTING LISBON

Above: Sporting Lisbon fans prepare for their European clash with Bayern Munich.

TEN YEAR EURO RECORD		
Season	Competition	Finished
1998–99	Uefa Cup	1st round
1999–00	Uefa Cup	1st round
2000–01	Champs League	Group*
2001–02	Uefa Cup	Last 32
2002–03	Champs League	3rd qual rd
	Uefa Cup	1st round
2003–04	Uefa Cup	2nd round
2004–05	Uefa Cup	Final
2005–06	Champs League	3rd qual rd
	Uefa Cup	1st round
2006–07	Champs League	Group
2007–08	Champs League	Group
	Uefa Cup	QF

* 1st of two group stages

Sporting struggle to get even

Sporting Lisbon float in a void. Almost guaranteed to be among the front-runners, having never finished outside the top five since the Portuguese league was formed in 1934, they have only twice been champions in the past 26 years. Furthermore, they are powerful enough to be one of the country's undisputed big three clubs yet are completely over-shadowed by one just down the road: Benfica. No wonder they were so excited by the chance to walk tall after reaching the 2005 Uefa Cup final.

That match was played in their own stadium against unfancied CSKA Moscow, yet they threw away a half-time lead to lose 3–1. Perhaps it was no surprise, given that it was 2005. Sporting's past ten league titles have come in even-numbered years, as was their only European trophy, the 1964 Cup Winners' Cup.

Their greatest period featured seven league titles in eight years from 1947, three of them under Englishman Randolph Galloway. Two of his coaching compatriots have also fared well. Malcolm Allison won the League and Cup double in 1982, which featured the club's last league title for 18 years, while Bobby Robson was controversially sacked when his team were joint top of the table (see opposite, below right).

Danish goalkeeper Peter Schmeichel inspired the league triumph of 2000, while Mario Jardel's 42 goals secured the title two years later, but, apart from a few Cup wins, Sporting have had to settle for taking pride in producing the likes of Luís Figo and Cristiano Ronaldo, wingers who have each won global individual player awards. Some sustained league success to match their size would be far more preferable for Sporting fans, though.

GREATEST PLAYERS

> FERNANDO PEYROTEO (1937–49)
One of Sporting's Five Violins forward line of the late 1940s – so-called because they played harmoniously – he scored 529 goals for the club, twice as many as any other player in their history.

> LUÍS FIGO (1989–95)
A midfield player who could dribble and cross the ball brilliantly, Figo won more than 100 caps for Portugal and was named Fifa World Player of the Year in 2001.

MATTER OF FACT

Name: Sporting Clube de Portugal
Stadium: Estádio José Alvalade (capacity 50,080)
Address: Rua Professor Fernando da Fonseca, 1600-616
To get there: Metro on yellow or green lines (station: Campo Grande). Buses 7, 36, 47, 108
Telephone: +351 21 751 6000
Email: lncaldeira@sporting.pt
Website: www.sporting.pt

Stadium tour (includes museum)
Open: Daily (except match day afternoons, the day after matches and team training days at the stadium): 11.30, 14.30, 16.00 (museum: daily 11.00–18.00)
Price: €8 (museum only: €6)
Contact: Tel: +351 21 751 6523 or email: eventos.visitas@sporting.pt

Home	Away

Trophies

1	European Cup Winners' Cup
18	Portuguese League
15	Portuguese Cup

Main rivals

City rivals Benfica (see pages 158–159) are the principal foes. Top division regulars Belenenses (tel: +351 21 301 0461, www.osbelenenses.com) are Lisbon's third team, based at Estádio do Restelo (Avenida Restelo, 1449-015).

Above: *Sporting Lisbon's Derlei shields the ball from Gerard Piqué of Barcelona.*

ROBSON'S UPS AND DOWNS

Bobby Robson had led Sporting to joint league leadership with Benfica in December 1993 but it was not enough for the club. They dismissed him, supposedly because of the Uefa Cup elimination by Salzburg, but more likely because they had Carlos Queiroz lined up as his replacement.

PORTO

Raise a glass to Porto

Port: yes, this is, unsurprisingly, where it comes from. We have all had a glass of this world-famous fortified wine (wine to which a spirit, usually brandy, is added) often as a mimic of the drink enjoyed by 'gentlemen' after a meal.

So if you like it, there is no better homage to your favoured drink then to have a taste in Porto, its home city. Euro guidelines in fact dictate that only fortified wine from this region can be called port, although the drink is produced in many other places around the world. Impress the locals by ordering a single *quinta* vintage, a port from a particular vineyard and particular year.

You'll need it too, to wash down the city's signature dish: tripe. The popularity of the dish stretches back, it is said, to 1415 when the city existed on tripe because its people gave the Portuguese fleet all their meat so they could go off and conquer new lands. Today you'll still find tripe soup and also tripe with white beans (*tripas à moda do Porto*).

Heavily industrialized Porto is the country's second city, with its population of about 240,000 settled along the Atlantic coast and River Douro. It is approximately 320 km (200 miles) north of the capital Lisbon. A popular place to head is the north bank of the river around Ribeira and the historic centre, which is a World Heritage Site.

Estádio do Dragão, Porto's home stadium, is about 3 km (2 miles) northeast of the centre, while Boavista's Estádio do Bessa is situated to the northwest.

Below: The historic north bank of Porto is a World Heritage Site.

3 THINGS YOU MUST DO...
(Apart from the football)

1 RIBEIRA

This relaxed riverside area is a great place during the day to simply stroll around the cobbled streets admiring the brightly coloured houses and boats, while after dark this is a busy nightlife centre. To get there: subway to São Bento.

2 SÃO PEDRO DA AFURUDA

A quaint fishing village to the south of the city for lazy hours wandering around or sitting in cafés watching the locals. To get there: buses 93 or 96 to Vila Nova de Gaia then a short walk.

3 RAMOS PINTO

You've tasted the port, now discover how it is made in these great cellars (Avenida Ramons Pinto 380, Villa Nova de Gaia, tel: +351 22 370 7000) and museum. Open: Jun–Sep Mon–Sat 10.00–18.00, Oct–May Mon–Fri 09.00–13.00 and 14.00–17.00. Closed public holidays. To get there: subway to Jardim do Morro.

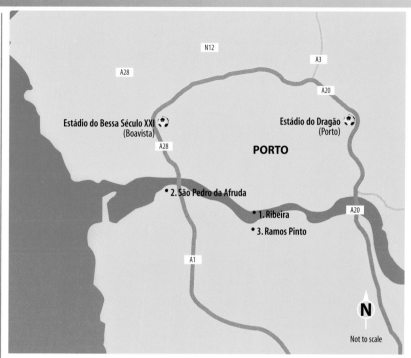

N12

A3

A28

A20

Estádio do Bessa Século XXI ⚽
(Boavista)

Estádio do Dragão ⚽
(Porto)

A28

PORTO

A20

• 2. São Pedro da Afruda

• 1. Ribeira

A20

• 3. Ramos Pinto

A1

N

Not to scale

BARS > CLUBS > RESTAURANTS

Bars > Just away from the bustle of the centre, the lounge of the upmarket **Solar do Vinho do Porto** (Rua de Entre Quintas, 220, tel: +351 22 609 4749) is a great place to sit back and enjoy a glass of the city's famed drink. For something completely different, there is always **Ryan's** (Rua Infante Dom Henrique 18, tel: +351 22 200 5366).

Clubs > Discoteque Aniki-Bóbó (Rua Fonte Tarina 36, tel: +351 22 332 4619) is a late venue that is relaxed and perfectly located in the Ribeira district. Meanwhile, the hip be-seen crowd can be found at **Indústria** (Avenida do Brasil 843, tel: +351 22 617 6806) in this busy street for nightlife.

Restaurants > You are going to try the city's favourite dish of tripe, aren't you? **Restaurante Tripeiro** (Rua Passos Manuel 195, tel: +351 22 200 5886) for tripe or a good selection of seafood.

Below: Intimate cafés and restaurants are everywhere in Porto.

Weather	Low (°C)	High
January	6	13
February	7	13
March	8	15
April	8	16
May	10	18
June	13	21
July	15	23
August	14	23
September	14	22
October	12	19
November	8	16
December	7	14

PORTO

Above: *The Porto team of 1904. A bit before José Mourinho.*

The all-powerful leaders

TEN YEAR EURO RECORD		
Season	Competition	Finished
1998–99	Uefa Cup	1st round
1999–00	Uefa Cup	1st round
2000–01	Champs League	Group*
2001–02	Uefa Cup	Last 32
2002–03	Champs League	3rd qual rd
	Uefa Cup	1st round
2003–04	Uefa Cup	2nd round
2004–05	Uefa Cup	Final
2005–06	Champs League	3rd qual rd
	Uefa Cup	1st round
2006–07	Champs League	Group
2007–08	Champs League	Group
	Uefa Cup	QF

* 1st of two group stages

Portugal's half-century of dictatorship collapsed in the 1970s but football soon created its own version of a one-party state. Previously marginalized, Porto grabbed power in the mid-1980s and have crushed most opposition since then, winning two-thirds of the league titles.

Their superiority is such that they can still prevail when punished. Docked six points in 2007–08 for bribing referees four seasons earlier – admittedly a flimsy penalty for such a crime – they barely noticed a difference as they still won the league by 14 points.

The monotony of domestic triumphs has increased Porto's interest abroad, where they have thrived. They won the 1987 European Cup and flourished again under coach José Mourinho, who collected the Uefa Cup and broke the major leagues' Champions League stranglehold to lift the 2004 trophy.

Mourinho then joined Chelsea, following the same route from Portugal to England that local wine trader António Nicholas de Almeida had taken on business trips when he discovered football and was inspired to found Porto in 1893. The club won three of the country's first six national championships from 1935, but decades of mediocrity lay ahead until Jorge Pinto da Costa took control in 1982.

His long-term presidency has had more than one whiff of corruption, however. In 1997 he resigned as head of the body which appoints referees after being accused of bribery and intimidation, a charge he denied. Then he received a two-year ban in 2008 over the aforementioned match-fixing scandal, again protesting his innocence. Let's hope Porto's record owes little or nothing to the kind of suppression of fairness that the country cast aside three decades ago.

GREATEST PLAYERS

> **MARIO JARDEL (1996–2000)**
The Brazilian scored 130 goals in 125 league games for Porto. He was the Portuguese league's top scorer in all four of his seasons there and Europe's leading scorer three times.

> **FERNANDO GOMES (1972–80; 1982–89)**
The Portuguese was a prolific scorer in both his spells at the club. He scored four times in their 9–0 win over Rabat Ajax *en route* to their 1987 European Cup triumph.

MATTER OF FACT

Name: Futebol Clube do Porto
Stadium: Estádio do Dragão
(capacity 50,399)
Address: Avenida Fernão de
Magalhães, 4350-158
To get there: Buses 21, 78. Metro line
E from airport or from Campanhã train
station (station: Antas)
Telephone: +351 22 557 0400
Email: geral-fcp@sportmultimedia.pt
Website: www.fcporto.pt

Stadium tour

Open: Thu–Sun (not match days),
10.00, 11.00, 12.00, 14.00, 15.00,
16.00, 17.00. Entrance 2, 28.
Bookings required
Price: €7
Contact: Tel: +351 22 707 28 1893
or email: apoioclientefcp@sport
multimedia.pt

Home   **Away**

Trophies

2	European Cup/ Champions League
1	Inter-Cities Fairs Cup/Uefa Cup
23	Portuguese League
17	Portuguese Cup

Main rivals

Benfica (see pages 158–159) are
Porto's greatest enemies. Boavista
(tel: +351 22 607 1004/5, www.
boavistafc.pt) are the strongest city
rivals. They play at Estádio do Bessa
Século XXI (Rua 1º de Janeiro, 4100).

*Above: Brazilian goalkeeper Helton
da Silva joined Porto in 2005.*

PITCH IMPERFECT

The Estádio do Dragão was opened
in November 2003 with a friendly
against Barcelona, but the pitch was
so poor that Porto were soon forced
into an embarrassing return to their
old Estádio das Antas while they
spent a few months getting the
grass to grow properly.

SPAIN

THE

3

MINUTE GUIDE

Capital: *Madrid.* **Language:** *Spanish, regionally Aranese, Basque, Catalan and Galician.* **Beer:** *Estrella Damm.* **Food:** Paella *(rice with meat or seafood),* chorizo *(spicy sausage),* gazpacho *(cold vegetable soup).* **National Anthem:** *La Marcha Real (The Royal March).* **Population:** *40,491,000.* **Time zone:** *GMT +1.* **Emergency number:** *112.* **Did you know?** *It is tradition to eat a grape with each strike of the clock at New Year.* **Football body:** *Real Federacion Española de Futbol Ramon y Cajal, s/n Apartado postal 385, Las Rozas 28230; tel: +34-91 495 9800, fax: +34 91 495 9801, email: rfef@rfef.es, website: www.rfef.es. Founded: 1909. Affiliated 1913.*

Below: The futuristic City of Arts and Sciences in Valencia.

Goodbye chokers, hello flair

You know the story. Spain go into a major tournament with a great group of players. They are everyone's second-favourite team (after their own country). They look good for the first few games, full of exciting promise. Then inexplicably they lose to a side with less skill and technique, and the players in red exit scratching their heads.

Spain are Europe's chokers, incapable of delivering when it matters. Or at least, that was the case until finally, in 2008, Spain won the European Championship, their first major trophy since 1964. It was won, fittingly with flair and freedom, the very talents that epitomize the game in Spain.

Domestically La Liga is one of the strongest and most-watched leagues in the world. Real Madrid and Barcelona, whose matches are dubbed *El Clasico* ('The Classic'), attract most of the attention both inside and outside the country, especially across Latin America. However, there is genuine competition, with, in recent years, clubs such as Deportiva La Coruña, Valencia, Sevilla, Atlético Madrid and even tiny Villarreal, ensuring that La Liga does not become a cosy two-club competition.

Regionally there is great rivalry, tinged by political and regional sentiment. Barcelona consider themselves the side of Catalonia while Athletic Bilbao are proud Basques, standing firm in a global game by refusing to choose players from outside their region. Both Catalonia and the Basque region have their own 'national' teams although they are not officially recognized by Fifa.

Above: Is this the biggest football flag ever? ***Below:*** There is intense regional rivalry in Spain.

THE TEN YEAR GUIDE

La Liga

Season	Winner	Runner-up
1998–99	Barcelona	Real Madrid
1999–00	Deportivo La Coruña	Barcelona
2000–01	Real Madrid	Deportivo La Coruña
2001–02	Valencia	Deportivo La Coruña
2002–03	Real Madrid	Real Sociedad
2003–04	Valencia	Barcelona
2004–05	Barcelona	Real Madrid
2005–06	Barcelona	Real Madrid
2006–07	Real Madrid	Barcelona
2007–08	Real Madrid	Villarreal

Copa del Rey

Season	Winner	Runner-up
1999	Valencia	Atlético Madrid
2000	Espanyol	Atlético Madrid
2001	Real Zaragoza	Celta Vigo
2002	Deportivo de La Coruña	Real Madrid
2003	Real Mallorca	Recreativo de Huelva
2004	Real Zaragoza	Real Madrid
2005	Real Betis	Osasuna
2006	Espanyol	Real Zaragoza
2007	Sevilla	Getafe
2008	Valencia	Getafe

MADRID

The royal city

Centrally located in the country at an altitude of 700 m (2,296 ft), Madrid is the highest of all European capital cities and is home to over three million people. Befitting a city with a long history yet one that is at home in the modern world, the backdrop to Madrid is varied and interesting.

You can see the signatures of historic Madrid in the form of landmarks such as the 18th century Baroque Royal Palace (official residence of the King of Spain), the nearby Catholic Almudena Cathedral and the peaceful green island that is the park El Retiro.

And you can see the modern in the form of the well-developed infrastructure and the architecture of the Cuatro Torres business area (built on the former site of Real Madrid's training ground), specifically the

Torre Espacio ('Space Towers') and, near the Charmartin railway station, the 'leaning' Puerta de Europa towers. It's impossible not to do a double take when you first see these two towers but don't worry, it's not your eyes; these 1996-built structures are built at a 15-degree incline.

On the nightlife front, it starts late and finishes late. Clubs especially don't warm up till well after midnight. Enjoy drinks and your choice of tapas in the Puerta del Sol area and the gay district of Chueca for bars, clubs and lively crowds.

Real Madrid's legendary Estadio Santiago Bernabéu is in the north of the city, while Estádio Vicente Calderon, home of Atlético Madrid, is to the southwest.

Below: Despite it's historic past, much of the city's modern architecture is bold and daring.

3 THINGS YOU MUST DO...
(Apart from the football)

1 PLAZA DE TOROS DE LAS VENTAS
Regarded as the home of Spanish bull-fighting, this bullring (c/Alcalá 237, tel: +34 90 215 0025 for tickets) can hold just over 23,000 people. Open: Mar–Oct on Sun and holidays from around 18.00. Price: from €2.20 to €125. To get there: subway line 2 or 5 to Las Ventas or buses 12, 21, 38, 53, 106, 110 and 146.

2 MUSEO DEL PRADO
Simply a world-class museum and art gallery (Paseo del Prado s/n, tel: +34 91 330 2800). Open: Tues–Sun 09.00–20.00. Price: adults €6, concessions €3 (some concessions free and everyone after 18.00 Tues–Sat and 17.00 Sun). To get there: subway to Banco de España and Atocha, buses 9, 10, 14, 19, 27, 34, 37 and 45.

3 REAL MADRID BASKETBALL
As hot as the football team with 30 national titles and eight European titles. Matches are played at Estadio Vistalegre (Calle Utebo 1, tel: +34 91 422 0781). When: Sat 19.00 or Sun 12.30 and Tues or Weds 19.00. Price: from €20. To get there: subway to Vista Alegre and Oporto, buses 17, 34, 35, 55, 81 and 118.

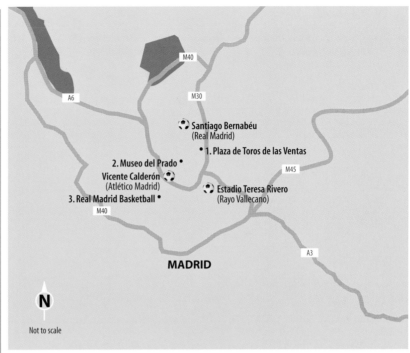

MADRID

Not to scale

BARS > CLUBS > RESTAURANTS

Bars > Café Commercial (Glorieta de Bilbao 7, tel: +34 91 521 5655) delivers a mixed and relaxed crowd and is a bar that has been serving drinks in the city for years. You should find yet more fun-loving people at **Del Diego** (C/de la Reina 12, tel: +34 91 523 3106).

Clubs > Splash out on food, cocktails and dancing, which can all be rolled into one in a great setting at **Fortuny** (34 Fortuny, tel: +34 91 319 0588). Or for something completely different, try the multi-levelled **Kapital** (Calle de Atocha 125, tel: +34 91 4202906) for less setting and more dancing.

Restaurants > Try **Casa Labre** (Calle Tetuán, 12, tel: +34 91 531 0081) and **El Sobrino de Botin** (Cuchilleros 17, tel: +34 91 366 4217) for some history with your food. The former has been around for more than 100 years, while the latter opened in 1725 and featured in a Hemingway novel.

Below: The after-dark action in Madrid starts late and continues on and on.

Weather	Low (°C)	High
January	0	10
February	1	12
March	3	15
April	6	18
May	8	21
June	13	27
July	16	32
August	16	32
September	12	27
October	9	20
November	3	14
December	1	11

ATLÉTICO MADRID

Above: Atlético Madrid in 1927. The stripes, which resembled army mattresses, earned the club the nickname of the Mattress Makers.

TEN YEAR EURO RECORD		
Season	Competition	Finished
1998–99	Uefa Cup	SF
1999–00	Uefa Cup	Last 16
2000–01	DNQ	
2001–02	DNQ	
2002–03	DNQ	
2003–04	DNQ	
2004–05	Intertoto Cup	Final*
2005–06	DNQ	
2006–07	DNQ	
2007–08	Intertoto Cup	Winners**
	Uefa Cup	Last 32

* 1 of three finals
** 1 of 11 winners

In the shadow of greatness

The picture startled the world: Jesús Gil, then president of Atlético Madrid, punching a senior official of Primera División rivals Compostela outside the Spanish League headquarters in 1996 over an apparent insult. It is easy for those associated with Atlético to nurture a sense of paranoia, of rebellion, of us-against-the-world. On an exclusive street across the city reside Real Madrid, more popular, successful and glamorous; Atlético are the poor relations, located next to a brewery and carrying the prosaic nickname of the Mattress Makers.

Alfonso Cabeza, Atlético president in the early 1980s, certainly perceived prejudice, criticizing the Spanish federation with such venom that they banned him for 16 months, but his reign was tranquil compared with later. Gil mixed barbs at authority with a dictatorial approach at his own club, appointing 23 coaches in

16 years. When the team lost away to Las Palmas, he declared: "I hope the plane crashes on the way back."

Atlético's impressive trophy haul has traditionally seen them labelled as Spain's third force after Real Madrid and Barcelona, but the description has fallen away recently. The club's double triumph of 1996 constitutes their only league title since 1977, and their only Spanish Cup victory since 1992.

The fans stuck with them in lean times, with attendances averaging around 50,000 in the second division in 2001–02, and they were rewarded when Enrique Cerezo replaced Gil and pumped money into the club. Qualification for the 2008–09 Champions League marked their first appearance in Europe's senior club competition in 12 years. The Mattress Makers – their red and white stripes resembled army mattresses – had a spring in their step again.

GREATEST PLAYERS

> ADELARDO (1959–76)
The Spaniard's strong tackling and skilful passing graced Atlético's midfield for 17 years from 1959 and helped inspire one of their greatest periods. With Adelardo in the ranks, the club won three league titles, five Spanish Cups and their only European trophy.

> FERNANDO TORRES (2001–07)
Appointed as Atlético captain at 19, Torres was such a talismanic figure that there was uproar whenever it was suggested that the striker might leave the club. After scoring 82 goals for the team, he was eventually prised away in 2007 by Liverpool for €25 million.

MATTER OF FACT

Name: Club Atlético de Madrid
Stadium: Vicente Calderón
(capacity 54,851)
Address: Paseo Virgen del Puerto
67, 28005
To get there: Metro: line 5 (stations:
Pirámides, Marqués de Vadillo). Buses:
17, 18, 23, 34, 35, 36, 50, 116, 118, 119
Telephone: +34 91 366 4707
Email: comunicacion@clubatletico
demadrid.com
Website: www.clubatleticode
madrid.com

Stadium tours

Open: Museum Mon–Sat
11.00–19.00. Match days 11.00 until
kick off. Tours at 12.00, 13.00, 16.30,
17.30. Turn up 15 minutes before to
buy ticket
Price: Museum €6, tour €8
Contact: Tel: +34 90 226 0403, or
email: museo@clubatleticode
madrid.com

Home   **Away**

Leading trophies

1	European Cup Winners' Cup
9	Spanish League
9	Spanish Cup

Main rivals

Real Madrid (see pages 172–173) are
overwhelmingly Atlético's biggest
rivals. Atlético have looked on
enviously as the city's 'establishment'
club have dominated football in the
city, across Spain and around Europe.
The city's third largest club is Rayo
Vallecano (tel: +34 91 478 2253,
www.rayovallecano.es), although
they have not played in the Primera
División since 2003. They are based in
an unappealing area of southern
Madrid at the Estadio Teresa Rivero
(Payaso Fofó, 28018).

Above: *Atlético Madrid's Maxi
Rodriguez celebrates scoring a
goal with his team mates.*

BUILDING TRAGEDY

Jesús Gil, Atlético's autocratic
president (1987–2003) and property
developer, was jailed in 1969 when
one of his constructions collapsed,
killing 58 people, because the
cement had dried and no architect
or surveyor was used. Gil was grant-
ed clemency by General Franco.

REAL MADRID

Above: The legendary Santiago Bernabéu.

TEN YEAR EURO RECORD		
Season	Competition	Finished
1998–99	Champs League	QF
1999–00	Champs League	Winners
2000–01	Champs League	SF
2001–02	Champs League	Winners
2002–03	Champs League	SF
2003–04	Champs League	QF
2004–05	Champs League	Last 16
2005–06	Champs League	Last 16
2006–07	Champs League	Last 16
2007–08	Champs League	Last 16

The club that reigns in Spain

Meet Spanish football's aristocrats. Based in a posh district of Madrid, blessed with a royal name and friends to Franco during the dictator's reign, they were never considered to be in danger of collapse when deep in the red early this decade because it was thought banks would not dare to call in their debts from a much-loved national institution.

But Real's global renown owes more to their efforts on the pitch. European champions a record nine times, their 31 domestic titles are the most among the continent's leading leagues. Such success has helped to establish them as the world's biggest-earning club.

The march to greatness began when Santiago Bernabéu became president in 1943, building the stadium that bears his name and pioneering the concept of a multi-national club team. The side of Hungarian Ferenc Puskás and Argentine Alfredo Di Stéfano lifted the first five European Cups from 1956, but those stylish triumphs brought huge expectations that have weighed heavily on modern-day coaches.

The club sacked John Toshack, Vicente del Bosque and Fabio Capello shortly after they won the title and dismissed Jupp Heynckes after he secured the Champions League. Juande Ramos, appointed in 2008, was their 21st coach during the managerial reign of Sir Alex Ferguson at Manchester United.

The club won three Champions League victories around the millennium, when the commercially driven Galácticos policy of signing one superstar per year began. Luís Figo, Zinedine Zidane, Ronaldo and David Beckham all arrived as Real seemed more intent on chasing pesetas than points. Rivals scoffed as trophies became scarce but, not surprisingly, given their history, Real were soon back among the honours.

GREATEST PLAYERS

> **ALFREDO DI STÉFANO (1953–64)**
Spain's football federation settled a dispute between Real Madrid and Barcelona over the Argentine by decreeing he would play for both in alternate seasons. Real eventually persuaded their rivals to relinquish their claim to him and reaped the benefit.

> **ZINEDINE ZIDANE (2001–06)**
Real broke the world transfer record by paying Juventus €76 million for the French attacking midfielder. The Fifa World Player of the Year on three occasions, he showed his outstanding technique with a brilliant volleyed goal in the 2002 Champions League final.

MATTER OF FACT
Name: Real Madrid Club de Fútbol
Stadium: Santiago Bernabéu
(capacity 80,400)
Address: Avenida de Concha Espina
1, 28036
To get there: Metro line 10 (station:
Santiago Bernabéu). Buses 14, 27, 40,
43, 120, 147, 150
Telephone: +34 91 398 4300
Email: realmadrid@club.
realmadrid.com
Website: www.realmadrid.com

Stadium tours
Open: Mon–Sat 10.00–19.30. Sun
and public holidays 10.30–18.30.
Matchdays: tour closes five hours
before kick-off. Closed: 1 Jan, 25 Dec
Price: (includes museum) €15; under
14s €10
Contact: Tel: +34 91 398 4370 or
window 10 (next to gate 7). Tour starts
gate 20

Home

Away

Leading trophies
9	European Cup Winners' Cup
2	Fairs Cup/Uefa Cup
31	Spanish League
17	Spanish Cup

Main rivals
Barcelona (see pages 176–177) are
480 km (300 miles) away but are
Real's biggest enemies, flaunting as
they do their Catalan identity and
holding the next best club record in
Spain after Real. Matches against city
neighbours Atlético Madrid (see pages
170–171) are also intense. Rayo
Vallecano (tel: +34 91 478 2253,
www.rayovallecano.es), whose latest
top-division stint ended in 2003, play
in a downmarket part of Madrid at
the Estadio Teresa Rivero (Payaso
Fofó, 28018).

A FUNNY BUSINESS
Real's training complex was in an
area banned from commercial use,
but city authorities (encouraged by
Real) re-zoned it in 2000, allowing
the club to sell it to developers and
wipe out their huge debts. Real's
rivals were angered by the
'convenience' of the arrangement.

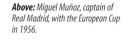
*Above: Miguel Muñoz, captain of
Real Madrid, with the European Cup
in 1956.*

BARCELONA

Gaudi not Gaudy

In many ways, Barcelona's famous Las Ramblas sums up the city: bright, cheerful, self-assured. Visitor honey pots in other cities – London's Covent Garden, Paris's Montmartre – might have the same collection of art stalls, knick-knacks for sale and inventive street performers, but somehow nowhere has the same languid self-confidence of Las Ramblas. Visitors are welcome, of course, but make no mistake, this is Barcelona's space. There's certainly no shortage of confidence in the living statues, the oh-so-cool performers who playfully engage with visitors who approach them nervously then pose for photographs.

It's all rather fitting, really, because displays are what this city is all about. From the iconic Gaudi- and Miró-inspired architecture, to bold and daring installations that other cities would shudder at even considering,

to the legacy of Picasso, is it any wonder the city's football fans demand style as well as victories? You can go in search of landmarks, such as where Picasso used to dine, in the hope that the city's genius might rub off on you, but it's more fun just strolling around and admiring how art has been worked into daily life.

The 1.2 km (0.7 mile) walkway of Las Ramblas, or simply Ramblas as it is often called, runs through the heart of the city. It runs from Placa de Catalunya, generally regarded as the centre of Barcelona and focused on a large square containing trees, fountains and major shops, to Monument a Colom ('Christopher Columbus Monument'). Ramblas borders the historic Barri Gotic, with its cobbled streets and old buildings.

Camp Nou, Barcelona's home, is 6.5 km (4 miles) west of the centre.

Below: *Gaudi's architectural influence is everywhere in Barcelona.*

3 THINGS YOU MUST DO...
(Apart from the football)

1 MUSEU PICASSO
Picasso moved to Barcelona as a teenager, and while some say the Picasso museum (Montcada 15–23, tel: +34 93 256 30 00) does not have the most extensive collection, you can have your fill of Gaudi and Miró by walking around the city. This is the city's second most popular museum. Number one? Barcelona FC, of course.

2 LAS RAMBLAS
Flower sellers, artists, performers entertaining crowds and arty shops abound in Barcelona's iconic artery. Just stroll along and soak it up, and get your portrait drawn in the street while everyone watches.

3 BARCELONETA BEACH
Is there really a better place to eat seafood than while people-watching, with the source of your food as a backdrop? Barcelona's beaches bring together a vibrant yet relaxed crowd and there are multiple beach huts to cater for them when they have had enough of the sun. Take your pick.

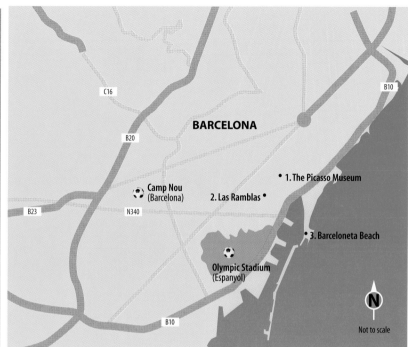

BARCELONA

C16
B10
B20
B23
N340
B10

Camp Nou (Barcelona)

2. Las Ramblas
1. The Picasso Museum
3. Barceloneta Beach

Olympic Stadium (Espanyol)

N

Not to scale

BARS > CLUBS > RESTAURANTS
Bars > Rita Blue (Placa Sant Augusti 3, tel: +34 93 342 4086) is perfectly situated near Ramblas. Enjoy a drink on its terrace in the sunshine then sink into its retro interior later. Or check out the different levels at the ultra-cool designer **Bestial** (C/Ramon Trias Fargas 2–4, tel: +34 93 224 0407).
Clubs > If you're looking for a really late one then try **Otto Zutz** (Lincoln 15, tel: +34 93 238 0722) where dancing continues on three levels through to morning. Or for later still (why stop, right?) head to **Tijuana Morning Café** (Passeig Maritim de la Barceloneta 32, tel: +34 93 423 1285).
Restaurants > For a taste of Catalan cuisine choose between stylish **El Tragaluz** (Passatge de la Concepció 5, tel: +34 93 487 0196) or the more relaxed **Can Gaig** (Passeig de Maragall 402, tel: +34 93 429 1017) which has been around for 150 years.

Below: A trip in the cable car offers spectacular views.

Weather	Low (°C)	High
January	4	12
February	5	13
March	6	15
April	9	17
May	11	20
June	15	23
July	18	27
August	19	27
September	17	25
October	12	21
November	8	16
December	5	13

BARCELONA

Above: Barcelona fans are among the most loyal in Europe.

Catalonia's beautiful club

TEN YEAR EURO RECORD		
Season	Competition	Finished
1998–99	Champs League	Group
1999–00	Champs League	SF
2000–01	Champs League	Group*
	Uefa Cup	SF
2001–02	Champs League	SF
2002–03	Champs League	QF
2003–04	Uefa Cup	Last 16
2004–05	Champs League	Last 16
2005–06	Champs League	Winners
2006–07	Champs League	Last 16
2007–08	Champs League	SF

* 1st of two group stages

So long does noise take to cross the vast Camp Nou stadium, that fans behind the far goal appear slow-witted as their roars of delight reach your ears a full second after your eyes have seen a goal. Size matters to Barcelona, who bill themselves as 'more than a club' because they have long guarded Catalan identity, notably so when former Spanish dictator Franco tried to crush such regional feelings. "We are more than a club because we have always defended the values of civility, solidarity and democracy," says club president Joan Laporta.

But while Laporta does his worthy defending, the team concentrates on attacking, a positive approach evident from the 1974 league title-winning side featuring Johan Cruyff, to the 1992 European champions coached by the same man and the 2006 Champions League winners inspired by Ronaldinho.

Despite their devotion to the Catalan cause, there is an international feel to the club that extends beyond the presence of 2,000 or so official supporters' clubs worldwide. Barcelona have not felt compelled to use local coaches in their pursuit of success: eight have been English, most recently Terry Venables and Bobby Robson, while their four longest-serving men in the dugout have been Dutch, one of whom, Johan Cruyff, has become Camp Nou's unofficial figurehead. Oh, and their founder in 1899 was a Swiss, Joan Gamper.

But enough of the cynicism – Barcelona are goodies. Owned by their fans, they have eschewed shirt sponsorship to retain the jersey's purity; when in 2006 they finally agreed to sport a name, it was that of Unicef, to whom they committed to pay €7.5million over five years. In a beautiful city boasting beautiful weather, the beautiful game thrives.

GREATEST PLAYERS

> **JOHAN CRUYFF (1973–78)**
The elegant Dutch forward immediately inspired Barcelona's first league title in 14 years when he arrived from Ajax in 1973, winning the European Footballer of the Year award for the third time in four years for good measure.

> **RONALDINHO (2003–08)**
A Real Madrid big-shot admitted that the Brazilian was too ugly for their 'brand', which required the looks of a David Beckham, so instead the toothy-grinned winger brought smiles to Barcelona fans. He was named Fifa World Player of the Year in 2004 and 2005

MATTER OF FACT

Name: Fútbol Club Barcelona
Stadium: Camp Nou (capacity 98,772)
Address: Carrer d'Arístides Maillol, 08028
To get there: Subway line 3 (stations: Maria Cristina, Palau Reial or Zona Universitaria) or line 5 (stations: Collblanc or Badal). Buses 7, 15, 33, 43, 54, 56, 57, 67, 68, 74, 75, 113, 157, 158, L12, L14, L50, L56, L62. Trams T1, T2, T3 (stops: Avinguda de Xile, Palau Reial, Pius XII)
Telephone: +34 902 189 900
Email: ticketsbarcelona@barcelona.com
Website: www.fcbarcelona.com

Stadium tours

Opening hours: Mon–Sat 10.00–17.30 (until 19.00, 14 Apr–12 Oct), Sundays and public holidays 10.00–13.30. Closed 1, 6 Jan, 25 Dec.
Price: €13 (incl museum); €8.50 for museum only
Contact: Tel: +34 934 963 600 or email: museu@fcbarcelona.cat

Home	Away

Leading trophies

2	European Cup/Champions League
4	European Cup Winners' Cup
3	Inter-Cities Fairs Cup/Uefa Cup
18	Spanish League
24	Spanish Cup

Main rivals

Real Madrid (see pages 172–173) are Barcelona's greatest foes. Barcelona have some enmity with Espanyol (tel: +34 932 927 700, www.rcdespanyol.com), who play at the Olympic Stadium (Passeig Olímpic, 7–19, 08038), scene of the 1992 Games, but plan to move to the new, 40,000-seat Estadi RCDE in Cornellà de Llobregat, near Barcelona.

ANYONE GOT A LIGHT?

Ricardo Zamora, the club's goalkeeper, was jailed and fined for trying to smuggle Cuban cigars in 1920 (Barcelona were so superior to opponents he could have smoked one during matches), and, two years later, received a year-long ban from football for tax evasion.

Above: *Barça fans prepare for another night of Champions League action.*

SEVILLE

Oh Macarena!

Seville sits at the heart of Andalucia on the River Guadalquivi in the south of Spain and is home to around 700,000 people. Head to the waterfront where you will find the former military watchtower Torre del Oro, a perfect starting point for wandering around the medieval city and its surrounds.

Many of the city's landmarks are clustered in and around the small old centre. These include one of the oldest churches in the world, the Seville Cathedral, built on the site of the city's former mosque, the University of Seville, the Alcázar (royal palace) and the impressive and sweeping Plaza de España, which has been used as the setting for numerous films.

A short distance away is the district of La Macarena, a largely working-class area, which has a fair share of its own attractions including a large part of the old medieval walls and a 16th century wooden statue of Virgen de la Macarena. But if nothing else, you'll want to go here just to hum the song of the same name, made famous by local music duo Los del Río. Just make sure no-one is around before breaking into those well-rehearsed dance movements.

Across the river (on an island) is the neighborhood of Triana, traditionally the district that was home to the gypsy population, although today that is changing as property prices have risen.

Sevilla's home Ramón Sánchez Pizjuán stadium is centrally located just east of the river, and Estadio Manuel Ruiz de Lopera, where Real Betis play, is a short distance to the south.

Below: Traditional transport entertains the tourists in Seville. A horse and carriage waits outside the cathedral for business.

3 THINGS YOU MUST DO...
(Apart from the football)

1 TAPAS
From prawns to ham to fried fish, there is no better way to taste Andalucia than with tapas. Centrally located and with views, dip in and enjoy at Restaurante & Tapas El Giraldillo (Plaza Virgen de los Reyes 2, tel: +34 95 421 4525). To get there: tram 1 to Archivo de Indias.

2 SHERRY
Before moving onto your drink of choice raise a glass of the region's famous fortified wine. At Bodega Santa Cruz, Las Columnas (Calle Rodrigo Caro 1, tel: +34 95 421 3246) you can enjoy the fresh air while waiting for more tapas. To get there: tram 1 to Archivo de Indias.

3 LA GIRALDA
Enjoy great city views from the bell tower of the Seville Cathedral (Plaza Virgen de los Reyes, tel: +34 95 421 4971). Open: Mon–Sat 11.00–17.00, Sun 14.00–18.00. To get there: tram 1 to Archivo de Indias.

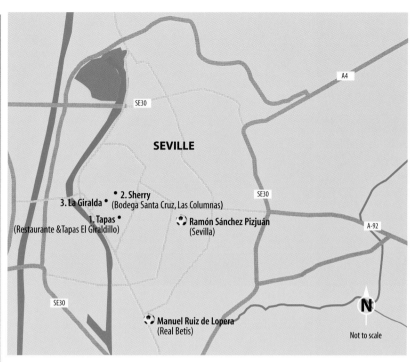

SEVILLE

3. La Giralda
• 2. Sherry
(Bodega Santa Cruz, Las Columnas)

1. Tapas •
(Restaurante &Tapas El Giraldillo)

Ramón Sánchez Pizjuán
(Sevilla)

Manuel Ruiz de Lopera
(Real Betis)

N

Not to scale

BARS > CLUBS > RESTAURANTS

Bars > Avelino (Plaza de los Andes 1, tel: +34 95 461 0489) is a good option away from the centre. Great tapas and prices. **Cervecería Internacional** (Calle Gamazo 3, tel: +34 95 421 1717) has a good beer selection and the best Russian salad in Sevilla. Local people, international drinks.

Clubs > Caramelo (Avda. San Francisco Javier-Edificio, tel: +34 95 463 4288) parties until six or seven in the morning. Nice staff and reasonable drinks prices. **Boss Betis**, (2, tel: +35 95 499 0104) can get crowded but has a nice mix of people and continues until seven.

Restaurants > Manolo León (8 Calle Guadalquivir, tel: +34 95 437 3735) in an elegant 19th century Andalucian house serves traditional Spanish food, especially fish and seafood from Cádiz and Huelva. **La Raza** (2 Avenida Isabel la Catolica, tel: +34 95 423 2024) has amazing views.

Below: Andalucian cuisine specializes in seafood; the restaurants specialize in relaxed elegance.

Weather	Low (°C)	High
January	5	16
February	6	17
March	7	20
April	10	21
May	12	26
June	16	30
July	18	35
August	19	35
September	17	32
October	13	25
November	9	20
December	6	16

SEVILLA

Above: Beating the drum for Sevilla.

Finally the real deal

TEN YEAR EURO RECORD		
Season	Competition	Finished
1998–99	DNQ	
1999–00	DNQ	
2000–01	DNQ	
2001–02	DNQ	
2002–03	DNQ	
2003–04	DNQ	
2004–05	Uefa Cup	Last 16
2005–06	Uefa Cup	Winners
2006–07	Uefa Cup	Winners
2007–08	Champs League	Last 16

White-shirted, a modern force, based in a posh part of town and playing at a stadium designed by the joint architect of the Santiago Bernabéu stadium, Sevilla seem to have much in common with Real Madrid. A glance at the trophy cabinet, however, discourages comparisons. While the club from the capital have been league champions 31 times, the side from the deep south have a solitary title.

It is not as if Sevilla have refused to think big. Many high-profile foreign players have been enticed with big wages, but few have prospered. Diego Maradona's contribution during his brief stay in 1992–93 amounted to several poor performances and two red cards.

After their 1958 move into the Sánchez Pizjuán stadium, created by Manuel Muñoz Monasterio in the Nervión district, Sevilla did not win a cup or finish in the league's top two until they were galvanized by the arrival of president Jose Maria del Nido in 2002.

A thriving youth system and transfer market astuteness have reaped dividends. Jose Antonio Reyes, a former trainee, was sold to Arsenal in 2004 for €15 million, while Brazilian pair Julio Baptista and Daniel Alves were signed for a combined €3 million and sold for €48 million. This approach is essential, given that their €29 million budget in 2006 was dwarfed by those of Valencia (€129 million), Barcelona (€235 million) and Real Madrid (€336 million).

Coached by Juande Ramos, the team flourished by adopting a high-speed game with two wingers, earning successive Uefa Cups – the first when thrashing Middlesbrough 4–0 in the final – a Spanish Cup and Champions League qualification. They could be mentioned in the same breath as Real Madrid at last.

GREATEST PLAYERS

> JUAN ARZA (1943–59)
The goalscoring feats of the Spanish forward stand out in the club's history. The only Sevilla player to have topped the Spanish league's goalscoring chart – 28 goals in 1954–55 – his haul of 182 league goals is 43 higher than the club's second most prolific player.

> DAVOR SUKER (1991–96)
So popular was the Croatian striker that, despite having announced he would leave Sevilla for Real Madrid in the summer of 1996, he was carried from the pitch by adoring fans after scoring a hat-trick against Salamanca in his final game to help the club avoid relegation.

MATTER OF FACT

Name: Sevilla Fútbol Club
Stadium: Ramón Sánchez Pizjuán (capacity 45,500)
Address: Avenida Eduardo Dato, 41005
To get there: Buses C1, C2, 27, 32
Telephone: +34 902 510 011
Email: sevillafc@sevillafc.es
Website: www.sevillafc.es

Stadium tours

Opening hours: Contact club to arrange time for tour
Price: €5
Contact: Email: prensa@sevillafc.es

Home	Away

Trophies

2	Inter-Cities Fairs Cup/ Uefa Cup
1	Spanish League
4	Spanish Cup

Main rivals

Sevilla and Real Betis maintain perhaps the most intense cross-city rivalry in Spain. Betis (tel: +34 954 610 340, www.realbetisbalompie.es) play at the Manuel Ruiz de Lopera stadium in the downmarket district of Heliopolis, south of the city centre (Avenida Heliópolis, 41012). In a derby game at Betis in February 2007, Sevilla coach Juande Ramos – once in charge of Betis – was knocked unconscious by a missile thrown from the crowd.

Above: Sevilla players Andrés Palop (left) and Daniel Alves with the Uefa Cup, which the club won in 2006 and 2007.

NO SUBSTITUTE FOR RIVALRY

Sevilla were accused of deliberately losing against Real Oviedo at the end of the 1999–2000 season to ensure bitter rivals Real Betis were relegated. When Sevilla goalkeeper Frode Olsen made several fine saves he was substituted, and the fans cheered their own team's defeat.

VALENCIA

The paella city

Paella, possibly the definitive dish of Spain to outsiders, is Valencian-born. There can be few Europeans who haven't tried this famous dish in their local Spanish restaurant or on their annual sun-seeking holiday to Spain. In truth, the seafood dish most of us know is actually a spin-off of the true Valencian dish which was originally meat (chicken, duck or rabbit) mixed with rice, snails, vegetables and seasoning. Either way, whether your preference is the original (meat) version or the other (seafood) version, most of the Hispanic world and beyond agree that this is one tasty dish, so thank you Valencia.

Once you've had your fill of paella (yes, pretty much every restaurant will serve it) you'll be looking for a party. The old centre of Valencia, Barri del Carme, as well as being a visitor magnet in the day, is also the place to be when the sun sets. The diversity of the crowd means that this is always a lively area with no shortage of bars, cafés, and nightclubs to keep visitors busy until the sun starts coming up again. You might even see some Spanish flamenco if that's your thing.

And if it's a real party you are after, you should be angling to be here in March for the Fallas festival for giant papier maché models and seemingly unlimited fireworks, or the messy La Tomatina festival in August (in nearby Buñol) where splattering ripe tomatoes on each other is the name of the game.

Mestalla, the stadium of Valencia, is centrally located to the east while Levante's Ciutat de Valencia stadium is a short distance to the north.

Below: Intricate carvings are a feature of the rich artistic traditions of Spain.

3 THINGS
YOU MUST DO...
(Apart from the football)

1 CIUTAT DE LES ARTS I LES CIÈNCIES

The City of Arts and Science (Avda. Autopista del Saler, tel: +34 90 210 0031) includes an oceanarium, science museum and planetarium. Open: 10.00–18.00 (sometimes later). Price: adults €31.60, concessions €24. To get there: metro line 3 and 5 to Alameda, buses 19, 35, 40, 95.

2 PAELLA

When you're in the USA it's burgers, when in London it's fish and chips. You're in Valencia so now's the time for paella. Try La Pepica (La Playa de las Arenas, tel: +34 96-371-03-66). Open: Mon–Sat 13.00–16.00 and 20.30–23.00. To get there: buses 1, 2, 19, 20, 21, 22, 30, 31 and 81.

3 IBIZA AND MALLORCA

Look, we're not suggesting that you go partying instead of returning to work, but Ibiza and Mallorca are only a few hours away... Ferry companies are Acciona Transmediterranea (tel: +34 902 45 46 45), Balearia (tel: +34 96 642 87 00) and Iscomar (tel: +34 97 143 7500).

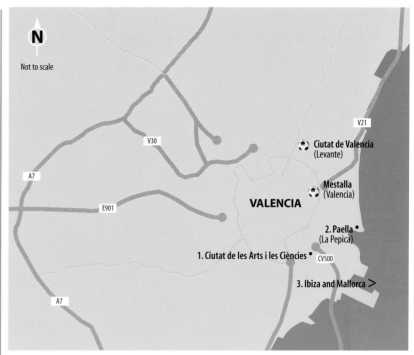

N

Not to scale

V21

V30

A7

E901

A7

VALENCIA

⚽ **Ciutat de Valencia** (Levante)

⚽ **Mestalla** (Valencia)

2. Paella ● (La Pepica)

1. Ciutat de les Arts i les Ciències ● CV500

3. Ibiza and Mallorca ⟩

BARS > CLUBS > RESTAURANTS

Bars > If you're looking for a mixed drinking crowd with decent music you'll find it at **Café Infanta** (Plaza Tossal 3, tel: +34 96 392 1235). The aptly named **Beer** (C/Salamanca 4, tel: +34 96 374 1431) offers a good selection and has a lively, mixed crowd enjoying it too.

Clubs > Classic dance music in a smartly designed club and the promise of a long night ahead are on offer at the simply named **Disco City** (16 Calle Pintor Zariñena, tel: +34 96 391 4151). Late nights continue at **Susos** (Martí 4, tel: +34 96 395 6509) a bar and club rolled into one.

Restaurants > **La Riua** (C/del Mar 27, tel: +34 96 391 4571) has paella and other good seafood dishes available at decent prices. Looking for smart and sleek? More Valencian cuisine is available at **El Alto de Colón Mercado** (Colón 19, tel: +34 96 353 0900) based in a covered market hall.

Below: *Relaxed drinking in the Spanish sun.*

Weather	Low (ºC)	High
January	5	15
February	6	16
March	7	18
April	9	19
May	13	22
June	17	26
July	21	30
August	20	29
September	17	27
October	13	23
November	8	18
December	6	15

VALENCIA

Above: Mestalla stadium blends into the cityscape of Valencia.

TEN YEAR EURO RECORD		
Season	Competition	Finished
1998–99	Uefa Cup	Last 32
1999–00	Champs League	Final
2000–01	Champs League	Final
2001–02	Uefa Cup	QF
2002–03	Champs League	QF
2003–04	Uefa Cup	Winners
2004–05	Champs League	Group
	Uefa Cup	Last 32
2005–06	Intertoto Cup	Final*
2006–07	Champs League	QF
2007–08	Champs League	

* One of three finals

The heartbeat of a city

When the River Turia burst its banks in 1957, Valencia's Mestalla stadium was left under-water, setting the club back on their heels. Half a century later many fear Los Che ('The Lads') are drowning in debt after Juan Villalonga, briefly a financial advisor to the club, announced that they were €789 million in the red. Older fans recall that Valencia, a European force of late, were relegated the last time they suffered a severe cash shortage in the 1980s.

That first-ever demotion shook the supporters, who maintained that Spain's third largest city contained the country's third biggest club (after Barcelona and Real Madrid). The din made by the locals at the Mestalla marks out Valencia as a football-mad location, and it is apt that the Spanish national team's most famous follower, the rotund, drum-playing

Manolo, owns a local bar that is a shrine to the team.

Argentines have featured strongly in Valencia's history. Alfredo Di Stéfano took over a demoralized team and swiftly won the 1971 title; Mario Kempes, a recent World Cup winner, led the attack in the 1980 European Cup Winners' Cup final victory over Arsenal; and Héctor Cúper finished as Champions League runners-up in his two seasons as coach around the millennium.

Rafael Benítez, a Spaniard, replaced Cúper and won two titles and a Uefa Cup, but his departure to Liverpool destabilized the club so much that they were nearly relegated. They escaped, but a challenge remains in the shape of their enormous debt, half of which was created by building the 75,000-capacity Nou Mestalla. The fans hope that Manolo's drum will still be beating with Valencian pride at the new stadium following its opening in 2009.

GREATEST PLAYERS

> **WALDO (1961–70)**
A pacy forward and free kick expert, the Brazilian scored 32 goals in European competition for Valencia, including nine *en route* to their Inter-City Fairs Cup triumph in 1962.

> **MARIO KEMPES (1976–84)**
The charismatic Argentine forward, known as El Matador, was the Spanish League's leading goalscorer two seasons in a row from 1976 to 1978.

MATTER OF FACT

Name: Valencia Club de Fútbol
Stadium: Mestalla (capacity 55,000)
Address: Avenida de Suecia s/n.
46010
To get there: Metro line 5 (station: Aragón) or line 3 (station: Facultats). Buses 10, 80
Telephone: +34 96 337 26 26
Email: callcenter@valenciacf.es
Website: www.valenciacf.es

Stadium tours
Opening hours: Mon–Fri
10.00–13.00, 16.00–19.00 (not match days, or day before or after a match)
Price: Depends on group size (minimum 15 people). No museum, but one planned for Nou Mestalla
Contact: Tel: +34 963 372 626 or email: jamoros@valenciacf.es

Home   Away

Trophies
1	European Cup Winners' Cup
3	Inter-City Fairs Cup/Uefa Cup
6	Spanish League
7	Spanish Cup

Main rivals
City neighbours Levante (tel: +34 902 220 304, www.levanteud.com), who play at the 25,400-seat Ciutat de Valencia stadium (San Vicente de Paul 44), were formed ten years before Valencia but have been less prominent, playing only five top-flight seasons, their last two coming before relegation in 2008. Even so, these derbys are intense, though Valencia reserve greater enmity for east coast rivals Barcelona (see pages 176–177). The recent emergence of Villarreal (see page 187), also based in the Valencian Community region, has brought another local rival.

Above: Valencia's Joaquin Sánchez (front) and Valladolid's Jonathan Sesma battle for the ball.

A NOSE FOR TROUBLE
When rival players jostled at the end of a Valencia versus Inter Milan Champions League match in March 2007, David Navarro, an unused substitute for the Spanish side, ran onto the pitch and punched Inter defender Nicolas Burdisso, breaking his nose. He was banned for six months.

VILLARREAL

Small but successful

With fewer than 50,000 inhabitants, this small town in the east of Spain does well to support any high-level football team, let alone one that has been able to challenge at the highest level in Europe.

The club's home, El Madrigal, lies just a short distance north of the small, grid-patterned centre, the ground's capacity able to hold half of the city's population should they wish to hold a particularly contentious city meeting. The wealth of the city (and the club's success) in recent times has been built on ceramic tiles, although it was true to footballing terminology that the city was built as a solid defence against Muslims when founded by King James I of Aragon in 1274.

The heart of this small town is the Plaça Major, and the small list of attractions – the city museum and Saint Jacques Tower – are nearby.

Weather	Low (ºC)	High
January	5	15
February	6	16
March	7	17
April	9	18
May	13	22
June	17	26
July	21	29
August	19	28
September	16	27
October	13	23
November	8	18
December	6	15

Below: The city's wealth is built on its ceramic tile industry.

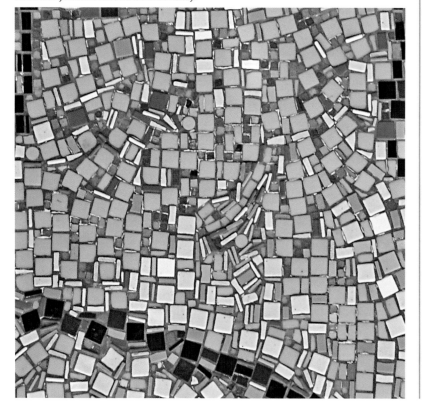

3 THINGS YOU MUST DO...
(Apart from the football)

1 PAELLA
The classic Spanish dish, originating from this region, consists of rice and vegetables with either meat or seafood. The Valencian version is with meat. Try Avenida 41 (Av Cedre 41, tel: +34 96 453 5047).

2 TAPAS
Dip into the amazing array of Spanish appetizers whether your preference is olives, squid or *potatas bravas*. Try Paradero Avenida (Av Francisco Tárrega 30, tel: +34 96 453 6454).

3 HEAD TO VALENCIA
Just over 60 km (37 miles) south of Villarreal are the bright lights of Valencia...

VILLARREAL

Above: *Villarreal's Robert Pirès (right) and Marcos Senna (left) battle for the ball with Barcelona's Sergi Busquets.*

MATTER OF FACT
Name: Villarreal Club du Fútbol
Stadium: El Madrigal
(capacity 22,000)
Address: Camino Miralcamp
(no number), 12540
To get there: Ten minutes' walk from the main train station
Telephone: +34 964 500 250
Email: villarrealcf@villarrealcf.es
Website: www.villarrealcf.es

Stadium tours: (no museum)
Open: Thu, Fri 10.00
Price: Free but must book
Contact: Email: elena@villarreal.cf.es

| **Home** | **Away** |

Leading trophies
None

Main rivals
Valencia (see pages 184–185) are just down the east coast and have become genuine rivals over the past decade after Villarreal's dramatic rise. Valencia edged their Uefa Cup semi-final meeting in 2004 but Villarreal can point to two 3–0 league wins in 2007–08. Valencia-based Levante (tel: +34 902 220 304, www. levanteud.com), whose Ciutat de Valencia stadium (San Vicente de Paul 44) is a similar size to El Madrigal, were relegated from the top division in 2008.

TEN YEAR EURO RECORD

Season	Competition	Finished
1998–99	DNQ	
1999–00	DNQ	
2000–01	DNQ	
2001–02	DNQ	
2002–03	Intertoto Cup	Final*
2003–04	Intertoto Cup	Winners**
	Uefa Cup	SF
2004–05	Intertoto Cup	Winners**
	Uefa Cup	QF
2005–06	Champs League	SF
2006–07	Intertoto Cup	Final***
2007–08	Uefa Cup	Last 32

* One of three finals
** One of three winners
*** One of 11 finals (Villarreal played in no previous round)

Minnows thriving in big pond

Nicknamed El Submarino Amarillo ('The Yellow Submarine') after their yellow shirts, Villarreal were not on Spanish football's radar until just before the millennium, when they first surfaced in the top division. Since then they have made waves not just in Spain but in Europe.

The club that almost reached the 2006 Champions League final have existed largely in regional leagues, seemingly a natural habitat for a club based in a town so small it fails to appear on many maps of Spain. Villarreal's population is around 47,000, yet the attraction of its football team is such that average league attendances in recent seasons at El Madrigal have approached 20,000.

Villarreal gained three promotions in the 1990s, the last in 1998 fuelled by the funds of new president and ceramic tile businessman Fernando Roig. A team packed with South Americans reached the semi-finals of the 2004 Uefa Cup and 2006 Champions League. Then, in 2007–08, the club recorded their highest league finish of second. Now they were on the map.

ITALY

<table>
<tr>
<td>

THE

3

**MINUTE
GUIDE**

</td>
<td></td>
<td>

Capital: *Rome.* **Language:** *Italian.* **Beer:** *Peroni, Nastro Azzurro.* **Food:** *Pizza, pasta,* antipasto.
National anthem: *Il Canto degli Italiani (The Song of the Italians).* **Population:** *58,145,000.*
Time zone: *GMT +1.* **Emergency number:** *112.* **Did you know?** *You can see the actual middle
finger of Galileo Galilei in the museum Museo di Storia del Scienza in Florence.* **Football body:**
*Federazione Italiana, Giuoco Calcio, Via Gregorio Allegri 14, Roma 00198; tel: +39 6 8491 2500,
fax: +39 6 8491 2526, email: international@figc.it, website: www.figc.it. Founded 1898.
Affiliated 1905.*

</td>
</tr>
</table>

Below: *A staircase in the Vatican, centre of the Catholic faith.*

Brilliant but troubled

In 1922 Italy had two champions; in 1927 and 2005 it had none. Tempestuous and scandalous, Italian football history is far from straightforward. The country has at various times possessed the world's greatest national team and its finest league, but skill has been accompanied by the odd schism and plenty of skulduggery.

Anger at the perceived growing influence of smaller clubs led Italy's heavyweights to form their own league in 1921–22, hence Pro Vercelli – giants at the time – are listed in record books as champions that season as well as little Novese, who won the official competition. Torino had their 1927 title revoked because of bribery, while Juventus were stripped of the 2005 honour in the wake of a referee-influencing scandal.

Yet Italian football has a remarkable capacity to bounce back from such calamities, as if strengthened by the feeling of being cleansed by investigations and punishments. The most recent scandal, Calciopoli – in which Juventus were forcibly relegated and gave up two titles (Inter were named champions in 2006 but the 2005 honour was not awarded) while others such as AC Milan were deducted points – disrupted Italy's preparations for the 2006 World Cup. Coach Marcello Lippi was even summoned by magistrates as a witness yet his team went on to win the tournament.

But Italy's footballing strength and fervour makes Serie A popular among fans worldwide. In the 1990s it was the world's most powerful league, boasting several clubs who enjoyed success in European competition.

Above: AC Milan fans fly the flag. *Below:* Football is Italy's other religion.

THE TEN YEAR GUIDE

* Juventus stripped of titles due to corruption

Serie A

Season	Winner	Runner-up
1998–99	AC Milan	Lazio
1999–00	Lazio	Juventus
2000–01	Roma	Juventus
2001–02	Juventus	Roma
2002–03	Juventus	Inter Milan
2003–04	AC Milan	Roma
2004–05	Not awarded*	AC Milan
2005–06	Inter Milan*	Roma
2006–07	Inter Milan	Roma
2007–08	Inter Milan	Roma

Coppa Italia

Season	Winner	Runner-up
1998–99	Parma	Fiorentina
1999–00	Lazio	Inter Milan
2000–01	Fiorentina	Parma
2001–02	Parma	Juventus
2002–03	AC Milan	Roma
2003–04	Lazio	Juventus
2004–05	Inter Milan	Roma
2005–06	Inter Milan	Roma
2006–07	Roma	Inter Milan
2007–08	Roma	Inter Milan

ROME

The seven hills of history

This legendary city, which was at the centre of the Roman Empire, is steeped in history. Famously built on seven hills, it is home to world-famous landmarks such as the sweeping Spanish Steps, linking Piazza Trinità dei Monti and Piazza di Spagna; the Trevi Fountain, where you can toss coins for luck and romance; the Colosseum, the former gladiatorial arena; and temple of the gods, the Pantheon.

Rome also encompasses the tiny city-state of Vatican City (the smallest country in the world), home to the head of the Catholic Church, the Pope. This is where you will find the skyline's iconic St Peter's Basilica, St Peter's Square, the Apostolic Palace and the Sistine Chapel. With these attractions clustered either centrally or inside the Vatican's walls a short distance across the river, you will find these well-trodden areas, but join the throngs in paying homage to the city's amazing history.

At the end of all the history, you'll be in need of food, and there is no better way to do it than to grab a huge slice of Italy's finest pizza from a vendor or café and eat it while watching the rest of Rome go about its business and pleasure. Wash it down with *gelato* (Italian ice cream) a refreshing Peroni beer or a glass of the country's excellent Chianti.

The capital of Italy is centrally located and sits on the River Tiber, with a population of about 2.7 million people. Olimpico, the stadium shared by AS Roma and Lazio is 6 km (4 miles) north of the city centre.

Below: Famous classical statue anyone?

3 THINGS YOU MUST DO...
(Apart from the football)

1 THE VATICAN CITY
Visit the world's smallest state, home to the Roman Catholic Church and its head, the Pope. It has a population of less than a thousand people and covers just 44 hectares. To get there: metro to Ottaviano or Cipro-Musei Vaticani, bus 40 and 64.

2 THE COLOSSEUM
See gladiators fight to the death and the Christians fed to the lions. In your imagination, anyway. The Colosseum (Piazza del Colosseo, tel: +39 6 3996 7700) gets busy so your imagine while you queue. Open: daily 09.00–16.00 (later some months). Price: €15.50, concessions €10.50 and €4.50. To get there: metro to Colosseo.

3 THE SPANISH STEPS
Get some exercise up the famous steps built between 1723–26 with the church Trinita dei Monti at the top. A lot of the designer shops are based around here, too. To get there: metro to Spagna.

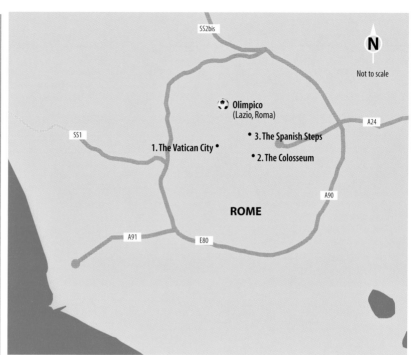

SS2bis

N
Not to scale

Olimpico
(Lazio, Roma)

SS1

1. The Vatican City •

• 3. The Spanish Steps

• 2. The Colosseum

A24

A90

ROME

A91   E80

BARS > CLUBS > RESTAURANTS
Bars > The Drunken Ship (20 Campo dei Fiori, tel: +39 06 6830 0535) is ever busy and ever popular with the city's young crowd. Meanwhile **Dulcarama** (449 Via Flaminia Vecchia, tel: +39 6 333 2108) offers a more relaxed setting, plus a terrace when the weather's good enough.

Clubs > It's not like you'll have trouble finding pretty people in this city wherever you go, but **The Gallery** (12 Via della Maddalena, tel: +39 6 481 8795) and **Alien** (13–19 Via Velletri Nuovo Salario, tel: +39 6 841 2212) are late-night venues that seem to specialize in them.

Restaurants > Take your pasta and antipasti pick from **Dal Bolognese** (Piazza del Popolo 1–2, tel: +39 6 361 1426), **Abruzzi** (Via del Vaccaro 1, tel +39 6 679 3897) or **Ristorante Il Matriciano** (Via dei Gracchi 55, tel: +39 6 321 2327), all well-located eateries.

Below: Cafés spill onto the streets everywhere in Rome.

Weather	Low (°C)	High
January	3	12
February	4	13
March	6	15
April	8	17
May	12	21
June	16	25
July	18	28
August	19	28
September	16	26
October	13	21
November	7	16
December	5	13

LAZIO

Above: Lazio's Pasquale Foggia (right) is congratulated by team mate Cristian Ledesma after he scores a goal.

MATTER OF FACT

Name: Società Sportiva Lazio
Stadium: Olimpico (capacity 81,903)
Address: Via Foro Italico, 00194
To get there: Metro line A (either station: Ottaviano, then bus 32; or station: Flaminio, then tram 225). Bus 280
Telephone: +39 06 9760 7111
Email: info.biglietteria@sslazio.it
Website: www.sslazio.it

Stadium tour
No stadium tour

Home	Away

Trophies
1	European Cup Winners' Cup
2	Italian League
4	Italian Cup

Main rivals
Lazio's biggest rivals by a distance are Roma (see page 193). They meet at their shared Stadio Olimpico, 6 km (4 miles) northwest of the city centre on the north bank of the River Tiber. Traditionally Lazio's fanbase is right-wing and from wealthy, suburban districts; Roma's is left-wing and from the poorer, inner-city areas.

TEN YEAR EURO RECORD
Season	Competition	Finished
1998–99	C Winners' Cup	Winners
1999–00	Champs League	QF
2000–01	Champs League	Group*
2001–02	Champs League	Group**
2002–03	Uefa Cup	SF
2003–04	Champs League	Group
2004–05	Uefa Cup	Group
2005–06	InterToto Cup	SF
2006–07	DNQ	
2007–08	Champs League	Group

* 2nd of two group stages
** 1st of two group stages

Staying at the top proves a tall order

Lazio's debt-induced decline after their league title of 2000 was a familiar tale for older fans. Just when the club threaten to establish themselves, they fall away. Their long-awaited debut trophy, the 1958 Italian Cup, was quickly followed by their first relegation, and their first title in 1974 led only to a decline that culminated in enforced demotion in 1980 because of a betting scandal.

Not that Lazio have lacked self-assurance. In 1927 they resisted the Fascist government's desire for them to join a newly merged Rome club – Roma – setting up a rivalry that remains perhaps Italy's strongest.

Lazio emerged from Roma's shadow after the arrival in 1992 of financier Sergio Cragnotti, who spent a fortune to turn the team into top-five regulars and then League and Cup double winners in 2000 under Sven-Göran Eriksson, whose team had lifted the European Cup Winners' Cup a year earlier. But, true to form, the collapse of Cragnotti's food group Cirio led to his departure, and most of the club's best players were sold.

ROMA

Above: The red half of the city is used to frustration as their side chase championships.

MATTER OF FACT
Name: Associazione Sportiva Roma
Stadium: Olimpico (capacity 81,903)
Address: Via Foro Italico, 00194
To get there: Metro line A (either station: Ottaviano, then bus 32; or station: Flaminio, then tram 225). Bus 280
Telephone: +39 06 501911
Email: info@asromaweb.com
Website: www.asroma.it

Stadium tour
No stadium tour

Home	Away

Trophies

1	Inter-Cities Fairs Cup/Uefa Cup
3	Italian League
9	Italian Cup

Main rivals
Roma contest a tempestuous city derby with Lazio (see page 192). In 2003 fans of both teams forced a half-time abandonment in the false belief that police had killed a supporter. Roma attract far larger attendances to the shared Stadio Olimpico. They also meet big rivals Napoli in the Derby of the South.

TEN YEAR EURO RECORD

Season	Competition	Finished
1998–99	Uefa Cup	QF
1999–00	Uefa Cup	Last 16
2000–01	Uefa Cup	Last 16
2001–02	Champs League	Group*
2002–03	Champs League	Group*
2003–04	Uefa Cup	Last 16
2004–05	Champs League	Group
2005–06	Uefa Cup	Last 16
2006–07	Champs League	QF
2007–08	Champs League	QF

* 2nd of two group stages

Eternal wait for titles

Eight minutes from the end of their league-clinching win over Parma in 2001, Roma players stood sheepishly in their underwear, fearing the title would be taken from them. With Roma 3–1 up, their fans stormed the pitch and grabbed shirts and shorts from their heroes. After a long delay, new kits were found and the game was concluded. Luckily, Parma, with nothing to play for, did not appeal for an abandonment.

Fabio Capello, their coach, had previously voiced the oft-expressed opinion that the presence in the capital of the national media and intensity of the local fans make it hard for clubs to thrive there. The fact that Roma have won just three titles, despite spending all but one season in Serie A, backs that claim.

Champions in 1942 and 1983, their third triumph was achieved by Capello's South American-packed squad. Roma then finished second five times in seven seasons. The red half of the Eternal City will hope that there is not another eternal wait for the next title.

MILAN

A beating heart of fashion

Situated in the north of Italy, a short distance from the Swiss border, Milan is one of the fashion capitals of the world. Central to this are a series of Milan Fashion Weeks to showcase menswear and womenswear, but that's really just the icing on the cake; the industry is well established here for design, manufacturing and retailing, and indeed Milan and the Milanese have become bywords for style in themselves.

Gucci, Versace, Prada, Armani… you'll find them all, plus many other high-end fashion houses and designer names, over and over again in Via Montenapoleone, the city's most celebrated shopping street. The street is close to many of the city's cultural attractions: Milan Cathedral, one of the world's most renowned opera houses, the Teatro alla Scala, plus the Santa Maria delle Grazie, a church that houses Leonardo da Vinci's famous painting, *The Last Supper*.

But if fashion and culture are at the heart of the city, then it is sport that is its soul. The city's main clubs AC Milan and Inter Milan are two of the world's most celebrated and have a host of Italian, European and world titles to their names (the San Siro, the city's football home which the clubs share is about 6 km/4 miles to the west of the centre). But there is another 'club' that rivals them for attention. Every year tens of thousands of Ferrari fans descend on the city for the annual Italian Formula One Grand Prix. The Monza track is about 20 km (12 miles) to the north. If that's not enough, Amatori Milano Rugby, the country's most successful rugby team, are also based here.

Below: A sculpted door at Milan Cathedral.

3 THINGS YOU MUST DO...
(Apart from the football)

1 A NEW SUIT
When in Milan, do as the Milanese do and get stylish. Try Armani Collezioni (Via Montenapoleone 2, tel: +39 02 7639 0068). To get there: metro or trams 1 and 2 to Montenapoleone.

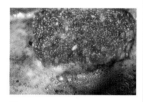

2 *COTOLETTA ALLA MILANESE*
Not unlike *wiener schnitzel*, this breaded veal cutlet is a regional favorite. Try Trattoria Milanese (Via Santa Marta 11, tel: +39 02 8645 1991). Open: Wed–Mon 12.00–15.00 and 19.00–01.00. To get there: metro to Cardusio.

3 AUTODROMO NAZIONALE MONZA
Take your own car and drive it around the famous Monza racetrack (Via Vedano 5, Parco di Monza, tel: +39 039 24821, email: infoautodromo@monzanet.it). Open: selected days between Nov–Mar. Price: €40 per half hour. To get there: drive north on A51 and A52, then Monza exit. Trains from Milano Centrale to Monza.

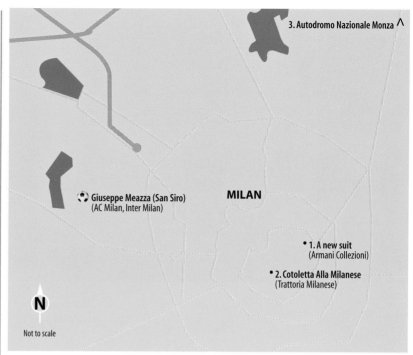

3. Autodromo Nazionale Monza ∧

⚽ **Giuseppe Meazza (San Siro)**
(AC Milan, Inter Milan)

MILAN

• **1. A new suit**
(Armani Collezioni)

• **2. Cotoletta Alla Milanese**
(Trattoria Milanese)

N

Not to scale

BARS > CLUBS > RESTAURANTS
Bars > It's no surprise in this city of fashion that you can find a bar like **Gold** (Via Carlo Poerio, tel: +39 02 757 7771). And it's no surprise you'll find the fashion crowd in this glitzy Dolce and Gabbana owned venue. Needless to say, gold features a lot. Another fashion hang out is the **Diana Garden** (Hotel Viale Piave 42, tel: +39 02 20581) in the Sheraton Diana Majestic Hotel.
Clubs > Rolling Stone (Corso XXII Marzo 32, tel: +39 02 733 172) is a live music venue that has been around for decades. There are more of the smart set at **Hollywood Rythmoteque** (Corso Como 15, tel: +39 02 659 8996).
Restaurants > Try fresh seafood at **Da Claudio** (Via Ponte Vetero 16, tel: +39 02 805 6857). For classic Italian pizza, go to **Premiata Pizzeria** (Via Alzaia Naviglio Grande 2, tel: +39 02 8940 0648).

Below: Style is the name of the game in Italy, everywhere you go.

Weather	Low (°C)	High
January	-3	6
February	-2	8
March	1	13
April	5	17
May	10	21
June	12	25
July	16	28
August	15	27
September	12	23
October	6	17
November	0	11
December	-3	7

AC MILAN

Above: *AC Milan's David Beckham (right) celebrates a goal scored by team mate Alexandre Pato.*

A gripping story

TEN YEAR EURO RECORD		
Season	Competition	Finished
1998–99	DNQ	
1999–00	Champs League	Group*
2000–01	Champs League	Group**
2001–02	Uefa Cup	SF
2002–03	Champs League	Winners
2003–04	Champs League	QF
2004–05	Champs League	Final
2005–06	Champs League	SF
2006–07	Champs League	Winners
2007–08	Champs League	Last 16

* 1st of two group stages
** 2nd of two group stages

A film and publishing millionaire ran AC Milan for most of their first golden era in the 1950s and early 1960s; then, floundering in debt in the mid-1980s, they were rescued and launched into their greatest period yet by a television mogul. The mass media has been kind to the club, but they have repaid the favour by creating a remarkable success story that has kept newspapers and TV companies happy.

Milan have been European champions seven times, five of those triumphs in the past two decades as satellite television has turned their stars into global household names. It is apt that Milan were dominating when Serie A came to televisions in the UK, because England exerted a huge early influence over a club that reverted proudly to their English name after Mussolini had ordered a patriotic change to Milano.

Formed in 1899 as Milan Cricket and Football Club, the team initially featured six Englishmen, including founder Alfred Edwards. They collected three early titles, during which they dropped their name's cricket reference, but only recaptured the crown in 1951. Four more titles followed under the presidency of Andrea Rizzoli, whose reign concluded in 1963 as Milan became Italy's first European Cup winners.

After an enforced relegation in 1980 for match-fixing and another (conventional) demotion in 1982, Silvio Berlusconi appointed Arrigo Sacchi, who led the side to European Cup success in 1989 and 1990. Fabio Capello, who followed Sacchi, recorded the only unbeaten season in Serie A history, the first of three titles in a row, and Carlo Ancelotti steered the team to three Champions League finals in five years this decade. The Milan tale continues to produce headlines.

GREATEST PLAYERS

> **MARCO VAN BASTEN (1987–93)**
Renowned for his agility and spectacular shooting, the Dutch forward was named European Footballer of the Year three times before an ankle injury ended his career at 28.

> **GUNNAR NORDAHL (1949–56)**
A muscular former fireman, Nordahl and fellow Swedes Gunnar Gren and Nils Liedholm inspired Milan in the early 1950s. The centre forward remains the club's leading goalscorer.

MATTER OF FACT

Name: Associazione Calcio Milan
Stadium: Giuseppe Meazza, or San
Siro (capacity 85,000)
Address: Via Piccolomini 5, 20151
To get there: Metro on line MM1
(station: Lotto Fiera 2). Tram 16
Telephone: +39 0262281
Email: press@acmilan.com
Website: www.acmilan.com

Stadium tours
(including museum)
Open: Daily 10.00–17.00 (subject to
change on event or match days).
Price: €12.50 (€7 museum only)
Contact: Tel: +39 02 404 2432, email:
tour@sansirotour.com or website:
www.sansirotour.com

Home   Away

Trophies
7	European Cup/ Champions League
2	European Cup Winners' Cup
17	Italian League
5	Italian Cup

Main rivals
Milan's greatest rivalry by far is played
out against Inter Milan (see pages
198–199). The pair meet in the Derby
della Madonnina, which refers to the
Blessed Virgin Mary statue on the
city's cathedral. Milan were
traditionally considered to have
a more left-wing fanbase than their
neighbours, a curiosity given that
their owner, three-times Italian Prime
Minister Silvio Berlusconi, occupies the
other end of the political spectrum.

NOT A BRIGHT IDEA
Milan were trailing Marseille on
aggregate in the closing moments of
the 1991 European Cup quarter-final
second leg in France when some
floodlights failed. The Italians walked
off, hoping to force a replay, despite
there being sufficient light. Marseille
were awarded victory and Milan
received a one-year European ban.

Above: *Arsenal's Philippe Senderos
outjumps AC Milan's Kaka during a
Champions League match.*

INTER MILAN

Above: A mural which appears in the changing rooms at Inter Milan.

TEN YEAR EURO RECORD

Season	Competition	Finished
1998–99	Champs League	QF
1999–00	DNQ	
2000–01	Champs League	3rd qual rd
	Uefa Cup	Last 16
2001–02	Uefa Cup	SF
2002–03	Champs League	SF
2003–04	Champs League	Group
	Uefa Cup	QF
2004–05	Champs League	QF
2005–06	Champs League	QF
2006–07	Champs League	Last 16
2007–08	Champs League	Last 16

Triumphs and turbulence

Inter Milan's roll of shame is lengthy. They conquered Europe in the 1960s with a dull approach amid claims of bribery and then, inviting ridicule rather than reproach, they were the huge-spending under-achievers of the 1990s.

Then there are the fans. Messina's Ivory Coast defender Marc Zoro tried to stop a match by walking off with the ball because of racist chanting in 2005; the same year, a flare that struck AC Milan goalkeeper Dida caused the forfeit of Inter's Champions League quarter-final; and in 2001 riot police had to prevent spectators from pushing a motorbike off the second tier of the San Siro.

But the case for the defence should also be stated. They are alone in spending every year in the top division since a nationwide league was formed in 1929. Furthermore there have been scandals aplenty in Italy, the latest of which in 2006 – clubs influencing refereeing appointments – left Inter untainted while others such as Juventus, Milan, Lazio and Fiorentina were punished. And racism and hooliganism have blighted many Italian clubs in recent years.

Inter's greatest period came in the 1960s, when Argentine coach Helenio Herrera took the *catenaccio* defensive system to its limit. They lifted the European Cup in 1964 and 1965, although suspicions have been aroused over the semi-finals in each year.

After winning the league in 1989, Inter only regained it with the first of three consecutive titles from 2006. Roberto Mancini returned them to the summit, and his replacement as coach by the outspoken José Mourinho in 2008 suggested that the club would continue to create controversy, in keeping with their turbulent history.

GREATEST PLAYERS

> GIUSEPPE MEAZZA (1927–40; 1946–47)
Skilful and cool in front of goal, Meazza is widely considered to be Italy's greatest ever player. He was in the Italian side that won the 1934 and 1938 World Cups and his 247 goals for Inter are 89 more than any other player for the club.

> GIACINTO FACCHETTI (1960–78)
The left back is credited with having revolutionized the full-back role by joining his side's attacks at every opportunity. Tall but possessing great ball control, he scored many goals and won four Serie A titles and two European Cups.

MATTER OF FACT
Name: Football Club
Internazionale Milano
Stadium: Giuseppe Meazza, or San
Siro (capacity 80,075)
Address: Via Piccolomini 5, 20151
To get there: Metro line MM1
(station: Lotto Fiera 2). Tram16.
Buses 49, 78
Telephone: +39 02 487 7761
Email: inter@inter.it
Website: www.inter.it

Stadium tours (including museum)
Open: Daily 10.00–17.00 (may
change when matches or events are
on), entrance gate 14
Price: €12.50, museum only €7
Contact: Tel: +39 02 404 2432, email:
tour@sansirotour.com or website:
www.sansirotour.com

Home　　　　**Away**

Leading trophies

2	European Cup/ Champions League
3	Inter-Cities Fairs Cup/Uefa Cup
16	Italian League
5	Italian Cup

Main rivals
Since 1947 Inter have shared the San
Siro stadium (officially renamed the
Giuseppe Meazza in 1979) with city
rivals AC Milan (see pages 196–197) –
San Siro is a district 6 km (4 miles)
west of the city centre. Milan is
Europe's most successful football city
in terms of continental club trophies,
with AC Milan leading the way, but
Inter's unique unbroken Serie A history
brings pride. Banners at the Milan
derby taunt: *Superiori da sempre, mai
stati in B* ('Always superior, we've never
been in Serie B'). Inter are also fierce
rivals of Juventus (see pages
202–203).

*Above: Inter Milan's Brazilian
wing-back Maicon.*

BLOWING THE WHISTLE
Journalists Brian Glanville and Keith
Botsford alleged that Inter bribed
referees of their victorious European
Cup semi-final second legs at home
to Borussia Dortmund (1964) and
Liverpool (1965).

TURIN

The honour of a legendary team

In 1949 a plane carrying the all-conquering Torino football team crashed into the Superga hill to the east of the city, killing 31 people including 18 players, most of whom formed the backbone of the Italian national team.

Torino had won Serie A in 1942–43 and returned after the end of the Second World War to win it for four times in a row from 1945–46. They were top of the league when the plane crashed, and had to field their youth team for the remaining four fixtures. In honour of Torino and the players that had died, their opponents did the same. Torino won those games and Serie A that season, but never fully regained their status at the top of the Italian game.

Turin is situated in the northwest of the country close to the French border and within striking distance of the Alps. The city, with a population of over 900,000, is the centre of Italy's car production, and the carmakers Alfa Romeo, Fiat and Lancia are all based here.

The 17th century Palazzo Reale, one of many palaces in the city, and its gardens, form a central point to many of Turin's landmarks. The most recognizable is the Mole Antonelliana, housing the National Museum of Cinema, while the most talked about is Turin Cathedral, home to the Turin Shroud, which millions believe to be the shroud of Jesus Christ. Also close by are the Palatine Towers, which served as one of the Roman city gates, and the much-visited Egyptian Museum.

Olimpico di Torino, the stadium shared by Juventus and Torino is southwest of the city centre.

Below: *The light dances through the arches of a covered walkway in Turin.*

3 THINGS YOU MUST DO...
(Apart from the football)

1 SUPERGA

About 10 km (6 miles) east of the city is the Superga hill where the Torino squad and many others lost their lives in an air crash in 1949. There is a small memorial at the Basilica of Superga. To get there: tram 15 to Sassi-Superga, then bus 79B to Geisser and a ten minute walk.

2 MOLE ANTONELLIANA LIFT

Ride in the glass lift of Turin's most distinctive building (Via Montebello 20, tel: +39 800 019 152) for great views from the viewing deck. Open: Tues–Fri 10.00–20.00, Sat 10.00–23.00. Price: adults €4.50, concessions €3.20. To get there: buses 13, 15, 55, 56, 61 to Via Po, 16 to Corso San Maurizio, 68 to Via Rossini.

3 EATALY TORINO

A giant food centre (Via Nizza 230, tel: +39 011 1950 6801) dedicated to the Slow Food movement, the opposite of all food that is fast, furiously eaten and globally distributed. Get tasting. Open: daily 10.00–22.30. To get there: train to Turin Lingotto, tram 10 to Porta Susa, buses 1, 18, 35.

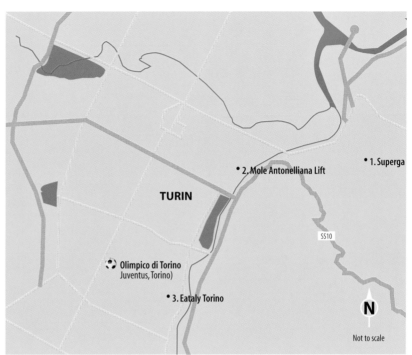

- • 1. Superga
- • 2. Mole Antonelliana Lift
- **TURIN**
- SS10
- ⚽ Olimpico di Torino (Juventus, Torino)
- • 3. Eataly Torino
- **N**
- Not to scale

BARS > CLUBS > RESTAURANTS

Bars > Ambhara Bar (via Borgo Dora 10, tel: +39 011 521 7346) offers Italian style and cocktails in long glasses. Or choose an Irish theme and large glasses of Guinness at **The Shamrock Inn** (Corso Vittorio Emanuele II 34, tel: +39 011 817 4950).

Clubs > For late nights in Turin take your pick from smooth and beautiful at **L'Hennessey** (Strada Traforo del Pino 23, tel: +39 011 899 8522) or city grunge and rock at the **Hiroshima Mon Amour** (Via Bossoli 83, tel: +39 011 317 6636).

Restaurants > Porto di Savona (Piazza Vittorio Veneto 2, tel: +39 011 817 3500) is a well-located and popular *trattoria* with plenty of local offerings. For more classic Torinese food and wine, head to **C'era una Volta** (Corso Vittorio Emanuele II 41, tel: +39 011 655 498).

Below: Seek out the smooth and stylish in Turin.

Weather	Low (°C)	High
January	-1	6
February	0	8
March	2	12
April	6	16
May	11	20
June	15	24
July	17	28
August	16	26
September	13	23
October	8	17
November	1	10
December	-1	7

JUVENTUS

Above: Juventus, based in Turin, but supported across Italy.

Italy's national club team

TEN YEAR EURO RECORD		
Season	Competition	Finished
1998–99	Champs League	SF
1999–00	InterToto Cup	Winners*
	Uefa Cup	Last 16
2000–01	Champs League	Group**
2001–02	Champs League	Group***
2002–03	Champs League	Final
2003–04	Champs League	Last 16
2004–05	Champs League	QF
2005–06	Champs League	QF
2006–07	DNQ	
2007–08	DNQ	

* One of three winners
** 1st of two group stages
*** 2nd of two group stages

Juventus had had enough. Having twice attracted fewer than 6,000 people to their Stadio Delle Alpi for Uefa Cup matches in 1994–95, they decided to continue their pursuit of the trophy elsewhere. Crowds of around 80,000 duly turned up at Milan's San Siro for their 'home' legs of the semi-final and final.

Whether measuring by league titles (a record 27) or support (an estimated one-fifth of the country's 60 million people), Juventus are Italy's biggest club by far, but their size only becomes clear when journeying outside Turin. They have been an institution since the 1930s, when they captured the loyalty of floating fans by winning the first five titles of the new national league, yet they have faced claims that local rivals Torino have more fans in the city. The Delle Alpi, at present being refurbished, was routinely half-empty

for games, although this was partly because of its inaccessibility on the edge of town, a lack of roofing and poor visibility.

Juventus's black and white jerseys are fitting for a club with few grey areas in terms of allegiance. Italians tend either to love or hate them, the second group motivated by envy of the finance provided by the Fiat-owning Agnelli family and by bitterness over a perceived helping hand from referees. The latter suspicion was given further fuel by the Calciopoli scandal (see opposite, below right), for which Juventus were relegated for the first time in 2006.

After that enforced demotion, they overcame an additional nine-point penalty to finish top of Serie B and then promptly booked a Champions League place. The Old Lady has quickly regained her pride.

GREATEST PLAYERS

> MICHEL PLATINI (1982–87)
The stylish Frenchman was Serie A's leading goalscorer for three seasons in a row from 1982–83 despite being a midfielder, each time earning the European Footballer of the Year award. He also scored the 1985 European Cup final winner against Liverpool.

> ZINEDINE ZIDANE (1996–2001)
So impressive was the French midfielder for Juventus that he was signed by Real Madrid in 2001 for €76 million, a figure that remained the world record transfer fee as the decade neared its end. Zidane possessed such fine balance that his movement was almost balletic.

MATTER OF FACT

Name: Juventus Football Club
Stadium: Olimpico di Torino
(capacity 27,500)
Address: Corso Galileo Ferraris
32, 10128
To get there: Metro, station: Lingotto.
Trams 4, 10. Buses 14, 14b, 17, 63,
1100, 1101, 1102, 1312
Telephone: +39 011 65631
Email: juventus@juventus.com
Website: www.juventus.it

Stadium tour
No tour available

Home	**Away**

Trophies
2	European Cup/
	Champions League
1	European Cup Winners' Cup
3	Inter-Cities Fairs Cup/Uefa Cup
27	Italian League
9	Italian Cup

Main rivals
Juventus face Inter Milan (see pages
198–199) in the intense Derby of
Italy: the nation's parliament was
suspended in 1998 when two deputies
came to blows over a controversial
recent match between the clubs.
Fiorentina became sworn enemies
when they were denied the 1982
league title by a dubious Juve penalty
on the last day of the season. There is
also strong rivalry with city neighbours
Torino (tel: +39 011 1970 0348,
www.torinofc.it), who groundshare
with Juve at the Stadio Olimpico.

*Above: Juventus have won Europe's
top trophy twice in their history.*

JUVE IN A FIX
Juve were forcibly relegated in 2006,
and stripped of their 2005 and 2006
league titles, after intercepted
telephone calls showed Luciano
Moggi, the club's general manager,
influenced match refereeing
appointments. Four other clubs were
deducted points.

GREECE

| THE **3** MINUTE GUIDE |  | **Capital:** *Athens.* **Language:** *Greek.* **Beer:** *Mythos.* **Food:** *Feta cheese,* horiatiki *(Greek salad),* souvlaki *(grilled meat on a skewer).* **National anthem:** *Ymnos eis tin Eleutherian (Hymn to Liberty).* **Population:** *10,723,000.* **Time zone:** *GMT +2.* **Emergency Number:** *112.* **Did you know?** *Greeks are the biggest smokers in the world, measured by cigarettes per head per day.* **Football body:** *Hellenic Football Federation, 137 Singrou Avenue, 3rd Floor, Athens 1712; tel: +30 210 930 6000, fax: +30 210 935 9666, email: epo@epo.gr, website: www.epo.gr. Founded 1926. Affiliated 1927.* |

Below: It's taken a while for Greece to move from Olympic glory to football glory.

Greece's Herculean feat

Athens inaugurated international sport's greatest competition when hosting the 1896 Olympics, but it took until the 21st century for Greek football to come of age on a global stage. Noise and passion have long marked club games but the national team finally gave fans something to shout about by winning Euro 2004.

Plagued by public indifference, with the domestic game holding a far stronger appeal, the Greece players had seemingly not been pulling their weight, having not won a game in their only two major tournament appearances, Euro '80 and the 1994 World Cup. But German coach Otto Rehhagel's defensive approach brought the surprise of qualification for Euro 2004 and then the miracle of victory, secured by beating hosts Portugal in the final.

Not that Greek clubs were being completely overshadowed by the national team. In that great sporting year of 2004, as Athens staged the Olympics for the second time, Greece had risen to sixth in Uefa's European rankings, earning them three Champions League places.

Domestic football does have its problems, however. The predictability of the league meant that for ten of the 11 seasons from 1997–98 the final table had Olympiakos top with the next two places filled, either way, by Panathinaikos and AEK Athens. The hooliganism that has long disfigured the game has, in recent years, seen a referee attacked by fans in the street over a Cup final decision and left another bloodied after an angry pitch invasion by fans and officials of Panathinaikos. Amid the shame, Rehhagel brought pride.

Above: Passions run high at a Panathinaikos game. *Below:* Celebrating Greece's Euro 2004 victory.

THE TEN YEAR GUIDE

Super League

Season	Winner	Runner-up
1998–99	Olympiakos	AEK Athens
1999–00	Olympiakos	Panathinaikos
2000–01	Olympiakos	Panathinaikos
2001–02	Olympiakos	AEK Athens
2002–03	Olympiakos	Panathinaikos
2003–04	Panathinaikos	Olympiakos
2004–05	Olympiakos	Panathinaikos
2005–06	Olympiakos	AEK Athens
2006–07	Olympiakos	AEK Athens
2007–08	Olympiakos	AEK Athens

Greek Cup

Season	Winner	Runner-up
1998–99	Olympiakos	Panathinaikos
1999–00	AEK Athens	Ionikos
2000–01	PAOK	Olympiakos
2001–02	AEK Athens	Olympiakos
2002–03	PAOK	Aris
2003–04	Panathinaikos	Olympiakos
2004–05	Olympiakos	Aris
2005–06	Olympiakos	AEK Athens
2006–07	Larissa	Panathinaikos
2007–08	Olympiakos	Aris

ATHENS

Home of the Olympics

The red and white of Olympiakos and the green and white of Panathinaikos are renowned as the main Greek and Athens footballing rivals. However, although Panathinaikos are based in the city itself (playing at the Olympic Stadium which they share with AEK), the red side of the city is actually located in the nearby port of Piraeus at the Stadion Georgios Karaiskakis.

It is a rivalry which nonetheless defines the footballing landscape in this, one of the world's most historic cities, and home to one of the world's great ancient civilizations. People have been living in what is today known as Athens for thousands of years and the city is home to a host of important landmarks, such as the ancient city of Acropolis, the ruins of the Temple of Olympian Zeus and the Panathinaiko Stadium,

site of the 1896 Olympics, the first in the modern era. This is the city that gave us the world's greatest sporting event, of course, and it was rewarded by being given the right to host the Summer Games in 2004.

It was an event that sparked large-scale regeneration of the city, especially in the transport infrastructure. So thank that upgraded system if you find yourself moving smoothly from the historic areas of the Acropolis, Monastiraki and Plaka, to Psiri, where you will find numerous bars and restaurants, and from the smart district of Nea Smyrni to the bustling port of Piraeus.

Below: Athens is one of Europe's oldest cities; people have been living here for thousands of years.

3 THINGS YOU MUST DO...
(Apart from the football)

1 THE ACROPOLIS AND PARTHENON
The very heart of Ancient Greece, the Acropolis (tel: +30 210 923 8175) dominates the skyline of modern day Athens. Open: daily 08.30–19.30 (1 Nov–31 Mar 08.30–15.00). Price: adults €12, concessions €6. To get there: subway to Akropoli.

2 ISLAND HOPPING
Got a few days to spare? Piraeus is the gateway to the numerous Greek islands. Try www.hellasferries.net for bookings. To get there: train to Piraeus.

3 CHANGING OF THE GUARD
See Greek soldiers wearing white tights and funny-looking shoes with pompoms just outside the Parliament building (2 Vasilissis Sophias). When: daily every hour, with a special ceremony Sun 10.00. Price: free. To get there: subway to Syntagma Square.

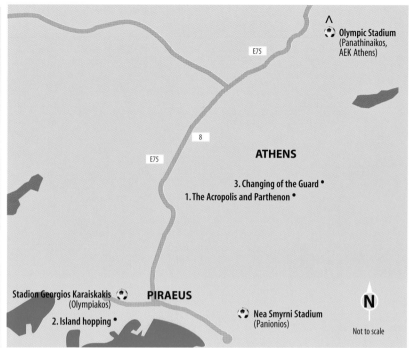

E75

E75

8

ATHENS

3. Changing of the Guard •
1. The Acropolis and Parthenon •

Olympic Stadium (Panathinaikos, AEK Athens)

Stadion Georgios Karaiskakis (Olympiakos) **PIRAEUS**

2. Island hopping •

Nea Smyrni Stadium (Panionios)

N

Not to scale

BARS > CLUBS > RESTAURANTS
Bars > Small but cool and very, very popular is the way to describe the **Guru Bar** (10 Theatrou, tel: +30 10 324 6530) where you can also pick up some food in a mixed, relaxed crowd. Or enjoy the laidback atmosphere of **Stavlos** (10 Irakleidon St, tel: +30 10 346 7206).

Clubs > If you want to move with the Athens smart and good-looking, check out **Wild Rose** (10 Panepistimiou St, tel: +30 210 364 2160) for late action on most nights of the week. Or head to stylish **Horostasion** (2 Skouleniou St, tel: +30 210 331 4330) for varied music on different levels.

Restaurants > All your Greek food and drink favourites from *moussaka* to *gyros* to *retsina* can be found at **Taverna Sigalas** (2 Plateia, tel: +30 210 321 3036) or at the nearby **Thanasis** (69 Mitropoleos, tel: +30 210 324 4705).

Below: Spend the day enjoying the culture of Athens then head out to discover its nightlife.

Weather	Low (°C)	High
January	6	12
February	6	12
March	8	15
April	11	18
May	15	23
June	18	27
July	22	30
August	22	31
September	19	28
October	15	22
November	11	17
December	8	14

OLYMPIAKOS

Above: Olympiakos's Michal Zewlakow (right) and Christos Patsatzoglou after the final whistle of the Uefa Champions League 2008.

MATTER OF FACT

Name: Olympiacos FC
Stadium: Stadion Georgios Karaiskakis (capacity 32,120)
Address: Karaoli Dimitriou & Sofianopoulou, 185 47 Neo Faliro
To get there: Metro line 1 (station: Neo Faliro)
Telephone: +30 210 414 3000
Email: info@olympiacos.org
Website: www.olympiacos.org

Stadium tour

Open: Mon—Fri to groups. Sat, Sun (not match days) to individuals.
Museum: Open Tue, Thu, Fri, Sat 10.00—18.00, Wed 12.00—20.00, Sun 10.00—16.00. Closed Mon, match days two hours before game
Price: €5 (museum only: €4)
Contact: Tel: +30 210 481 9440 or email: mouseio@olympiacos.org

Home   Away

Trophies

36	Greek League
23	Greek Cup

Main rivals

Olympiakos play Panathinaikos (see page 209) in the Derby of the Eternal Enemies. AEK Athens (tel: +30 210 610 1371, www.aekfc.gr) play at the Olympic Stadium (Grammou str. 69—71, Marousi 151 24). Panionios (tel: +30 210 931 1189, www.pgss.gr) play at the Nea Smyrni Stadium (1, I Chrisostomou str, Nea Smirni 17122).

TEN YEAR EURO RECORD

Season	Competition	Finished
1998–99	Champs League	QF
1999–00	Champs League	Group*
	Uefa Cup	Last 32
2000–01	Champs League	Group*
	Uefa Cup	Last 32
2001–02	Champs League	Group*
2002–03	Champs League	Group*
2003–04	Champs League	Group*
2004–05	Champs League	Group
	Uefa Cup	Last 16
2005–06	Champs League	Group
2006–07	Champs League	Last Group
2007–08	Champs League	Last 16

* 1st of two group stages

Fired-up supporters

When Olympiakos's 1996 title hopes were destroyed by defeat to Panathinaikos, their fans smashed and burned seats. A year later, already champions, supporters marked the final league match by throwing fireworks and invading the pitch. Emotions run high in good times and bad for Greece's most successful club.

The atmosphere at the Stadion Georgios Karaiskakis seems to affect visiting teams. While Olympiakos failed to win any of their first 31 away games in the main stages of the Champions League, they were unbeaten in their first 13 at home.

Champions four times in a row in the early 1980s, they declined after president George Koskotas was convicted in 1988 of embezzling money from his Bank of Crete, leaving the club deep in debt. Technology magnate Socrates Kokkalis has proved a better president, his appointment of Bosnian coach Dusan Bajevic in 1996 sparking a run of 11 titles in 12 years, and he has overseen the rebuilding of their stadium.

PANATHINAIKOS

Above: The Panathinaikos players celebrate a rare league title in 1996.

TEN YEAR EURO RECORD

Season	Competition	Finished
1998–99	Champs League	Group
1999–00	Uefa Cup	Last 32
2000–01	Champs League	Group*
2001–02	Champs League	QF
2002–03	Uefa Cup	QF
2003–04	Champs League	Group
	Uefa Cup	Last 32
2004–05	Champs League	Group
	Uefa Cup	Last 32
2005–06	Champs League	Group
2006–07	Uefa Cup	Last 32
2007–08	Uefa Cup	Last 32

* 2nd of two group stages

A civil exchange

A thens gave the world Western civilization, and Panathinaikos have scoured the globe to earn payback for the city. Their 19-title haul has been gathered by coaches from nine foreign countries as well as Greece: Argentina, Austria, England, Bulgaria, Czechoslovakia, Hungary, Israel, Poland and Yugoslavia. The last was won in 2004 by Israeli Itzhak Shum, the first of eight successive coaches from eight different nations.

In all Panathinaikos have recruited coaches from 19 countries and, given this cosmopolitan approach, it is apt that the club have impressed abroad more than other Greek sides. They lost the 1971 European Cup final and reached the 1985 and 1996 semi-finals.

Panathinaikos were champions four times in the 1990s – inspired by Krzysztof Warzycha, who has scored nearly 100 goals more than anyone else for the club – but won just one of 12 titles after 1996.

A new 46,000-capacity stadium is planned to open in 2010 but average attendances have rarely risen above 10,000 over the past decade.

MATTER OF FACT
Name: Panathinaikos Athlitikos Omilos
Stadium: Olympic Stadium (capacity 71,030)
Address: Irodou Attikou 12A, Maroussi 151 24
To get there: Metro line 1 (station: Irini). Bus 14
Telephone: +30 210 809 3630
Email: paepao@hellasnet.gr
Website: www.pao.gr

Stadium tour
Contact club for details

Home   Away

Trophies
19   Greek League
16   Greek Cup

Main rivals
The biggest foes are Olympiakos (see page 208). AEK Athens (tel: +30 210 6121371, www.aekfc.gr) play at the Olympic Stadium (Grammou str 69–71, Marousi 151 24). Panionios (tel: +30 210 9311189, www.pgss.gr) play at the Nea Smyrni Stadium (1, I Chrisostomou str, Nea Smirni 17122).

TURKEY

Capital: *Ankara.* **Language:** *Turkish.* **Beer:** *Tekel Birasi, Efes Pilsen.* **Food:** *Kebab (meat on a skewer),* köfte *(meatball).* **National anthem:** *Istiklâl Marfli (The March of Independence).* **Population:** *71,893,000.* **Time zone:** *GMT +2.* **Emergency numbers:** *Police 155, medical 112, fire 110.* **Did you know?** *St Nicholas (Santa Claus) was born in modern-day Turkey.* **Football body:** *Türkiye Futbol Federasyonu, Konaklar Mah, Ihlamurlu Sok 9 4, Levent, Istanbul; tel: +90 212 282 7020, fax: +90 212 282 7016, email: tff@tff.org.tr, website: www.tff.org. Founded 1923. Affiliated 1923.*

Below: The shapes and colours of Turkey's Cunda Island in the Aegean Sea.

Turkey shoots are over

The late 1980s overhaul of coaching in Turkey was a matter of urgency, with memories fresh of two 8–0 thrashings by England. In the match in Istanbul the home side did not impress *The Times* of London, which reported that 'their goalkeeper was inept, their defence was disorganized, their midfield was inefficient and their attack was anonymous. They showed no heart either.' England manager Bobby Robson added: "It's not often you score eight and feel you've let your opponents off the hook."

Signs that Turkey's coaching reappraisal was paying off came when they were crowned European Under-19 champions in 1992 and then qualified for their first major tournament in 42 years at Euro '96. Better was to follow, as they reached the quarter-finals of Euro 2000 and the semi-finals of both the 2002 World Cup and Euro 2008, losing the latter match to Germany despite totally outplaying their opponents with an under-strength team.

While the international game thrives, there are concerns closer to home. In 2007 two club sponsors withdrew their financial backing citing corruption in domestic football; a year earlier two-thirds of fans polled in the country said they thought bribery was a part of the Turkish game. Even so, supporters continue to show great commitment, often creating a tremendous atmosphere long before kick-off. Besiktas, for example, open their stadium gates about four hours before the start of normal matches and up to seven hours early for derbies. At last such Turkish passion is being rewarded on the global stage.

Above: Sparks fly during a Besiktas game. *Below:* Celebrating a win against Croatia in Euro 2008.

THE TEN YEAR GUIDE

Süper Lig

Season	Winner	Runner-up
1998–99	Galatasaray	Besiktas
1999–00	Galatasaray	Besiktas
2000–01	Fenerbahçe	Galatasaray
2001–02	Galatasaray	Fenerbahçe
2002–03	Besiktas	Galatasaray
2003–04	Fenerbahçe	Trabzonspor
2004–05	Fenerbahçe	Trabzonspor
2005–06	Galatasaray	Fenerbahçe
2006–07	Fenerbahçe	Besiktas
2007–08	Galatasaray	Fenerbahçe

Türkiye Kupasi

Season	Winner	Runner-up
1998–99	Galatasaray	Besiktas
1999–00	Galatasaray	Antalyaspor
2000–01	Gençlerbirligi	Fenerbahçe
2001–02	Kocaelispor	Besiktas
2002–03	Trabzonspor	Gençlerbirligi
2003–04	Trabzonspor	Gençlerbirligi
2004–05	Galatasaray	Fenerbahçe
2005–06	Besiktas	Fenerbahçe
2006–07	Besiktas	Kayseri Erciyesspor
2007–08	Kayserispor	Gençlerbirligi

ISTANBUL

At the crossroads

One of the world's oldest cities (famously dubbed 'the crossroads or bridge of civilizations'), Istanbul is also one of the fiercest in Europe when it comes to football rivalry, with the demand of its clubs – Galatasary, Besiktas, Fenerbahçe – for constant success relegating other cities (except possibly Trabzon's Trabzonspor) to perennial also-rans. As if to keep the rivalry charged, the clubs are not even all based on the same continents. Sükrü Saracoglu, home of Fenerbahçe, is on the eastern bank of the Bosporus (Asia geographically), while across the water on the western bank (Europe) is Besiktas's Inönü venue and Galatasaray's planned new stadium.

Although the more than 11 million people who live in Istanbul spread far and wide into both Europe and Asia, it is the few districts either side of the Bosporus that contain a large part of the residents and the attractions. Eminönü and Fatih are the old city districts in the lower part of what is known as the Golden Horn, which juts into the Sea of Marmara and the mouth of the Bosporus; they essentially form what was once Constantinople. It is just north of here you that you will find Fenerbahçe and Besiktas.

Facing them across the water are Üshüdar and Kadiköy, two Asian districts with a high density of residential buildings and business activity. On both sides you will see expensive homes lining the waterfront. It is the walled city of the Golden Horn that remains popular with visitors, with attractions such as the Blue Mosque, Topkapi Palace and Hagia Sophia.

Below: The city spans the Bosporus and is at the crossroads of east and west.

3 THINGS YOU MUST DO...
(Apart from the football)

1 KAPALIÇARSI

Get lost among a quarter of million people all looking for a bargain in one of its many thousands of shops. The Grand Bazaar of Istanbul is one of the world's greatest covered markets. Open: Mon–Sat. 08.30–19.00. To get there: tram to Beyazit.

2 BLUE MOSQUE

With its six minarets, the Blue Mosque (At Meydani 21, Sultanahmet, tel: +212 518 1319) is one of the iconic buildings of the city. Thousands of blue tiles on its ceiling give it the name. Open: daily 09.00–18.00, except during prayer times and noon Fri. Price: free. To get there: tram to Sultanahmet.

3 TURKBALON

See the city from 200 m (656 ft) up from the Asian side in a balloon. (Kadiköy Dock, tel: +216 347 6703). The balloon is tethered by a rope and takes people up every few minutes. Open: 09.00–18.00. Price: 15ytl. To get there: ferry to Kadiköy.

Türk Telekom Arena (Galatasaray)
Inönü (Besiktas)
Atatürk Olympic Stadium (Istanbul BB)
01
ISTANBUL
03
1. Kapaliçarsi
2. Blue Mosque
D100
N
Not to scale
3. Turkbalon
Sükrü Saracoglu (Fenerbahçe)

BARS > CLUBS > RESTAURANTS

Bars > After a day in this hectic city, sink back in the spaciousness of **Nifl** (Abdi Ipekci Cad Azer Is Merkezi 44/3, tel: +212 296 9555) where you can enjoy smart design, good food and sexy people. If you are looking for views of the Bosporus as well as sexy bodies, it has to be **Vogue** (Spor Caddesi, BJK Plaza A Blok Kat 13, tel: +212 227 4404), one of the city's most popular spots.

Clubs > It's classy and open very late. Head to **Wanna** (Tepebasi Meflrutiyet Caddesi No 151, tel: +212 243 1794). Or try **Babylon** (Seyhbender Sokak 3, tel: +212 292 7368).

Restaurants > The laid-back **Borsa Lokantasi** (Yaliköskü Cad, Yaliköskü Han 60–62, tel: +212 511 8079) is well located and has been serving Turkish specialities since the 1920s. **Hamdi Et Lokantasi** (Kalçin Sokak 17, tel: +212 528 0390) is for meat lovers.

Below: Istanbul nightlife. It's not often you can go out in two continents in the same night.

Weather	Low (ºC)	High
January	2	7
February	3	8
March	4	10
April	8	16
May	12	20
June	16	25
July	19	27
August	19	27
September	16	24
October	12	19
November	8	13
December	5	10

BESIKTAS

Above: Besiktas fans light up a night game.

MATTER OF FACT

Name: Besiktas Jimnastik Kulübü
Stadium: Inönü (capacity 32,125)
Address: BJK Plaza, Akaretler
Süleyman Seba Caddesi, No. 92,
Besiktas 80680
To get there: Subway or bus to
Besiktas or Taksim Square or ferry
to Besiktas or Kabatas (Üsküdar
and Kadiköy)
Telephone: +90 212 310 1000
Email: bilgi@besiktasjk.com.tr
Website: www.bjk.com.tr

Stadium tour
Open: Contact the club to book
Cost: Free
Contact: On email above or fax: +90
212 258 8194

Home	Away

Trophies
10	Turkish League
7	Turkish Cup

Main rivals
Fenerbahçe (see page 215) and
Galatasaray (see pages 216–217) are
the main rivals. Istanbul BB (tel: +90
212 587 4549, www.ibbspor.com) play
at the Atatürk Olympic Stadium
(Halkali Konutlari Arkasi, Altin Sehir
Yolu Uzeri, Küçükçekmece- Ikitelli).

TEN YEAR EURO RECORD		
Season	Competition	Finished
1998–99	C Winners' Cup	2nd round
1999–00	Champs League	2nd qual rd
2000–01	Champs League	Group*
2001–02	DNQ	
2002–03	Uefa Cup	QF
2003–04	Champs League	Group
	Uefa Cup	Last 32
2004–05	Uefa Cup	Group
2005–06	Uefa Cup	Group
2006–07	Uefa Cup	Group
2007–08	Champs League	Group

* 1st of two group stages

Enjoying old age

One title in 13 seasons around the millennium is a poor return for one of Turkey's big three, but at least Besiktas picked the best year to triumph. The 2003 crown came in their centenary, a landmark they had trumpeted as it underlined their status as the country's oldest sports club. They even beat Göztepe 7–3 on their 100th birthday.

That scoreline might imply a carefree attitude, but success was built on a formidable defence, as it was when they won three consecutive titles from 1989–90. Their run of one defeat in 73 league games included becoming the only unbeaten Turkish champions in history in 1991–92.

That added to their many boasts. The oldest club are alone in having the Turkish flag on their emblem as recognition for filling the entire national side in a game against Greece in 1952. Furthermore, the Bosporus and its Asian shores, along with the Dolmabahçe Palace, are visible from their Inönü stadium. During these lean years, the fans have had something decent to look at after all.

FENERBAHÇE

Above: Fenerbahçe players celebrate with the league trophy in 2005.

MATTER OF FACT

Name: Fenerbahçe Spor Kulübü
Stadium: Sükrü Saracoglu
(capacity 52,056)
Address: Maraton Girisi, Kiziltoprak,
Kadiköy 34724
To get there: Bus 4. Train (station:
Sö ütlüçeflme)
Telephone: +90 216 542 1907
Email: aysesu@fenerbahce.org
Website: www.fenerbahce.org

Stadium tour
Contact club for details

Home	Away

Trophies
17	Turkish League
4	Turkish Cup

Main rivals
Galatasaray (see pages 216–217) are
the big rivals while Besiktas (see page
214) complete the Big Three. Istanbul
BB (tel: +90 212 587 4549, www.
ibbspor.com) play at the Atatürk
Olympic Stadium (Halkali Konutlari
Arkasi, Altin Sehir Yolu Uzeri,
Küçükçekmece- Ikitelli).

Prime movers

TEN YEAR EURO RECORD		
Season	Competition	Finished
1998–99	Uefa Cup	1st round
1999–00	Uefa Cup	1st round
2000–01	DNQ	
2001–02	Champs League	Group*
2002–03	Uefa Cup	2nd round
2003–04	DNQ	
2004–05	Champs League	Group
	Uefa Cup	Last 32
2005–06	Champs League	Group
2006–07	Champs League	3rd qual rd
	Uefa Cup	Last 32
2007–08	Champs League	QF

* 1st of two group stages

Turkey founder Mustafa Kemal Atatürk is claimed to have been a
Fenerbahçe supporter who attended matches; 1940s Prime Minister
Sükrü Saracoglu doubled as the club's president; and Tayyip
Erdogan, the long-term leader this decade, is a fan and nearly had
a trial with them. They are the nation's most popular team.

Saracoglu's memory lives on through the arena that bears his name.
Unbeaten in 15 European matches there before losing to Arsenal in 2008,
Fenerbahçe won all 17 home games *en route* to the 2001 title and 16 out
of 17 in becoming 2005 champions. But perhaps their greatest result was
away, when they ended Manchester United's 40-year undefeated
European home record in 1996. Unlike Galatasaray and Besiktas, their
Europe-based city rivals, Fenerbahçe reside in Asia but they have thrived
by recruiting from a third continent, South America. Brazilian coach Zico,
aided by four Brazil-born players, won the league in 2007. The club with
friends in high places remain high achievers.

GALATASARAY

Above: *Galatasaray fans have got used to success.*

TEN YEAR EURO RECORD		
Season	Competition	Finished
1998–99	Champs League	Group
1999–00	Champ League	Group*
	Uefa Cup	Winners
2000–01	Champs League	QF
2001–02	Champs League	Group**
2002–03	Champs League	Group*
2003–04	Champs League	Group
	Uefa Cup	Last 32
2004–05	DNQ	
2005–06	Uefa Cup	1st round
2006–07	Champs League	Group
2007–08	Uefa Cup	Last 32

* 1st of two group stages
** 2nd of two group stages

Germans lead the way

When Galatasaray chose Michael Skibbe to lead the team in 2008, they doubtless felt on safe ground in appointing a German. Coaches from that country have helped establish them as Turkey's most successful club in the period since 1984, when Jupp Derwall, formerly in charge of West Germany, surprised his compatriots by accepting a job in a nation that was then a footballing backwater.

Derwall introduced fresh tactical training ideas and engineered Galatasaray's first title for 14 years in 1987. Karl-Heinz Feldkamp then led a side with three German players to the 1993 title, and Rainer Hollmann's team retained the crown a year later having also knocked Manchester United out of the Champions League.

Skibbe is the sixth German coach in this era, not that Turkey have been unrepresented. Indeed, Mustafa Denizli led the team to the 1989 European Cup semi-finals and Fatih Terim lifted the 2000 Uefa Cup, Turkey's only European club trophy. In that year Galatasaray also won their second successive domestic double and their fourth consecutive league title, which all came in Terim's remarkable four-year stewardship.

Those triumphs would have delighted Ali Sami Yen, one of the club's founders and its first president, who gave his name to Galatasaray's stadium. The intimidating atmosphere at the ground and around the city shocked Sir Alex Ferguson when he took Manchester United there in 1993. The manager said the fixture "exposed us to as much harassment and hostility as I have ever known on a football expedition."

Galatasaray plan to relocate to the new Türk Telekom Arena, due to open in 2009. The club will hope the fans' passion survives the move.

GREATEST PLAYERS

> **GHEORGHE HAGI (1996–2001)**
The Romanian attacking midfielder was a brilliantly creative player, inspiring Galatasaray to success during their great era of the late 1990s. His left-footed free kicks were especially dangerous.

> **HAKAN SÜKÜR (1992–95; 1995–2000; 2003–08)**
The striker enjoyed three spells at the club, reaching a peak during the second, when he was Turkey's leading league goalscorer for three consecutive seasons from 1996 to 1999.

MATTER OF FACT

Name: Galatasaray Spor Kulübü
Stadium: (Due to open Oct 2009) Türk Telekom Arena (capacity 52,647). Previous stadium: Ali Sami Yen (capacity 23,785).
Address: Halkali Konutlari Arkasi, Altin Sehir Yolu Uzeri, Kucukcekmece-Ikitelli
Telephone: +90 212 444 1905
Email: gssite@galatasaray.org
Website: www.galatasaray.org

Stadium tour
Contact club for details

Home	Away

Trophies
19	Turkish League
14	Turkish Cup

Main rivals
Besiktas (see page 214) and, especially, Fenerbahçe (see page 215) are the biggest rivals. Istanbul BB (tel:+90 212 587 4549, www.ibbspor. com) play at the Atatürk Olympic Stadium (Halkali Konutlari Arkasi, Altin Sehir Yolu Uzeri, Küçükçekmece-Ikitelli).

Above: Galatasaray lift the Uefa Cup in 2000 after winning a penalty shoot-out against Arsenal in the final.

FLAG DAY

After Galatasaray's extra-time winner in the second leg of the 1996 Turkish Cup final against Fenerbahçe on their bitter rivals' own ground, victorious coach Graeme Souness greeted the final whistle by planting a Galatasaray flag in the centre circle. The gesture nearly caused a riot.

ISRAEL

THE

3

MINUTE
GUIDE

Capital: *Jerusalem.* **Languages:** *Hebrew and Arabic.* **Beer:** *Maccabee, Goldstar.* **Food:** *Kebabs, hummus.* **National anthem:** *HaTikvah (The Hope).* **Population:** *7,112,000.* **Time zone:** *GMT +2.* **Emergency number:** *Police 100, medical 101, fire 102.* **Did you know?** *The Dead Sea, between Israel, Jordan and the West Bank is the lowest lake in the world at 417 m (1,368 ft) below sea level.* **Football body:** *The Israel Football Association, Ramat-Gan Stadium, 299 Aba Hilell Street, Ramat-Gan 52134; tel: +972 3 617 1500, fax: +972 3 570 2044, email: r.dori@ israel-football.org.il, website: www.israel-football.org.il. Founded 1928. Affiliated 1929.*

Below: The Dead Sea. Not too dead.

Divided we stand

Israel's history in world football has been, unhappily, characterized by numerous political, religious and geographical divisions.

For a start, Israel has played World Cup qualifiers in three different continents. When they played first in the Asian and then Oceanian qualifiers, there was so much political unrest they were forced to seek out the more welcoming playing arena of Europe (from 1994).

Domestically you'll see the same names crop up again and again; about 80 per cent of them are prenamed either Maccabi or Hapoel. In the early 20th century the World Maccabi Organization represented Jewish sporting interests around the world, but there was a split, and the more left-leaning Hapoel (Labour) Organization sprung up.

Just about every club formed in Israel ever since has been affiliated to one or other of these organizations. To this day the rivalry at a derby game between Maccabi Tel Aviv and Hapoel Tel Aviv is fierce… except that in the interim, the right-wing Beitar Jerusalem and a new kid on the Israeli Premier League block, Bnei Sakhnin, an Arab team, have struck up a similar rivalry.

Domestically, Israeli Premier League clubs are enjoying rude health with money pouring in from sugar-daddies and oligarchs from around the world. Consequently, Israeli players are starting to be taken note of across Europe.

Above: A sea of Israeli supporters. *Below:* The Ramat Gan stadium in Tel Aviv.

THE TEN YEAR GUIDE *Premier League replaced Liga Leumit which became second tier, in 1999–00

Premier League*

Season	Winner	Runner-up
1998–99	Maccabi Haifa	Maccabi Tel Aviv
1999–00	Maccabi Tel Aviv	Maccabi Haifa
2000–01	Maccabi Haifa	Maccabi Tel Aviv
2001–02	Maccabi Haifa	Maccabi Tel Aviv
2002–03	Maccabi Tel Aviv	Maccabi Haifa
2003–04	Maccabi Haifa	Maccabi Tel Aviv
2004–05	Maccabi Haifa	Maccabi Petah Tikvah
2005–06	Maccabi Haifa	Hapoel Tel Aviv
2006–07	Beitar Jerusalem	Maccabi Netanya
2007–08	Beitar Jerusalem	Maccabi Netanya

State Cup

Season	Winner	Runner-up
1998–99	Hapoel Tel Aviv	Beitar Jerusalem
1999–00	Hapoel Tel Aviv	Beitar Jerusalem
2000–01	Maccabi Tel Aviv	Maccabi Petah Tikvah
2001–02	Maccabi Tel Aviv	Maccabi Haifa
2002–03	Hapoel Ramat Gan	Hapoel Be'er Sheva
2003–04	Bnei Sakhnin	Hapoel Haifa
2004–05	Maccabi Tel Aviv	Maccabi Herzeliya
2005–06	Hapoel Tel Aviv	Bnei Yehuda
2006–07	Hapoel Tel Aviv	Hapoel Ashkelon
2007–08	Beitar Jerusalem	Hapoel Tel Aviv

HAIFA

The Middle East's European football city

This industrial and port city jutting out into the Mediterranean Sea is on the northwest coast of Israel, but in the football world, Haifa, as with other Israeli cities, finds itself located in Europe for political reasons. It has a large population from the Soviet Union, with around one in four of its 265,000 population being Jewish immigrants from that former state.

The oldest district is Walid Salib in the lower city near the port, while the main Arab settlement is the nearby Wadi Nisnas. The upper city comprises the neighbourhoods on Mount Carmel, and is linked to the lower part of the city by the old commercial centre Hadar Hacarmel. The German Colony, now restored, is a popular area for nightlife.

The Kiryat Eliezer Stadium, home to both Maccabi Haifa and Happoel Haifa, is just north of Wadi Salas near the top of the city by the sea.

Weather	Low (ºC)	High
January	11	17
February	11	15
March	13	18
April	16	21
May	19	23
June	22	26
July	24	28
August	25	29
September	23	28
October	21	26
November	17	22
December	12	17

Below: The view of Haifa from Mount Carmel.

3 THINGS YOU MUST DO...
(Apart from the football)

1 BAHA'Í GARDENS
A holy site for the Baha'í faith, it's unlikely you'll find gardens more perfectly manicured than the Baha'í Gardens (80 Hatzionut Avenue, tel: +972 4 831 3131). Open: daily except Wed 09.00–17.00 but the hour-long tours must be booked at least 24 hours in advance. Price: free. To get there:buses 22, 23, 25 or 26.

2 THE GERMAN COLONY
Dating back to the 1870s, the German Colony is a hive of shops, bars, clubs and restaurants. Head to Ben Gurion Avenue, the main street that runs down to the port. Try the upmarket restaurant and bar Hashmura1872 (15 Ben Gurion Ave, tel: +972 4 855 1872). To get there: it's next to Baha'í Gardens.

3 HAIFA FUNICULAR
For amazing views of Mount Carmel and across the sea, take the funicular from Bat Galim (Bat Galim Funicular station, tel: +972 4 837 6861) to Stella Maris and back again. Open Sat–Thur 06.00–22-00, Fri 06.00–15.00 and 19.00–22.00. To get there: buses 3a, 41, 42.

MACCABI HAIFA

Above: Already an Israeli international, Maccabi Haifa's Avi Ran was killed aged just 23 in a motorboat accident as the team celebrated winning the title in 1987.

MATTER OF FACT
Name: Maccabi Haifa Football Club
Stadium: Kiryat Eliezer Stadium (capacity 14,002)
Address: 16 Tzahal Street, 35157
To get there: Buses 1, 2, 8
Telephone: +972 4 834 6626
Email: info@maccabihaifafc.com
Website: www.maccabi-haifafc. walla.co.il

Stadium tour
Contact club for details

Home	Away

Trophies
10	Israeli League
5	Israeli Cup

Main rivals
Hapoel Haifa (tel: +972 4 866 4000, www.hhaifa.com), who have played in the second division in recent seasons, share the Kiryat Eliezer Stadium with Maccabi Haifa.

TEN YEAR EURO RECORD

Season	Competition	Finished
1998–99	C Winners' Cup	QF
1999–00	Intertoto Cup	1st round
2000–01	Uefa Cup	1st round
2001–02	Champs League	2nd qual rd
2002–03	Champs League	Group
	Uefa Cup	Last 32
2003–04	Uefa Cup	2nd round
2004–05	Champs League	3rd qual rd
	Uefa Cup	1st round
2005–06	Champs League	2nd qual rd
2006–07	Champs League	3rd qual rd
	Uefa Cup	Last 16
2007–08	Intertoto Cup	2nd round

Fighting for recognition

The embarrassment was acute. Asked to assess Maccabi Haifa ahead of their Champions League match with his Manchester United side in 2002, Sir Alex Ferguson said: "We cannot underestimate them. Beating Lokomotiv Moscow, Parma and AC Milan last season was a big step up." The manager confused them with Israeli rivals Hapoel Tel Aviv.

The error underlined Israeli football's lack of prominence at the time, but Haifa, the country's first club in the Champions League group phase, soon improved matters, beating United 3–0 in one of the sides' two clashes that season. The club's Champions League efforts have been hampered by frequent orders to move home matches outside Israel for security reasons. They beat United at 'home' in Cyprus and lost a qualifying tie narrowly to Liverpool in 2006–07 after a 'home' leg in Kiev.

Despite their trailblazing, Haifa were a minor team in Israel before winning the first of their ten titles in 1984. Now the challenge is to earn the kind of success to ensure the likes of Ferguson remember who they are.

TRAVEL RESOURCES

Electrical sockets used across Europe

A   B   C

1   2   3   4   5   6   7   8

Country	Voltage	Plugs and sockets		Country	Voltage	Plugs and sockets	
Austria	230	A 1		Italy	220	A 4	
Belgium	230	A 2		Netherlands	230	A 1	
Bulgaria	220	A 1		Norway	230	A 1	
Croatia	220	A 1		Poland	220	A 1	
Czech Republic	230	A 2		Portugal	230	A 1	C 8
Denmark	220	A 3		Russia	220	A 1	
England	230	B 7		Scotland	230	B 7	
Estonia	220	A 3		Serbia	220	A 1	
France	230	A 2		Spain	220	A 1	
Germany	230	A 1		Sweden	220	A 1	
Greece	220	A 3		Switzerland	220	A 1	A 5
Hungary	220	A 1		Turkey	220	A 2	
Israel	230	A 6		Ukraine	220	A 3	